Nickolas P. Roubekas rediscovers the long shadow cast by Euhemerus of Messene over the history of conceptualizing the divine from Hellenistic times to the present. While building on classical studies on Euhemerus and his reception, Roubekas presents scholarship on religion with a timely appropriation of Euhemerus and the discourse he elicited on the origins of gods and the divine for the contemporary study of religion. This study of Euhemerus provides the necessary ground work for retrieving the discursive processes of manufacturing divinity that lie at the foundation of the history of European Christianity.

—Professor Gerhard van den Heever,
University of South Africa

# An Ancient Theory of Religion

*An Ancient Theory of Religion* examines a theory of religion put forward by Euhemerus of Messene (late 4th–early 3rd century BCE) in his lost work *Sacred Inscription*, and shows not only how and why euhemerism came about but also how it was—and still is—used.

By studying the utilization of the theory in different periods—from the Graeco-Roman world to Late Antiquity, and from the Renaissance to the twenty-first century—this book explores the reception of the theory in diverse literary works. In so doing, it also unpacks the different adoptions and misrepresentations of Euhemerus's work according to the diverse agendas of the authors and scholars who have employed his theory. In the process, certain questions are raised: What did Euhemerus actually claim? How has his theory of the origins of belief in gods been used? How can modern scholarship approach and interpret his take on religion? When referring to 'euhemerism,' whose version are we employing? *An Ancient Theory of Religion* assumes no prior knowledge of euhemerism and will be of interest to scholars working in classical reception, religious studies, and early Christian studies.

**Nickolas P. Roubekas** is a postdoctoral research fellow at the School of Ancient Languages and Text Studies, North-West University, South Africa. He received his Ph.D. in Religious Studies from the Aristotle University, Greece, and held research and teaching positions at the University of South Africa and the University of Aberdeen, UK.

# Routledge Monographs in Classical Studies

# An Ancient Theory of Religion

Euhemerism from Antiquity to the Present

Nickolas P. Roubekas

Routledge
Taylor & Francis Group

NEW YORK AND LONDON

First published 2017
by Routledge
711 Third Avenue, New York, NY 10017

and by Routledge
2 Park Square, Milton Park, Abingdon, Oxon OX14 4RN

*Routledge is an imprint of the Taylor & Francis Group, an informa business*

*British Library Cataloguing-in-Publication Data*
A catalogue record for this book is available from the British Library

*Library of Congress Cataloging-in-Publication Data*
Names: Roubekas, Nickolas P. (Nickolas Panayiotis), 1979– author.
Title: An ancient theory of religion : Euhemerism from antiquity to the
present / Nickolas P. Roubekas.
Other titles: Euhemerism from antiquity to the present
Description: Abingdon, Oxon ; New York, NY : Routledge, 2017. |
Series: Routledge monographs in classical studies | Includes bibliographic
references and index.
Identifiers: LCCN 2016025447 | ISBN 9781138848931 (hardback :
alk. paper) | ISBN 9781315725871 (ebook)
Subjects: LCSH: Euhemerus, of Messene, active 4th century B.C. |
Euhemerism.
Classification: LCC PA3972.E9 R68 2017 | DDC 201/.3—dc23
LC record available at https://lccn.loc.gov/2016025447

ISBN: 978-1-138-84893-1 (hbk)
ISBN: 978-1-315-72587-1 (ebk)

Typeset in Sabon
by Florence Production Ltd, Stoodleigh, Devon, UK

To my mother Mary, for her love, support, and for being the first who taught me how to think.

To my brother Chris, for always being there, no matter what, ready to help.

Now every theory tacitly asserts two things: firstly, that there is something to be explained; secondly, that such and such is the explanation.
—Herbert Spencer, *First Principles*

*Our evaluations.*—All actions may be tracked back to evaluations, all evaluations are either original or adopted—the latter being by far the most common.
—Friedrich Nietzsche, *Daybreak: Thoughts on the Prejudices of Morality*

οἶδα μὲν οὖν πάνυ πολλούς αὐτῶν ἐπιστρέψων, ἐνίοις δὲ καὶ πάνυ ἐπαχθὴς δόξων, καὶ μάλιστα ὁπόσοις ἀποτετέλεσται ἤδη καὶ ἐν τῷ κοινῷ δέδεικται ἡ ἱστορία. εἰ δὲ καὶ ἐπήνηται ὑπὸ τῶν τότε ἀκροασαμένων, μανία ἂν εἴη ἡ ἐλπίς, ὡς οἱ τοιοῦτοι μεταποιήσουσιν ἢ μετεγγράψουσί τι τῶν ἅπαξ κεκυρωμένων καὶ ὥσπερ ἐς τάς βασιλείους αὐλάς ἀποκειμένων.
—Λουκιανὸς, *Πῶς δεῖ Ἱστορίαν συγγράφειν*

# Contents

# Acknowledgments

Both before and during the process of writing this book, I was fortunate to have a number of friends and colleagues that helped, offered ideas, and dedicated precious time and energy in making what follows better. First and foremost, I would like to thank my two teachers and now good friends, Panayotis Pachis and Robert Segal. It was due to Panayotis that I first encountered the work of Euhemerus back in 2006 as a Ph.D. student at the Aristotle University of Thessaloniki, an interest that turned into a doctoral thesis completed in 2011 under his guidance and supervision. His knowledge of the Graeco-Roman world and the Hellenistic religions is unsurpassable, and a lot of what follows comes from studying as well as chatting with him about these issues on numerous occasions. Additionally, he diligently went over the whole manuscript and offered ideas and made various suggestions—I must further thank him for spotting a mistake that, if it had gone unnoticed, could have literally ruined the book.

I was also fortunate to study with Robert Segal and, a few years later, work with him as his colleague at the University of Aberdeen. His specialization and authority on theories of religion and myth is indisputable. I learned from him as much in the classroom as I did over the numerous dinners we had, as well as during the countless hours we spent discussing the study of religion in his office. Moreover, he went over many of the chapters, and helped me clarify some points that were either ambiguous or confusing. His generosity, friendship, and readiness to help have been inspiring and I wholeheartedly thank him.

I would also like to thank Albert Baumgarten, Franco De Angelis, Chris De Wet, Gerhard van den Heever, Phil Tite, Luther H. Martin, Sam Newington, Yannis Papadogiannakis, Lukas Pokorny, Katerina Stathi, and Dimitris Xygalatas for their support, and for providing me with bibliographical references otherwise impossible to obtain. I am greatly indebted to Claire Hargaden who went over the whole manuscript in such short notice and saved me from numerous mistakes. I would also like to thank Russell McCutcheon, who read part of the book and, as always, had meaningful suggestions to make. Lastly, I must thank the anonymous reviewers whose input helped me to polish my argumentation and take into consideration aspects that I had initially overlooked.

I must also express my thanks and appreciation to the people at Routledge and the production team: Laura Sterns, who enthusiastically embraced this idea back in 2014; my editor Amy Davis-Poynter; the production editor Anna Dolan; Amy Thomas for her excellent copy-editing work; Tamsyn Hopkins for her professionalism and help throughout the production process; and especially Lizzi Thomasson, who tolerated my delays, dealt with numerous practical matters, and was always ready to answer even my most foolish questions.

Last but not least, my gratitude goes to my mother Mary and my brother Chris, for so many things that cannot possibly be enumerated here. This book is dedicated to them.

\*    \*    \*

Some of the material in the following pages was previously published in other forms elsewhere. Some parts of the Introduction and Chapter 1 originally appeared in "What is Euhemerism? A Brief History of Research and Some Persisting Questions," *Bulletin for the Study of Religion* 43.2 (2012): 30–37 © Equinox Publ., Sheffield, U.K. Parts of Chapter 5 were previously published in "*Post Mortem* Makes a Difference: On a Redescription of Euhemerism and Its Place in the Study of Graeco-Roman Divine Kingship," *Religion & Theology* 19.3/4 (2012): 319–339 © Brill, The Netherlands. Lastly, Chapter 7 is based on "Which Euhemerism Will *You* Use? Celsus on the Divine Nature of Jesus," *Journal of Early Christian History* 2.2 (2012): 80–96 © Taylor and Francis, U.K. I am grateful to the publishers for granting me permission to include reworked and revised parts of these materials here.

\*    \*    \*

Note: I am primarily relying on the LOEB translations of the ancient texts that appear in the book. However, I often intervene, whereas in many instances I adopt other translations, which are noted in the endnotes. For the translation of Diodorus's fifth book and Eusebius's summary of Diodorus's sixth book, I primarily use—with many changes—the translation by Diskin Clay and Andrea Purvis (*Four Island Utopias*, 1999). For Lactantius's 'excerpts' of Ennius's Latin translation of the *Sacred Inscription*, I resort to the translation by Anthony Bowen and Peter Garnsey (Lactantius, *Divine Institutes*, 2003). The abbreviation W. refers to the ancient available testimonies on Euhemerus, which have been toilsomely collected by Marek Winiarczyk (*Euhemerus Reliquiae*, 1991).

# Introduction

## Why Study Euhemerism?

Euhemerism is not an indigenous term. On the contrary, it is a modern coinage referring to an ancient theory formulated by a largely unknown figure of the early Hellenistic period, namely Euhemerus of Messene. His theory held that there were two groups of gods: the earthly (Olympian) and the heavenly ones. The latter were eternal and could be observed in nature; the former, benevolent and powerful kings. The most notorious of the gods, Zeus, was deified while he was alive, whereas his ancestor, Uranus, was deified posthumously. Given the nature of his theory (tackling one of the most fundamental questions humans have speculated upon—that of the origin of belief in gods), Euhemerus's approach managed to exceed its temporal and spatial limits and survived throughout antiquity, late antiquity, middle ages, Renaissance, and Enlightenment, finding its way into our modern scholarly works and discussions. Nevertheless, this has been a journey full of turbulence, often so intense that the theory we today adopt or refer to seems in many respects alienated from its *most ancient* forms. I deliberately do not refer to an 'original form' here because any discussion about Euhemerus's original text is a futile pursuit. The so-called *Sacred Inscription*, Euhemerus's work in which he promoted his theory of the origins of the gods, is only survived in secondary 'pagan' and early Christian sources,[1] which do not copy verbatim from the original but, on the contrary, either summarize, modify, or even translate into Latin the original Greek, whereas one of our sources merely incorporates parts of that translation into his own work. As I will discuss in the chapters that follow, this journey of Euhemerus's theory is not only neglected but, most importantly, seems to be unknown to most of the authors and scholars who choose to refer to or implement the theory in their own works.

In his masterful study of how Darwin's theory was received, interpreted, and utilized in different settings, David Livingstone notes:

> As the theory diffused, it diverged. In different venues, both Darwin's name and Darwinism were made to mean different things. In one

place his theory of evolution was seen as an individualist assault on collectivism, in another as a justification for colonial supremacy; elsewhere it was taken to be a subversive attack on racial segregation, yet elsewhere as a symbol of progressive enlightenment.[2]

Yet, Darwin's theory was an idea explicitly stated in his works. Why so much confusion? Wouldn't a simple reading of his works decipher the meaning, scope, and end results of his scholarly output? Livingstone traces those discussions, representations, assessments, and misinterpretations, noting the peculiar way in which ideas travel from one place to another, from one reader to another, and from one group of people to another. Although this is seemingly straightforward, Livingstone reminds us that

> [a]s ideas circulate, they undergo translation and transformation because people encounter representations differently in different circumstances. If theories must be understood in the context of the period and place they emerge from, their reception must also be temporally and spatially situated.[3]

While most scholars today take Euhemerus's theory to be one thing—that is, the deification of dead people—this has not always been the case from the third century BCE onwards, as this book endeavors to demonstrate.

There are at least three moments in euhemerism's temporal itinerary: The Hellenistic euhemerism has Zeus as its protagonist and narrates how kings were deified while they were *still* alive. The deification of previous dead kings plays a secondary role in the narrative, mentioned only in passing in one or two lines of text; the *Sacred Inscription* is about Zeus. At the same time, this ancient euhemerism makes an explicit distinction between earthly or human (Olympian) and heavenly or celestial gods, with Euhemerus maintaining that it is the latter group that is truly divine—a position which is not easily identified in the available testimonies (an issue I address in Chapter 1). The early Christian euhemerism, on the other hand, concentrates on Euhemerus's earthly gods in order to primarily show the superiority of the Christian God, but also seeks to establish an unequivocal classification of all previous 'false' religions versus the one 'true' religion. Lastly, modern euhemerism maintains that every case of deified dead people constitutes euhemerism and should be treated as such. Considering however the nature of our sources, it becomes evident that what we are dealing with is not so much Euhemerus's euhemerism but, as it turns out, the reception of his theory already from antiquity onwards. As such, the study of Euhemerus's theory is first and foremost not the examination of his own conception and articulation of what came to be known as 'euhemerism,' but rather the way in which it has been presented, changed, modified, corrupted, manipulated, and utilized in the works of later authors—both ancient and modern, 'pagan' and Christian, religious and secular. In a sense, as Brennan Breed put it in another context, "[r]eception history, or the study of things other than the original text in its original context, may be all that has ever existed."[4]

However, a book on euhemerism may seem to many readers as beating on an open door, especially after the publication, initially in German (2002) and recently in an English translation (2013), of Marek Winiarczyk's monograph *The Sacred History of Euhemerus of Messene*. Undoubtedly, Winiarczyk's work is not only extremely valuable but, as Benjamin Garstad put it, it "has laid the groundwork for all future study of Euhemerus."[5] Nevertheless, Winiarczyk is writing from a Classics perspective, following a strict philological and textual approach, and on numerous occasions makes sure to remind his readers of this. This, of course, is not anathema in and of itself—it is simply the way traditional classicists work. Winiarczyk's book is indeed the groundwork for anyone interested in Euhemerus, and for this reason I eagerly employ his work throughout mine, often agreeing with his assessments, but also diverging from some other points he makes. My approach, however, is distinctively different. Writing from the field of religious studies, I am interested in the ancient context and textual background but, primarily, I am intrigued by the theoretical issues that emerge through the study of what is now known as 'euhemerism.' From this perspective, Winiarczyk and I have considerable differences both in our approaches and hypotheses. It may surely be the case that a traditional historical account might be (or might seem) more scientific than a theoretical one, since the former avoids speculations and deals with what we have available. However, I personally subscribe to Neville Morley's and John Arnold's approach to the study of history and antiquity. Morley has eloquently showed that it is theory

> that enables us to make sense of the evidence and use it to create an account of the past. Historical sources do not 'speak' or present us with their intrinsic meaning and significance; rather, we give them meaning and significance by interpreting them.

Arnold, on the other hand, argued some years ago that "[f]or every historian, what is at stake is what actually happened—and what it might *mean*."[6] Thus, my approach is mainly directed to both the ancient context and the earliest forms of the theory as well as to how that theory has been slowly transformed into a generalization of 'euhemerism equals dead deified people.' The possible meaning of the theory and its interpretations preoccupies me in the first five chapters of the book, whereas the problem of how ancient and modern readers have interpreted and used the theory is mostly addressed in the last three chapters.

The generalization that stems from particular interpretations is not something unique with euhemerism within the study of reception history of ancient ideas as one might already know or perhaps imagine. In a short but extremely interesting volume, Page Dubois addresses a modern trend in the

U.S., according to which popular presses publish works by conservative authors, like William Bennett and Allan Bloom, who utilize the Graeco-Roman civilizations with "a reductive, one-dimensional, shallow interpretation" that seeks to "justify their political platform for America."[7] One could readily object to Dubois's argument by pointing out the rich bibliography, older and more recent, on antiquity—which, by the way, Dubois herself acknowledges.[8] This, however, virtually means nothing when seen against the actual reality, which is the transformation or selective utilization of ancient ideas in order to serve modern agendas. This hardly differs from what ancient euhemerism underwent in the works of the early Christian authors. Classicists are well aware, to return to the book's objective, of what, say, Diodorus or Lactantius—two figures I will be addressing in Chapter 3—tell us about Euhemerus's work, but they hardly provide any justification of why, in which context, and to what ends those two authors chose to use Euhemerus in the first place. This becomes even more complicated when we shift our focus toward the early Christian authors. Although those Church-related figures (cf. Chapter 6) never actually read either the lost original or the authors who saved Euhemerus's ideas (in whatever final form) from oblivion, they nevertheless utilized Euhemerus in their own way, in a selective and corrupted version, in order to address issues themselves and the early Christian communities were facing. In this manner, a new kind of euhemerism was created, which was further alienated from its most ancient version by later (primarily Christian) postclassical and modern thinkers. If we add to this the emergence of disciplines such as anthropology and sociology, in which 'euhemerism'—now a theory with a name—enjoyed wide reception, we come to the conclusion that today's euhemerism seems like an abstract reference to a theory that has nothing in common with its ancient progenitor.

Modern scholarship on euhemerism resembles, no doubt with exceptions, the way the early Christian authors dealt with Euhemerus's theory. This essentially means that most modern scholars resort to secondary or even tertiary sources about what euhemerism is, which are themselves largely influenced by the way the theory was altered in the first centuries of Christian domination. As I will argue, Euhemerus's euhemerism cannot be solely understood as a theory of deification of dead humans. The earliest available testimonies, that is, the first authors who included the (most likely modified) summaries or the translation of the lost original into their own works, offer us substantial information regarding that original's content that, practically, negates the common view of what euhemerism is all about. Like the early Christian authors, modern scholars still have little, if any, knowledge of the exact content of Euhemerus's euhemerism in those earliest sources. On the contrary, both parties have something in common: they are eminent examples of what Pierre Bayard describes as having knowledge of a work's *location* rather than its content.[9] To illustrate this further, imagine this: most people today have no difficulty classifying certain regimes under specific rubrics. As such, Castro's Cuba or Stalin's U.S.S.R. or Mao's People's Republic of China immediately invoke the term 'communist countries.' However, how many of those people can readily reply to the question of how communistic those regimes were when seen against Karl Marx's *Capital* or *Manifesto of the Communal Party*? Similarly, for many nowadays, Richard Dawkins and Sam Harris are exponents of atheism. Yet, the ancient philosopher Socrates is more often than not seen as an atheist. Are both Socrates and Sam Harris atheists in the same fashion? Hardly. To return to Bayard's point, what often determines our classification of works is not so much our personal contact with those works but what is said about them by other people: "To a significant extent, our discourse about books [and ideas] focuses on the discourse of other people about those books [and ideas], and so forth ad infinitum."[10] As such, the early Christian authors based their evaluations and interpretations of Euhemerus's theory on what their own sources claimed about Euhemerus (Chapter 6) and, surprisingly enough, modern scholars somehow perpetuate that tradition (Chapter 8).

This is a problem that is not restricted to the study of Euhemerus's theory. In his recent work on Orphism, Radcliffe Edmonds III deals with a similar case and addresses the problem of invoking Orpheus's name in texts or rites, thereby considering them as part of a wider tradition of 'Orphism' which, in his view, is more a fabrication of a category than an existing classification that shares a unilinear path:

> Who is labeling something as "Orphic" or describing it in terms that categorize it with other things labeled "Orphic"? What is the context for this classification? Even if the state of the evidence from antiquity often makes these questions difficult to answer, we can nevertheless try to determine whether the label is self-applied or applied by another.[11]

The problem of self- or external application of the term 'Orphic' is, in many respects, similar to the problem this book addresses regarding euhemer*ism*: a fabricated -ism, which seeks to bring together diverse cases without, however, taking into consideration the available ancient testimonies, nor the contexts within which many generations of authors, philosophers, religious people, and scholars adopted this classificatory -ism in order to serve their own particular agendas. After all, in any study of a theory or idea, it is far more productive not to merely name it but, to recall Jonathan Z. Smith's words, to locate it "within a history of tradition and to provide some sort of explanation for the processes of continuity and change."[12]

However, in order to proceed, I need to address the very title of the book, and especially what is here meant by theory of *religion*. Contrary to the various different interpretations and motivations that scholars have identified in the study of Euhemerus's theory,[13] I take his work as a straightforward case of a theory of religion; that is, as an attempt to provide an answer to either one or both of the questions that theories of religion generally seek to address—that of the origin and the function of religion (see Chapters 1 and 2). Nevertheless, the issue of what is here meant by 'religion' begs for some further elaboration. I have no interest in offering a definition of religion of my own, which as recent scholarship has demonstrated, it is not only difficult but also highly problematic as a scholarly pursuit.[14] If one adds to this the peculiarity of the very term 'religion' and its history, which is full of ideological baggage stemming from a (Protestant) Christian-centric milieu and supplemented by colonialism,[15] it becomes evident that there is so much disagreement among contemporary scholars that the attempt to find a common definition seems at present to be a lost cause. Throughout the book, however, I am referring to Euhemerus's theory of the origin of belief in gods, almost always adding the phrase "and religion."[16] As I will discuss in Chapters 1 and 2, the question of the origin of gods for the ancient philosophers was linked to the issue of 'belief in those gods.' People come to believe in the existence of gods for different reasons, as both Euhemerus and other thinkers—like Critias, Prodicus, and Democritus to name a few—claimed. In this sense, the concept of gods originates because people, for varied reasons as we will see, fulfill a specific need via the creation of and belief in the existence of gods. In this regard, many ancient thinkers—and definitely Euhemerus as well—took religion to be 'belief in gods.' This, however, does not mean that I am arguing that belief in supernatural agents is an appropriate or, worse, a universal definition of religion. Rather, I maintain that for some ancient thinkers, including Euhemerus, religion was *about* belief in gods. This, in turn, is a stipulative definition of ancient religion which does not claim any universality and I am fully aware that by employing such a definition I cannot simultaneously talk about everything in the world, across time and space, which is labeled, for various reasons and by different people, 'religion.' Thus, it goes without saying that this ancient definition, which is virtually implied rather than stated in the theory of euhemerism as well as in other ancient theories, cannot be applicable to other phenomena or traditions, which do not predicate their existence and function on such an assertion.

Nowhere does Euhemerus mention the Greek terms εὐσέβεια or θρησκεία, which are usually employed by modern authors to refer to—or, better, translate as—what for the ancient Greeks was the equivalent of what we conventionally call 'religion' in the modern world. So, why a theory of religion and not of gods? For many years, ancient Greek religion was seen as purely ritualistic, where belief had virtually no place in the study of Greek antiquity or was of secondary importance. However, Henk Versnel's publication of his *Coping with the Gods* (2011), attacked such an assertion furiously and for good reasons.[17] As he pointed out,

> the fact that Greek religion was basically a matter of ritual action in no way implies the consequence that Greeks did not believe in (the existence) of their gods. This would indeed imply a contradiction: how

does one communicate with divine beings through prayer, gift-giving, and attributing them a full scale of anthropomorphic (and allomorphic) features that we have been discussing throughout the present book, *without* believing (that is taking as true) that these beings exist (in whatever sense of the word 'exist')? The prerequisite of all these actions, especially prayer, is the belief that gods have power and are willing to interfere in human life. How would they do that in the perception of the worshippers without existing? Stating that Greek religion is ritualist [. . .] is either nonsense or a kind of sophistry run wild, which should be banished from scholarly discourse.[18]

In other words, Versnel's view, which I unreservedly share, advocates ancient Greek *thrēskeia* (θρησκεία) being predicated on the very existence of the gods, toward whom the actions/rituals were addressed. So, why a theory of 'religion'? I could perhaps propose an alternative title: *An Ancient Theory of Thrēskeia*. This suggestion reveals, however, a persistent problem in the study of ancient Greek practices and beliefs that are coined as 'religious,' which unfortunately has little to do with our sources or the way ancient Greeks dealt with their supernatural agents, and a lot to do with the scholarly problem of anachronism. But even more so, Versnel's reaction highlights another issue that is hardly addressed by scholars of religion—and justifiably so. All the works dealing with the problem of 'religion' and its definition, are exactly that: works on *religion*. In other words, they deal with a Latin term (*religio*), from which the English term 'religion' originates. The North American and Western European approach to the category 'religion,' somewhat *hegemonic* nowadays, although in many respects accurate to its observations, fails to acknowledge its own linguistic limitations, let alone the circularity of its approach, similar in a way to the very criticism it prides itself of putting forth: if seventeenth century colonials had Christianity in mind when classifying non-European traditions as religion, magic, superstition, etc., then modern Western scholars of religion see themselves as the 'only' valid critics of what the term 'religion' is and how and if it must be used, neglecting however a series of other concepts and terms, often more ancient and with a longer history than *religio* (and 'religion') has. Consider the following examples:

One of the implications of this approach is that 'religion' and other categories are not neutral descriptive and analytical terms but are on the contrary prescriptive and normative. [. . .] It is a classificatory device, a function of Euro-American world making, but it has acquired an appearance of being immutably in the nature of things. [. . .] A further methodological point is that confining the focus to English-language documents as I have done is an artificial procedure because the Latin root of 'religion' and its co-opting by the Catholic church means that the problem I am investigating is equally fundamental in all European languages that have significant descent from Latin. However, it is also surely true that the same methodological principles and approaches can be followed equally in other European languages.[19]

Further, I am not arguing that the phenomena generally described as 'religious' did not exist before the modern period, but instead (in a Foucauldian vein) that they did not exist in the same aggregate form that has come to define current uses of the term. On even a cursory analysis, the similarity of the words for 'religion' in contemporary European languages is striking (German [Ger.], *Religion*; Dutch [Du.], *religie*; French [Fr.], *religion*; Italian [It.], *religione*; Spanish [Sp.], *religión*; Portuguese [Pg.], *religião*; Romanian, *religia*; Polish, *religia*; Russian, религия, *religiia*). This parallel vocabulary demonstrates the terms' shared philology.[20]

Because the contemporary concept of religion is native to the European modern period and is constitutive of our modern Western social order, its application in interpretations of other contexts—for example, ancient Rome, nineteenth-century Japan—is conceptually anachronistic. Conceptual anachronism is not inherently problematic; we could rightly point to 'ideologies' or 'social hegemonies' in cultures that did not use such terms so long as these are recognized as our technical terms, doing our work in the analysis of others. However, in contexts where the term was not constitutive of the social order, scholars run the risk of carrying over connotations that are completely alien to the context under analysis.[21]

These are merely a few instances of how 'religion' is by definition approached in modern English-speaking scholarship—which, of course, can be further supported by publications in other Latin-based languages that share this methodological and theoretical approach. Naturally, when seen from this perspective, Greek 'religion' is indeed an anachronistic term. But so is every term that we utilize when studying ancient Greek (or Egyptian, Mesopotamian, Jewish, and so on) practices, ideas, customs, ideologies, trends, laws, norms, etc. Was ancient 'Athens'—which, by the way, is another Western term, this time an unfortunate transliteration, considering the actual name of the *polis* or *astu* being Ἀθῆναι (*Athēnai*)—a city? If so, in what manner? Historians, as Morley reminds us, "are happy to use a word such as 'city,' although it has rather different overtones and associations from such ancient terms as *polis*, *astu*, *municipium* and *urbs*." As he immediately adds, "[w]e do not have the option of a neutral, transparent, 'normal' language; we simply have to choose from a range of possible vocabularies, some more precise and technical than others but all equally time-bound and laden with anachronistic baggage."[22] Where does this leave us? Definitely not in an isolated place that will eventually lead to the dismissal of our ability to actually study those ancient peoples and their practices. Some modern works on the academic study of religion have argued that what scholars of 'religion' need to address is not whether the term 'religion' can be used but how it must be approached in order to avoid the ideological (Christian-centric) baggage it carries. The focus now has shifted from the applicability of the term to its utilization; that is, focusing on the differences between describing and redescribing:

> In this context, to describe is to give a practice a name that the practitioners themselves use; thus one is simply describing what they understand themselves to be doing, and one describes a practice as a religion when the practitioners themselves use or import that concept. But when one gives it a name not used by the practitioners themselves, one is redescribing or interpreting their practice.[23]

In this regard, I employ the term 'religion' throughout the book keeping in mind two important conditions: first, this is a book written in English, and a theory of *thrēskeia* would probably make little sense to interested readers, given its applicability only within the Greek-speaking world, ancient and modern;[24] second, I do not use the term as a descriptive but as a redescriptive tool without making any claim that the ancient Greeks themselves understood belief in gods as constituting 'religion,' that is, a genus somehow distinct from the rest of Greek culture. Moreover, I do not maintain that Greek religion had a uniform and standardized form throughout the ancient Greek-speaking world or in each stage of the vast and diverge Greek history, which was based on such a 'belief in gods.' I am arguing, however, that this is how it was approached by some ancient thinkers, including Euhemerus, who decided to address this phenomenon. Given that to talk about Greek religion means to invoke Greek mythology and the gods (either individually or as a system exemplified in the Greek pantheon), an ancient theory of 'religion' in such a context addresses *those* stories about *those* gods. Euhemerus's theory, thereby, does not comprise a universal theory of religion, although it was (and still is) universalized in the process, often constituting today a theoretical tool of the origin of the gods across time and space (cf. Chapter 8). In other words, I agree with William Cavanaugh's assessment that "[r]eligion is not simply an objective descriptor of certain kinds of practices that show up in every time and place. It is a term that constructs and is constructed by different kinds of political configurations,"[25] and one such construction was a specific, mainly Homeric and Hesiodic, Greek religious worldview that Euhemerus addressed by theorizing about it.

So, why study euhemerism? First and foremost, in this book I wish to demonstrate that, just as with atheism, as Tim Whitmarsh argued recently (see Chapter 4), theorizing about religion is not a 'modern' achievement. The questions of origin and function of religion preoccupied the most ancient thinkers, with Euhemerus being one of the most prominent. With very few exceptions, the vast majority of works on theories of religion begin their surveys with the seventeenth-century-onwards famous theorists, like David Hume, Friedrich Max Müller, Edward B. Tylor, Émile Durkheim and others, who are also deemed the founders of the scientific study of religion. Although allusions to ancient Greek philosophers are often present in such works, those ancient thinkers are hardly taken as exponents of a scientific study of religion. There are many reasons for such a view. First, a scientific study of religion is considered modern, whereas pre-modern explanations or dealings with religion are reduced into philosophical treatises that stem from a non-secular milieu. Unfortunately, the distinction between modern and ancient is not solely a chronological but chiefly a qualitative one in this context.[26] In this regard, ancient theorists are acknowledged as precursors of the study of religion but rarely, if at all, as full-fledged theorists of religion. In both Chapters 1 and 2 I discuss some ancient thinkers, primarily Euhemerus, as theorists of religion that deserve our attention. Consider, for example, the opening lines of David Hume's *The Natural History of Religion* (1757):

> As every enquiry which regards religion is of the utmost importance, there are two questions in particular which challenge our principal attention, to wit, that concerning its foundation in reason, and that concerning its origin in human nature. [. . .] But the other question, concerning the origin of religion in human nature, is exposed to some more difficulty.[27]

It is exactly that second question, the 'challenging and difficult' one, that Euhemerus—like others before and after him—attempted to answer. The success or failure of his theory has little value here. It is the very need to theorize about these issues that should be stressed and further examined.

Second, since the beginnings of modernity, antiquity has been the field of classicists and historians, especially in any discussion about ancient religion. Scholars of religion have, either forced by their lack of expertise, or agitated by the overwhelming data, deliberately left ancient history to historians and classicists, and simply utilized their findings. However, there is a disciplinary chasm present that is either not taken into consideration or simply ignored. Classicists and ancient historians, obviously with exceptions, tend to under-theorize rather than theorize about their data. This becomes even more apparent in any meta-theoretical examination of the ancient Greek world in general and ancient Greek religion in particular. Although I might seem to be generalizing, a survey of works on, say, ancient Greek religion, demonstrates the tendency to rely heavily on the sources and avoid any theoretical discussions, as if the field of ancient religion is in danger if a different approach, hooked more on theory rather than data, is employed. The present volume is basically an attempt to bring the two disciplines closer and show, to both camps, that there is more at stake. By employing the case of 'euhemerism,' I indicate how this lack of cooperation has led scholars to misinterpret and occasionally misuse Euhemerus's theory from antiquity onwards—and even more so today. The easiness of adopting unreflectively another -ism, has led to a diverse and often contradictory view of Euhemerus's theory, which is unfortunately expanded in other disciplines like sociology and anthropology or even political sciences. Hopefully, this book will manage to reevaluate and rectify one of the most ancient theories of religion and its reception from antiquity to the present. Considering the vast number of references employing 'euhemerism' in modern publications, it goes without saying that addressing every single one would result in a massive volume. Yet, my purpose is not to give an exhaustive list of usages and misusages of euhemerism but, rather, to point out the very existence of such usages and misusages.

Last but not least, I do not assert holding *the* true interpretation of euhemerism. The scarcity of our sources, the enigmatic figure of Euhemerus, the lack of any detailed ancient evaluation—positive or negative—of his theory all contribute to a rather difficult enterprise. Given that much of what I claim about Euhemerus's euhemerism in the following pages will probably raise some (or many) eyebrows, I am concluding this short introduction by resorting, once again, to John Arnold's words:

> [H]istorians, like everyone else, can misread, misremember, misinterpret, or misunderstand things. But in a wider sense, historians always get things 'wrong'. We do this first because we cannot ever get it totally 'right'. [. . .] We also get it 'wrong' because we cannot always agree with each other; we need to get it 'wrong' in our own ways.[28]

## Notes

1 I use the term 'pagan' within quotation marks throughout the book in order to indicate that I do not employ it in the Christian derogatory sense. Since, however, the term has been established in scholarship, I am using it as merely a classificatory term for lack of another, more persuasive term. For a recent discussion, see Jones 2014. The term 'early Christians' is equally problematic, considering that it is not a designator those late first- and early second-century actors employed. For example, see the discussion in McCutcheon 2015.
2 Livingstone 2014, 197.
3 Livingstone 2003, 11–12. Cf. 2014, 1.
4 Breed 2014, 100.
5 Garstad 2003, 311.
6 See Morley 2004, 3; Arnold 2000, 13, emphasis in the original.
7 Dubois 2001, 4.
8 Ibid., 8–9.
9 See Bayard 2007, 11.
10 Ibid., 45–46.
11 Edmonds III 2013, 77.
12 Smith 1993, xi.
13 Winiarczyk 2013, 99–108 successfully summarizes the interpretations of the theory suggested by various scholars, without however going beyond the mere description of those interpretations—this crucial section in his book is exhausted in just nine pages, where he covers seven different interpretations.
14 For an overview, see Asad 1993, 29; Arnal and McCutcheon 2013, 17–30; Martin 2014, 2–6; Murphy 2014, 1–9.

15 For a genealogy of the term, see Nongbri 2013. Cf. the discussion in McCutcheon 2007; Jensen 2014, 13–37. On the way colonialism determined what religion is and how a phenomenon is qualified as a religion, see, among others, the essays in Lopez 1995; King 1999; Gottschalk 2013; Chidester 2014. Cf. the interesting discussion in Pennington 2005, who follows another path, which takes the 'invention' of Hinduism as a collaboration between Hindus and British colonials. Contrary to the popular idea of colonialism as having absolute power, Pennington sees colonialism in India as a powerful regime which, nevertheless, sought to address "the needs and desires of certain classes of Indians whose support it required," thus seeing Hinduism as "the result of continuous historical processes that include but by no means are reducible to interventions by Orientalists, missionaries, and British administrators" (4; 6).

16 As I discuss in Chapter 1, Euhemerus's theory of the origin of belief in gods is not an attempt to seek the historical origin, that is, when does religion emerge for the first time in a universal human history, but the recurrent origin. I often use the phrase 'origins of gods' when referring to euhemerism, with which I refer to the origins of belief in gods.

17 See my discussion in Roubekas 2015.

18 Versnel 2011, 552, emphasis in the original. See the examples he mentions in 544–545. Even one of the most important exponents of the ritualist school, William Robertson Smith, argued over a century ago that

> [m]en would not be men if they agreed to do certain things *without having a reason for their action*; but in ancient religion the reason was not first formulated as a doctrine and then expressed in practice, but conversely, practice preceded doctrinal theory.
>
> (1927, 20, emphasis added)

19 Fitzgerald 2007, 24; 44–45. However, I disagree with Fitzgerald's last sentence. It is one thing to talk about the Latin-based languages and the Protestant or even Catholic utilization (and manipulation) of the term 'religion' and yet another when addressing European non-Latin based terminology. After all, in the latter case we do not anymore talk about 'religion' and, thus, different methodologies and approaches are indeed needed, focused on the specificity of each one of those languages and their particular semantic idiosyncrasies.

20 Josephson 2012, 9. Although Josephson is discussing extensively the relevant Japanese terminology, the linguistic/philological examples he employs here are bounded by the Latin term *religio*.

21 Martin 2015, 298.

22 Morley 2004, 26.

23 Schilbrack 2014. Cf. Nongbri 2008, 443; 2013. Voices for a complete abandonment of the term still remain, however, with Fitzgerald 2000 being the classical example.

24 I have here in mind Jan Bremmer's essay in an edited volume in honor of Walter Burkert, who although begins with the question of "[w]hat does the term 'religion' mean and what does that meaning imply for a contemporary history of Greek religion?" he nevertheless approaches the topic by resorting to the history of the term *religio* and refers to ancient authors like Cicero, Lucretius, Vergil, Lactantius and others, all coming from the Latin-speaking world (see Bremmer 1998, 10 ff.). It is, in a sense, unfortunate that modern scholarship on ancient Greek religion needs to constantly address the issue of 'religion' solely to satisfy a particular branch of the English-speaking scholarly world. It is worth remembering here Ivan Strenski's (2011, 284) words:

In an age with post-colonial sensibilities such as ours, the question naturally arises of why we might not instead be students of *dharma* or *sasana* instead, rather than *religion*? Why don't we organize our field in terms of notions original to other cultures? [. . .] After all, in a way, we already do so in terms of fields such as algebra and chemistry, words translating disciplines taken first from Arab culture (*al-jabr* and *al-kimiya*, respectively). Why wouldn't it make sense then to refer to what we call religious studies as dharmatology? We would then see what we call religion against the template of the Hindu notion of dharma, instead of doing as we do—reading dharma against the template of religion.

25  Cavanaugh 2009, 58.
26  See the discussion in Morley 2009, 4–5.
27  Hume 1889, 1.
28  Arnold 2000, 12.

# References

Arnal, William and Russell T. McCutcheon. 2013. *The Sacred Is the Profane: The Political Nature of "Religion"*. New York and Oxford: Oxford University Press.

Arnold, John H. 2000. *History: A Very Short Introduction*. Oxford: Oxford University Press.

Asad, Talal. 1993. "The Construction of Religion as an Anthropological Category." In *Genealogies of Religion: Disciplines and Reasons of Power in Christianity and Islam*, 27–54. Baltimore, MD: Johns Hopkins University Press.

Bayard, Pierre. 2007. *How to Talk about Books You Haven't Read*. Translated by Jeffrey Mehlman. New York: Bloomsbury.

Breed, Brennan W. 2014. *Nomadic Text: A Theory of Biblical Reception History*. Bloomington, IN and Indianapolis, IN: Indiana University Press.

Bremmer, Jan N. 1998. "'Religion', 'Ritual' and the Opposition 'Sacred vs. Profane'." In *Ansichten griechischer Rituale: Geburtstags–Symposium für Walter Burkert*, edited by Fritz Graf, 9–32. Stuttgart and Leipzig: B. G. Teubner.

Cavanaugh, William T. 2009. *The Myth of Religious Violence: Secular Ideology and the Roots of Modern Conflict*. New York and Oxford: Oxford University Press.

Chidester, David. 2014. *Empire of Religion: Imperialism and Comparative Religion*. Chicago, IL and London: University of Chicago Press.

Dubois, Page. 2001. *Trojan Horses: Saving the Classics from Conservatives*. New York and London: New York University Press.

Edmonds III, Radcliffe G. 2013. *Redefining Ancient Orphism: A Study in Greek Religion*. Cambridge: Cambridge University Press.

Fitzgerald, Timothy. 2000. *The Ideology of Religious Studies*. New York and Oxford: Oxford University Press.

Fitzgerald, Timothy. 2007. *Discourse on Civility and Barbarity: A Critical History of Religion and Related Categories*. New York and Oxford: Oxford University Press.

Garstad, Benjamin. 2003. "Review of M. Winiarczyk: *Euhemeros von Messene. Leben, Werk und Nachwirkung*." Classical Review 53 (2): 309–311.

Gottschalk, Peter. 2013. *Religion, Science, and Empire: Classifying Hinduism and Islam in British India*. New York and Oxford: Oxford University Press.

Hume, David. 1889 [1757]. *The Natural History of Religion*. London: A. and H. Bradlaugh Bonner.

Jensen, Jeppe S. 2014. *What is Religion?* New York and London: Routledge.

Jones, Christopher P. 2014. *Between Pagan and Christian*. Cambridge, MA and London: Harvard University Press.

Josephson, Jason A. 2012. *The Invention of Religion in Japan*. Chicago, IL and London: University of Chicago Press.

King, Richard. 1999. *Orientalism and Religion: Postcolonial Theory, India and the 'Mystic East'*. London and New York: Routledge.

Livingstone, David N. 2003. *Putting Science in its Place: Geographies of Scientific Knowledge*. Chicago, IL and London: University of Chicago Press.

Livingstone, David N. 2014. *Dealing with Darwin: Place, Politics, and Rhetoric in Religious Engagements with Evolution*. Baltimore, MD: Johns Hopkins University Press.

Lopez, Donald S. (Ed.). 1995. *Curators of the Buddha: The Study of Buddhism Under Colonialism*. Chicago, IL and London: University of Chicago Press.

Martin, Craig. 2014. *A Critical Introduction to the Study of Religion*. London and New York: Routledge.

Martin, Craig. 2015. "Theses on the Critique of 'Religion'." *Critical Research on Religion* 3 (3): 297–302.

McCutcheon, Russell T. 2007. *Studying Religion: An Introduction*. London and Oakville, CT: Equinox.

McCutcheon, Russell T. 2015. "Why Do You Seek the Living Among the Dead? (Luke 24:5)." In *A Modest Proposal on Method: Essaying the Study of Religion*, 125–139. Leiden and Boston, MA: Brill.

Morley, Neville. 2004. *Theories, Models, and Concepts in Ancient History*. London and New York: Routledge.

Morley, Neville. 2009. *Antiquity and Modernity*. Malden, MA and Oxford: Wiley-Blackwell.

Murphy, Tim. 2014. *Representing Religion: Essays in History, Theory and Crisis*. London and New York: Routledge.

Nongbri, Brent. 2008. "Dislodging 'Embedded' Religion: A Brief Note on a Scholarly Trope." *Numen* 55: 440–460.

Nongbri, Brent. 2013. *Before Religion: A History of a Modern Concept*. New Haven, CT and London: Yale University Press.

Pennington, Brian K. 2005. *Was Hinduism Invented? Britons, Indians, and the Colonial Construction of Religion*. New York and Oxford: Oxford University Press.

Roubekas, Nickolas P. 2015. "Belief in Belief and Divine Kingship in Early Ptolemaic Egypt: The Case of Ptolemy II Philadelphus and Arsinoe II." *Religio: Revue pro religionistiku* 23 (1): 3–23.

Schilbrack, Kevin. 2014. *Philosophy and the Study of Religions: A Manifesto*. Malden, MA and Oxford: Wiley-Blackwell.

Smith, Jonathan Z. 1993. *Map Is not Territory: Studies in the History of Religions*. Chicago, IL and London: University of Chicago Press.

Smith, William R. 1927. *Lectures on the Religion of the Semites*. 3rd edition. New York: MacMillan.

Strenski, Ivan. 2011. "Dharma, the Sacred, and Durkheim's Definition of Religion." *Relegere: Studies in Religion and Reception* 1 (2): 283–295.

Versnel, Henk S. 2011. *Coping with the Gods: Wayward Readings in Greek Theology*. Leiden and Boston, MA: Brill.

Winiarczyk, Marek. 2013. *The Sacred History of Euhemerus of Messene*. Translated by Witold Zbirohowski-Kościa. Berlin and Boston, MA: De Gruyter.

# 1    Euhemerus's Euhemerism

Theories of religion are attempts to interpret and explain phenomena identified and categorized as religions. They are generalizations about the category 'religion' rather than explanations of particular religions. There exists a certain classification of types of theories related to the presumptions adopted by the theorist who decides to address the issue of religion. This classification derives from the acceptance or not of the truth of religion, that is, whether God or gods actually exist. An affirmative reply takes religion to be a matter of revelation or divine intervention and does not question the existence of the supernatural or transcendent reality. Such a religionist (or, religious) approach to religion is effectively a theological one and thus prone to rejection when one examines religion as a social creation or human by-product.[1] On the other hand, theories that either deny or simply do not broach the question of the truth of god(s), but rather approach religion as a human creation that addresses specific human needs, are commonly categorized as naturalistic (or social scientific) approaches to religion.

The emergence of naturalistic theories of religion triggered, more or less, the modern formation of a scientific study of religion as a discipline distinct from theology; a historical and intellectual development that has recently been extensively studied and discussed.[2] This shift, from religion as the result of divine intervention or manifestation into the world to religion as a human creation was accompanied by several questions associated with the phenomenon of religion across time and space. As Jeppe Jensen put it in his discussion of the emergence of the scientific study of religion,

> [i]f religion does not emanate from God, where, then, does religion come from? In which human domain does religion have its origin? Is religion primarily an intellectual phenomenon concerned with human thought and reason? Or is it principally an ethical and moral matter concerned with duties and obligations toward the gods and fellow human beings? Or, again, is religion an emotional and aesthetic disposition concerned with the sense of beauty and harmony?[3]

These were questions that preoccupied the philosophers and thinkers of the Enlightenment and post-Enlightenment periods that virtually created the space for a naturalistic theorizing about religion. A more careful look at these questions, however, reveals the basic and fundamental issues that theorists need to address when formulating their theory of religion: those of the origin and function of religion. Both questions address the same critical issue; that is, religion arises due to a need and its function is to fulfill precisely that need.[4] Whereas the need varies from theorist to theorist, what remains common and unaffected is the principle that religion is the creation of human beings rather than 'something' in the world revealed by one or more non-human agents. A theory of religion may address both origin and function or simply one of the two questions, but the significance of a need is apparent in all theories, no matter how elusive it might be. As such, in modern theorizing about religion, prominent theorists such as, among others, Karl Marx, Sigmund Freud, Edward B. Tylor, Émile Durkheim, and Friedrich Max Müller approached the issue of origin and/or function as a result of different needs that vary widely, from shelter, clothing, and food to psychological processes pertaining to repressed sexual urges, and from the togetherness sought within a social group to explaining the workings of the universe.[5]

Theorizing about religion is not exhausted, however, to the issues of origin and function. Michael Stausberg has listed, along with his reservation regarding origin and its differentiation from beginnings,[6] two further questions that need to be addressed by a theory of religion; namely specificity (whether there is anything special or unique about religion) and structure (what is the role of the various elements typically identified as parts of religion, such as rituals, myths, institutions, etc.).[7] Although specificity and structure are certainly critical when one studies religion, they do not however hold a key role in formulating a theory of religion. Rather, both issues are central to the question of defining or determining what counts as religion to begin with. Although one may argue that a definition is necessary for the development of a theory of religion, some theorists do not offer a definition at all, whereas others do indeed begin their inquiries by proposing one.[8] However, in order for a theory of religion to qualify qua theory, the introduction of a definition of the subject matter is of course appreciated but not required. The issue of the existence of a need that elicits the emergence of religion, however, effectively implies a definition even if it is absent or not explicitly articulated by the theorist. As such, pre-modern or ancient theories of religion, as we shall see in this and the next chapter, primarily dealt with the issue of origins whereas some addressed the function of religion as well, but they were not preoccupied with specificity and structure. Furthermore, those theories did not include an explicit definition but they did imply one. The vast majority of those thinkers in antiquity—if not each and every one— saw religion largely defined as belief in gods, evocative of Edward B. Tylor's famous minimum definition of religion as "belief in spiritual beings."[9]

It goes without saying that neither ancient nor modern theories of religion actually answer in a satisfactory manner both questions of what is religion and how and why it emerged. There is no agreement among scholars of religion when dealing with these questions and all available theories have certain problems, unfilled gaps, and blind spots. A reason for this is that theorists are scholars who approach religion from within their own area of expertise or interest, thus offering an interpretation, explanation, or definition of religion that is usually restricted by the very examples of 'religion' that prompted them to deal with this troublesome phenomenon in the first place. Additionally, the problem of religion as a category remains a persisting one, given the lack of the category's homogeneity and the disagreement among scholars of religion. The very history or genealogy of the term is disputable and justifiably so, whereas what gets to count as religion and how that classification takes place has generated numerous debates within academic settings. It is for such reasons that theories of religion are rarely offered or dealt with nowadays and, when they are, they usually receive severe criticisms.[10] The same ensued in antiquity, with philosophers that offered naturalistic theories of religion being targeted as atheists, while their explanations either fell into oblivion or were utilized by other authors, both contemporary and subsequent ones, in order to serve their own agendas, and thereby were changed, altered, or misrepresented in the process. However, the inability of a theory to explain religion across time and space does not mean that theories of religion are to be scorned or discounted; their success or failure is irrelevant. The process of theorizing about religion is what established the discipline of religious studies itself, since those very attempts were—and still are—the reason that revealed the problematic nature of the category and called for a more scientific and wary study of religion. As Ivan Strenski recently put it, "[u]ntil the time thinkers started studying religion in order to understand and explain it, studying religion was the main business of the religions themselves."[11] Even if theories of religion today seem imperfect attempts, they constitute the very reasons why the study of religion has in recent years detached itself from the 'insider' perspective—or, at least, attempts to do so—a project that was initially conceived by thinkers of antiquity in the Greek-speaking world, such as Euhemerus of Messene, the introducer of the theory known today as euhemerism.

## Euhemerus's Euhemerism as a Theory of Religion

We know next to nothing about who Euhemerus was, when and where he lived, or what or who prompted him to address the issue of religion. The majority of the ancient sources indicate the city of Messene as Euhemerus's birthplace, whereas in three other cases other locations are cited (Tegea in the Peloponnese, Kos in the Aegean Sea, and Acragas in Sicily).[12] Messene (Μεσσήνη), however, can refer to either the city located in the southwest part of the Peloponnese in the province of Messenea, or to the homonymous colony in Sicily. Recent scholarship places Euhemerus in the Sicilian context, without however excluding the possibility of having visited the Greek metropolis. Franco De Angelis and Benjamin Garstad published a lengthy article in 2006 arguing in favor of the Sicilian context, providing solid arguments that urge us to accept the Sicilian cultural background of Euhemerus.[13] The issue of dating Euhemerus is, however, even more difficult to resolve. Scholars have offered various alternatives but what can be said with some certainty is that Euhemerus lived in the second half of the fourth and the first half of the third century BCE, which situates him in the early Hellenistic period.[14]

Euhemerus wrote a work comprising at least three volumes and entitled *Hiēra Anagraphē* (= *Sacred Inscription*; Greek: Ἱερὰ Ἀναγραφή).[15] It is unfortunate that it is not preserved in its entirety but only in fragmentary form and, mainly, through summaries and alleged verbatim renditions offered by later authors. The main source is Diodorus Siculus, the first-century-BCE historian, who preserved parts of the *Sacred Inscription* in the fifth (5.41.4–46.7) and sixth book (6.1) of his voluminous *Historical Library*. Unfortunately, the text from Diodorus's sixth book has not survived as well; instead, we find a summary in Eusebius of Caesarea, the Christian writer of the third and fourth century CE. Author of the monumental *Church History*, Eusebius preserved a summary of Diodorus's text in the second book of his *Preparation for the Gospel* (2.2.59b–61a). Quintus Ennius (239–169 BCE), the father of Roman poetry, translated the *Sacred Inscription* into Latin with the title *Euhemerus sive Sacra Historia*.[16] The source problems, however, do not cease here. Ennius's work is lost and we can only access it through Lactantius, the third- and fourth-century-CE Christian author, who incorporated fragments of Ennius's translation in the first book of his *Divine Institutes*. Thus it becomes evident that the *Sacred Inscription*, written around the end of the fourth or during the first decades of the third century BCE, is only accessible through the writings of authors who lived in a period that expands from the third century BCE to the fourth century CE. This roughly 700-year period of utilization and, subsequently, dissemination of Euhemerus's work (and theory) holds an equally important role as the theory itself as I will argue in Chapter 3. A summary of what we do have available regarding the content of the *Sacred Inscription* is offered below.

Euhemerus was a member of the royal court of King Cassander of Macedonia and he embarked on a journey into the Indian Ocean at the behest of the King. During his journey, he reached an unknown archipelago, of which the main island was called Panchaea, situated at the east of Arabia Felix. Panchaea was inhabited by different peoples, such as the autochthonous Panchaeans, Oceanites, Indians, Scythians, and Cretans. The capital city of the island was called Panara. The main site of the city was a temple dedicated to Zeus Triphyllius (that is, of the three tribes). There was a dominant tripartite social system, with certain duties, rights, and roles distributed among the population: the priests comprised the first group, with the artisans assigned next to them. The second group consisted of the farmers, and the third one of the soldiers, which also included the herdsmen. The priests constituted the group in charge of all the other social groups, and it was they who distributed the goods to the people of Panchaea. There was no private ownership, except home and garden. The prominent feature of Panchaea was its sacred character. Euhemerus makes a distinction between the heavenly or celestial and the earthly or human gods. For him, the former are eternal and thus immortal, whereas the latter are mortal. In the first group we find the sun, the stars, the moon, and the winds (that is, natural elements and phenomena). In the second group we encounter exemplary individuals who received immortal honor and glory due to their benefactions or power. The sanctuary of Zeus Triphyllius was established by Zeus himself when he was king of the whole inhabited earth. In the temple Euhemerus found a ceremonial couch of the god on which stood a large golden stele, containing in inscribed Panchaean characters (hieroglyphs) a summary of the deeds of Uranus, Cronus, and Zeus. In subsequent periods, the deeds of Artemis and Apollo were added by Hermes. Uranus, the first king, was a gentle and benevolent man, who was familiar with the movements of the stars. He was the first to honor the heavenly gods with sacrifices. His grandson, Zeus, travelled to different places of the known world. He went to Babylon, where he became the guest of Belus and then returned to the island of Panchaea, where he erected an altar honoring his grandfather. Returning from Panchaea, he visited Syria, Casius, and arrived to Cilicia, where he conquered the ruler Cilix after a battle. Zeus also visited many other nations, being honored by them and acknowledged as a god. In the last years of his life, and after having travelled around the world five times, he returned to the island of Crete, his birthplace, where he died and was interred.

Euhemerus's theory of religion is primarily preserved in the works of Eusebius and Lactantius (who follows Ennius) and secondarily in Diodorus, given that the sixth book of the *Historical Library* has only survived in fragmentary form. In order to determine whether Euhemerus can be deemed a theorist of religion we first need to break down his approach into its two constituent parts, namely the discussion regarding the origins of belief in the celestial or heavenly and the earthly or human gods.

## The Celestial Gods

The first branch of Euhemerus's theory addresses the existence of celestial gods that are acknowledged as such by Uranus. Those agents, who are identified for the first time through observing the celestial objects, are recognized as gods not simply because they exist in the heavens but primarily because they follow trajectories by moving in the empyrean. Uranus, who receives his name (Οὐρανός, literally 'heaven') from recognizing these heavenly gods (οὐρανίους θεούς), establishes the practice of sacrificing to them by performing the first rituals himself. The initiation, thus, of rituals offered to the celestial gods, who remain unnamed throughout the available sources, is to be found in the actions of one primordial beneficent and lenient king.[17] Thus, the origin of belief in the celestial gods and consequently the origin of religion as the combination of belief and practice is the result of one man's actions. The question of function remains somehow unanswered in the narrative. What is the need the emergence of belief in the celestial gods fulfills? Euhemerus, or the authors who decided to incorporate his writings in their works, neither explicitly explains nor addresses this question. A speculative answer could be that religion originates from the feelings of awe that humans experience from observing the ways the universe functions. However, this does not offer us a need for the emergence of religion but merely the process of the emergence itself. The need, in such a scenario, is for explanation. Uranus is credited not only for acknowledging the celestial objects as gods but also for introducing the very concept of gods. By understanding the movement of the stars, he assigns agency to them and subsequently introduces the rituals that are offered to those agents. The need is the explanation of the workings of the universe resulting from mere observation. If the celestial objects follow a routine movement in the heavens, as they indeed do, the question is why that is so. The answer is not a scientific but a religious one: the movement of the stars is due to one or many agents that have set those objects in motion and regulate their trajectories.

It is not clear, however, whether Euhemerus claimed that Uranus thought each star was itself divine and thereby a god or, alternatively, each one had a god 'behind' it, orchestrating and regulating its movement in the heavens. A solution could be given by Diodorus-via-Eusebius, who clarifies Euhemerus's theory by arguing that "each of these [objects] has an ever-lasting genesis and duration" (ἀίδιον ἔχειν τὴν γένεσιν καὶ τὴν διαμονήν).[18] However, the phrase can be interpreted in two fashions: either that each star/planet is self-created, or that it was created by an everlasting source.[19] The former implies that each star is a god, whereas the latter asserts the existence of a god behind every star, or even a group of stars; that is, a god who causes the movement of a celestial object or even a group of celestial objects. Yet, in the same excerpt, Eusebius, in citing Euhemerus, claims that Diodorus also adds the winds to the list of natural phenomena observed by Uranus. Furthermore, in Diodorus's fifth book, which does survive, we read:

προσηνῶς ἐνδιατρίβειν ἐν τῷδε τῷ τόπῳ, καὶ ἀπὸ τοῦ ὕψους ἐφορᾶν τόν τε οὐρανὸν καὶ τὰ κατ' αὐτὸν ἄστρα.

[Uranus] took great pleasure in this place [the mountain], and from its height he observed the heaven and its array of stars.[20]

Why Diodorus himself does not repeat here what comes out of this observance generates a great deal of confusion. Not only it is not mentioned that Uranus acknowledges those objects as the so-called heavenly gods, but the institution of sacrifices on the mountain is eventually established not by him but by priests, without providing an explanation as to whether those sacrifices were in honor of the heavenly gods or of Uranus himself as a commemoration of his greatness and his introduction of the concept of god(s).[21] Given, however, that the fifth book was dedicated to utopias and islands and their social organization, whereas the lost sixth book presumably focused on the issue of religion, one could argue that Diodorus simply chose not to expand on the issue of how religion emerges when discussing the social realities of Panchaea. Additionally, the inclusion of winds found in Eusebius's summary is not mentioned by Diodorus. This, however, causes fewer problems, since the inclusion of winds or other natural phenomena does not alter the need for the explanation of the workings of the universe, for which religion emerges according to the available texts. It could well have been the case that Euhemerus included, even in passing, more natural phenomena among Uranus's heavenly gods, but the celestial objects must have been at the crux of his theory.

The question of the establishment of sacrifices as a medium of honoring the gods is not sufficiently explained by our sources, nor is the goal of those rituals. The given explanation, that is, paying homage to the heavenly gods, does not insinuate that they also had some other practical objective. In other words, the offered sacrifices were mere offerings and not ways to manipulate the celestial objects and/or the natural phenomena; that is, to make requests pertaining to either interrupting their routine, or acting in favor of the petitioners. Uranus, in Euhemerus's explanation and always as transmitted to us by Eusebius, is thus the introducer of the concept of gods, belief in the gods, and rituals; namely, what would qualify as religion when the category is defined as the combination of primarily belief in gods and, secondarily, practices stemming from that belief. The establishment of kingship by Uranus, which is presented here as appearing for the first time in Greek history as a political system according to our testimonies, must be appreciated as closely related to religion. All of our sources agree on presenting Uranus as the first king.[22] Euhemerus is claiming that Zeus's grandfather was the first king on earth, which in turn means that he introduces monarchy in the form of kingship along with religion. The same scheme applies, as we will see, to the second branch of Euhemerus's theory, although in that case the relationship between politics and religion is more explicitly oriented toward the exercise of power rather than to benefaction.

It is evident that Uranus was known with another name before introducing to the world the concept of heavenly gods. Unfortunately, his initial name is not mentioned in our sources, while Uranus is obviously a name assigned to him after his introduction of the celestial gods. We can only infer that he received that name from his fellow citizens as an honorary title, since the introduction of the concept of gods was apparently a cultural development that was welcomed by his people. There is, however, an inconsistency encountered in our sources pertaining to the chronological sequence of the facts being presented by Diodorus, Eusebius, and Lactantius. In his fifth book, Diodorus does not mention a name-change but is restricted to calling Uranus an ancient king of the whole world.[23] Eusebius, as we have seen, asserts that Uranus received that name (Οὐρανός) for acknowledging and honoring the gods of heaven (τοὺς οὐρανίους θεούς). Lactantius, however, complicates this issue. In citing Ennius, he argues that:

> *in Sacra Historia sic Ennius tradit: deinde Pan eum deducit in montem, qui vacatur Caeli sella, postquam eo ascendit, contemplatus est late terras ibique in eo monte aram creat Caelo primusque in ea ara Iuppiter sacrificavit. in eo loco suspexit in caelum quod nunc nos nominamus, idque quod supra mundum erat, quod aether vocabatur, de sui avi nomine caelum nomen indidit idque Iuppiter quod aether vocatur placans primus caelum nominavit eamque hostiam, quam ibi sacrificavit, totam adolevit.*

> Ennius in his *Sacred History* reports as follows: "Then he was taken to the Panchaean mountain which is called the Pillar of Heaven. When Jupiter had climbed it, he gazed all over the lands, and there on the mountain he built an altar to heaven, and he was the first to sacrifice on the altar. There he looked up at what we now call heaven, and he gave the name heaven to what is above the world, which used to be called aether, naming it after his grandfather, and Jupiter was the first to call what used to be called aether heaven, doing so in a placatory spirit; the sacrificial victim that he offered there he burnt entire."[24]

Lactantius's alleged verbatim citation of Ennius's Latin translation of the *Sacred Inscription* contradicts what Eusebius tells us regarding how Uranus received his name. If until the time of Zeus, the heavens were known as aether, then we must assume that Uranus did not have another name before introducing the very idea of gods. Lactantius's version does indeed agree with Diodorus's narration in the fifth book of the *Historical Library*, but not as well with what Eusebius claims that was mentioned in the lost sixth book. If we take Eusebius's version as the correct one, then the renaming of aether to heaven was probably that first king's deed, who was then named Uranus, but now for introducing not only the concept of heavenly gods and honoring them with sacrifices but also the very term 'heaven,' that is, οὐρανός. There is no possible way to reconcile our sources and assign a chronological order to the facts presented in order to determine whether Uranus did have another name, or Zeus is to be credited for renaming the sky from aether to heaven. This source problem has one further consequence, which threatens the euhemeristic terminology itself and on which the theory is based. If Lactantius is correct, we must then assume that those celestial or heavenly gods, mentioned in Eusebius, were not indeed called as such. The widely accepted οὐράνιοι θεοί (heavenly gods) must have had another rendition, such as aether gods or something in those lines.

## The Earthly Gods

The second branch, which came to be known as mainstream or ancient euhemerism, deals with the earthly or human gods. Undoubtedly, Euhemerus is primarily known for this aspect of his approach to religion as indicated by a quick look in the numerous works that cite his name or theory. The discussion on that group of gods is revolving around the figure of Zeus, who is obviously presented as the protagonist of the *Sacred Inscription*.

Euhemerus approaches the traditional Greek gods, and particularly the most powerful and known god of Mt. Olympus, not as real divine agents but as mere humans that were eventually seen as gods. The central role of the traditional Greek deities in the *Sacred Inscription* is evident and undisputable in our sources: heroes or other mythological figures are not broached. Eusebius presents Diodorus saying that the book itself was written to address the earthly gods rather than both divine groups. The motive behind the writing of the *Sacred Inscription* seems to be the "monstrous set of tales concerning the gods" as were invented by Homer, Hesiod, Orpheus, and other poets.[25] It was already known from the fifth century BCE that it was the poets who gave the details regarding the Olympian gods to the people, as Herodotus eloquently put it:

ἔνθεν δὲ ἐγένετο ἕκαστος τῶν θεῶν, εἴτε δή αἰεὶ ἦσαν πάντες, ὁκοῖοί τε τινές τὰ εἴδεα, οὐκ ἠπιστέατο μέχρι οὗ πρώην τε καὶ χθὲς ὡς εἰπεῖν λόγῳ. Ἡσίοδον γὰρ καὶ Ὅμηρον ἡλικίην τετρακοσίοισι ἔτεσι δοκέω μευ πρεσβυτέρους γενέσθαι καὶ οὐ πλέοσι. οὗτοι δὲ εἰσὶ οἱ ποίσαντες θεογονίην Ἕλλησι καὶ τοῖσι θεοῖσι τὰς ἐπωνυμίας δόντες καὶ τιμάς τε καὶ τέχνας διελόντες καὶ εἴδεα αὐτῶν σημήναντες.

However, it was only the day before yesterday, so to speak, that the Greeks came to know whence each of the gods originated, whether all of them had always existed, and what they were like in their visible forms. For I take it that Homer and Hesiod lived no more than four hundred years before my time. They are the poets who composed a theogony for the Greeks and gave the gods their names and epithets, distinguished their honors and functions, and indicated their visible forms.[26]

This historization not of the gods themselves, in this case, but of the creation by the poets of what would be the official Greek beliefs regarding the characteristics of those agents, could have motivated Euhemerus to write the *Sacred Inscription* and respond to that construction. This explanation, however, makes Euhemerus an advocate of anti-anthropomorphism—similar to the teachings of Xenophanes of Colophon to whom I will turn in the next chapter—rather than a denier of the divine nature of those gods. On the contrary, Euhemerus is not merely interested in denuding the traditional gods of their anthropomorphic depiction but is primarily focused on stripping them of divinity per se.

In the *Sacred Inscription* Zeus is credited for the creation of the traditional pantheon. According to the narrative, he built the massive temple in Panchaea and erected the golden column upon which he wrote the deeds of his ancestors along with his own activities and exploits. Eusebius mentions that on the stele one could find the deeds of Uranus, Cronus, and Zeus, while Diodorus in the fifth book does not include Cronus but appends the names of Hermes, Artemis, and Apollo as chronologically later additions. Lactantius, on the other hand, argues that Zeus only inscribed his achievements on the gold column, without mentioning any of the other traditional gods.[27] The lack of agreement in our sources creates certain problems when attempting to reconstruct the content of the golden stele. The absence of any information regarding the length and height of the column is not of much help either. Eusebius claims that what was encountered on the stele was merely a summary rather than a detailed biography of those figures. One has to assume that what truly mattered was the narration of the deeds and achievements of the characters in question rather than a detailed description of their lives. Eusebius insists on that in his summary of Diodorus's sixth book, where he gives a very brief genealogy starting from Uranus down to Zeus.[28] Cronus is here mentioned in passing as the connecting link between Uranus and Zeus, which coincides with the complete absence of his name in Diodorus's fifth book. On the contrary, Lactantius gives us a much more detailed genealogy, which echoes more what the traditional poets would claim than what Euhemerus himself would have said.[29] Surprisingly, Lactantius's citation of Ennius is primarily focused on Cronus rather than Uranus or Zeus. In a Hesiodean fashion, Lactantius has Cronus plotting to have Zeus killed, which results in Zeus's finding out about the conspiracy and chasing Cronus, who eventually ends up in Italy where he hides himself to avoid Zeus's armed men.[30]

If we should see the *Sacred Inscription* as a work primarily interested in the origins of belief in gods to be found in the deification of kings, then Eusebius's and Diodorus's versions seem more properly located within this context. Lactantius's—or, better, Ennius's—version creates a weak link in the succession of prominent kings who managed to be deified, which puts into jeopardy the idea itself. Deification here should be seen as a characteristic of kings, even though the absence of a divine Cronus from all available sources could be an indication of divine status not being assigned to a king automatically or merely due to his title, but only if the person in question had earned it.[31]

The deification process is a twofold one. According to the *Sacred Inscription*, Uranus is posthumously deified by Zeus, who establishes an altar in honor of his grandfather and offers the first sacrifice to him.[32] It is not clear whether Zeus deifies Uranus due to being the first to acknowledge and honor the celestial gods, or simply out of respect and admiration for his ancestor.

The latter seems more plausible given the lack of explanation in our sources; if Zeus would have wanted to deify Uranus for being the one to introduce the celestial gods to the world, then, I think, such information would have been preserved in all or at least some of our sources. In this first level of deification as an explanation of the origins of anthropomorphic gods, there is no clear indication of the why of origin that would also offer an answer to the question of the function of religion. There is no hint or discussion of Uranus being able to affect the living, which would transform this first level of origins into an ancestor cult, encountered in many traditions around the world. In that case, religion would have originated in order to placate the ancestral spirit—now transformed into the god Uranus—that would in turn provide us the need for which religion originates and functions.

Zeus's deification, however, follows a radically distinctive path. The protagonist of the *Sacred Inscription* is deified ante mortem. We encounter two different ways in the sources according to which his deification took place. According to Eusebius, Zeus's deification followed a bottom-up sequence: he is seen as traveling to various places of the known world and encountering local potentates, who either accept him or face him in battle, only to be eventually defeated by the powerful king. Among the figures mentioned are Casius in Syria, Cilix in Cilicia, and Belus in Babylon. Zeus's deification was immediate: "he travelled to numerous other nations as well all of which paid honors to him and publicly proclaimed him a god."[33] Eusebius does not provide more information regarding the actual processes of deification. Lactantius, on the other hand, informs us that the process involved a top-down sequence, with Zeus setting up shrines dedicated to himself by conceptualizing and executing a cunning plan. To each place he visited, upon departure,

> *iubebat sibi fanum creari hospitis sui nomine, quasi ut posset amicitiae ac foederis memoria conservari [. . .] quod ille astutissime excogitavit, ut et sibi honorem divinum et hospitibus suis perpetuum nomen adquireret cum religione coniunctum [. . .] hoc modo religionem cultus sui per orbem terrae Iuppiter seminavit et exemplum ceteris ad imitandum dedit.*

> gave orders for a shrine to be built to him in the name of his host, as if a memory of the friendship and agreement could be so preserved [. . .] It was a very clever idea of his: he acquired for himself divine honors and for his hosts a name for ever, linked with a religious cult [. . .] In this way Zeus spread the celebration of his cult throughout the world and made it an example for everyone else to follow.[34]

If we take Lactantius's words as actually representing the deification process missing from Eusebius, then Zeus is virtually self-deified. One could claim that Eusebius is offering merely the result of Zeus's actions, whereas Lactantius a more detailed description of the deification process.

In order to deal with this branch of Euhemerus's approach as a theory of religion, we need to address the issue of the need in response to which religion originates and aims to fulfill. Based on the process, that is, bottom-up or top-down deification of Zeus, Euhemerus's second branch of his theory may or may not qualify as a fully fledged theory of religion. But there are certain problems that need to be addressed, especially when this branch of Euhemerus's approach is seen as a theory of religion. First, this explanation is not a generalization but rather a theory of the origins of Greek gods—still, one that refuses their divinity. By claiming that the traditional deities were mere humans, Euhemerus apparently denied their divine nature and not merely their anthropomorphic descriptions. Or, possibly, he accepted the Homeric and Hesiodic anthropomorphism but ruled out the divine nature of those agents. Greek traditional religion, in this way, is based not on belief in gods but, rather, it is seen as a case of misrepresentation of events that occurred deep into the distant past. Second, whether the proclamation of his divine nature was the result of a decision taken by the various nations that he visited or due to Zeus's own arrogance, religion pre-exists in both plausible contexts. That is, if we solely accept Eusebius's narration, then the peoples who honored and proclaimed Zeus to be a god already had the concept of religion as 'belief in gods,' which implies that we either need to see their proclamation as merely an honorary but not a religious action—which, in turn, would make Zeus a god-like figure but not a real god—or argue for a second stage of religion. Still, in order to have a second stage we would also have a new need, which does not preclude the coexistence of the two stages.[35] If Eusebius is right, then the need is on the part of the group; religion is created by a group of people in order to express their gratitude toward and possibly secure the protection of a powerful king. If, on the other hand, we take Lactantius's more detailed description of the deification process at face value, then the problem is that self-deification cannot be seen as an answer to a need apart from satisfying a potentate's arrogance. As such, in the first case, the commemoration of Zeus's actions and power and his subsequent proclamation as god does fulfill a specific need. However, one could argue that if humans already have the concept of gods, it is clear that they already have individual gods, which makes this secondary stage of religion as merely introducing new members in their pantheon, and thereby cannot be seen as a new theory of religion but simply as a second stage of religion. In the second case, on the other hand, the origin of religion as self-deification and its subsequent imposition is not fulfilling the need of those who accept and practice religion but only of the individual who imposes it—that can simply be the result of one's vanity. Still, apart from arrogance (*insolentia*), as Lactantius argues, Zeus does not gain anything more than simply the pleasure of his self-deification, given that following the establishment of the joint cults he permanently departs from each country, only to return much later without knowing what exactly he did in his second, third, etc. visits. The result would be that religion would simply die out after Zeus's departure or his death. The power of religion, according to theories of religion, is its persistence rather than its immediate extinction that begs for a theory in the first place. The need must be strong enough that will make religion a persisting phenomenon rather than a one-off incident in human history, in a specific place, and involving a particular group of people, no matter how extensive that group might be. This problem inevitably prompts us to consider the importance of the first group of gods, that is, the celestial or heavenly agents, as the means through which we can explain the second group of gods in Euhemerus's theory.

\* \* \*

The twofold approach to religion that Euhemerus promoted has many similarities and differences with some of the most known modern theories of religion. It is evident that the distinction between heavenly or celestial and earthly or human gods that Euhemerus argued about cannot be used interchangeably. It is only the former part of his approach that can qualify as a fully fledged theory of religion, that is, a generalization about the category itself, whereas the second part balances between two options. It is unclear and thus debatable whether for Euhemerus the first branch of his approach does not entail the denial but, rather, the acceptance of the divinity of those gods. With the need being that of an explanation of the workings of the universe, Euhemerus's theory is seemingly quite close to the one offered by the Victorian anthropologist Edward B. Tylor (1832–1937) and his theory of animism. For Tylor, animism emerges from the determinant difference between the living and the dead, that is, the universal fact of motion and mobility. The logical conclusion is that everything in the world has an anima (soul), which eventually leads to the notion of spiritual beings as personalities, who are to be found everywhere except for humans. The result is that spiritual beings

> are held to affect or control the events of the material world, and man's life here and hereafter; and it being considered that they hold inter-course with men, and receive pleasure or displeasure from human actions, the belief in their existence leads naturally, and it might almost be said inevitably, sooner or later to active reverence and propitiation.[36]

Within this context, we could argue that Uranus's observance of the stars and the acknowledgment that they are controlled or set in motion by divine beings, is not too far detached from Tylor's notion of spiritual beings affecting or controlling "the events of the material world." Furthermore, Uranus's establishment of sacrifices to those celestial gods agrees with Tylor's eventual "reverence and propitiation." Additionally, by arguing that spiritual beings, that is, gods for Tylor, are not to be found in humans, Tylor's theory of animism seems compatible to Euhemerus's second group of gods and his denial of their divinity. It is surprising that, even though Tylor mentions euhemerism, albeit in its later form and solely when discussing mythology, he does not consider Euhemerus's explanation as a theory of religion and only deals with it as an explanation of myths, although an erroneous one.[37]

It must be noted, however, that for Tylor the truth of religion is simply denied. The notion of spiritual beings and the ensuing ideas are merely "theological systems devised by human reason, without supernatural aid or revelation."[38] In other words, his naturalistic theory of religion does not agree with Euhemerus's seemingly religionist view of religion in its first instance. However, the scarcity of sources does not allow for a better understanding of Euhemerus's theory regarding this issue. If Uranus's introduction of the celestial gods was accompanied by Euhemerus's criticism, in a way similar to Tylor's, then it must be seen as a naturalistic rather than a religionist theory. If, on the other hand, what Euhemerus implies is the reality of those gods, then he deviates considerably from Tylor's view of religion.

Accepting the latter as a possible explanation, we should count Euhemerus's theory among the religionist ones. Uranus's introduction of the celestial gods is the result of an unexpected encounter with them, similar to the German-born philologist and orientalist Friedrich Max Müller's (1823–1900) theory of religion: "Thus sunrise was the revelation of nature, awakening in the human mind that feeling of dependence, of helplessness, of hope, of joy and faith in higher powers, which is the source of all wisdom, the spring of all religion."[39] Among the various things in the world that can be related to gods "it is the intangible objects 'such as the sky, the stars, the sun, the dawn, the moon' that are sublime enough to produce outright *deities*."[40] Those gods, however, remain unnamed by Uranus but the origin of belief in gods is indeed the result not of longing for contact with gods but merely of experiencing their existence in the natural world in general, and in the celestial phenomena in particular. Nevertheless, any proposed similarity between Euhemerus and Müller must be restricted to this basic principle.

An anticipated criticism here is whether Euhemerus's view of religion is actually universal, that is, a generalization about the category of gods and, subsequently, religion. It is obvious that Euhemerus only addresses the Greek pantheon and beliefs. This, in turn, means that he is eventually offering a theory of the origin and function of the Greek gods (and, thus, religion) rather than a theory of religion across time and space. Although such an argument is valid and extremely difficult to dispute, as we will see, euhemerism has been universalized by later readers and scholars. This has transformed the Greek-centric ancient euhemerism into a full theory pertaining to the origins of gods and religion wherever and whenever they are to be found. Nevertheless, we should not easily disregard the common view in antiquity of the centrality of the Greek culture in the Mediterranean world, partly exemplified in the known dipole of Greeks and barbarians. In this sense, one could argue that Euhemerus's view of the Greek pantheon and religious beliefs was a criticism of the most noble and superior form of religion, that is, *the* religion, which could therefore be applied throughout the rest of the ancient world.

Euhemerus's theory of religion, with its twofold development, was not however as innovative as one might think. The distinction between heavenly or celestial and earthly or human gods is one fairly popular idea in antiquity, which has offered some theories that precede the author from Messene and which, most likely, influenced his own approach to religion.

## Notes

1 Known religionist approaches were promoted by, among others, Mircea Eliade (1959) and John Hick (2005). For a discussion, see Clarke and Byrne 1993.
2 There are numerous publications on this topic. For example, see Capps 1995; Sharpe 2005; Stroumsa 2010; 2015; Turner 2014, 357–380.
3 Jensen 2014, 15.
4 Segal 2005, 50.
5 There are many works on theories of religion that discuss in detail the approaches employed by theorists and the answers they offer to the questions of origin and function, from the now classic Evans-Pritchard 1965 to more contemporary ones, such as Preus 1987; Kippenberg 2002; Deal and Beal 2004; Pals 2014; Strenski 2015.
6 Segal 2005, 49 describes the difference between beginnings and origins as recurrent ("why religion arises whenever and wherever it arises") and historical ("where and when religion first arose") origin.
7 Stausberg 2009, 3–6. For a thorough postmodern discussion on the problem of studying origins in the academic study of religion, see Masuzawa 2015; for a similar approach from the discipline of Classics, see López-Ruiz 2015, 369.
8 The former group is represented by Max Weber and his discussion in the *Sociology of Religion*, while the latter by Émile Durkheim in his *The Elementary Forms of Religious Life* and Edward B. Tylor in his *Primitive Culture*. However, there are theorists, such as Sigmund Freud, who in different works offer different definitions of religion.
9 Tylor 1883, 383.
10 See Stausberg 2010 for a detailed discussion of why theories of religion are generally avoided within the academic study of religion. On the history or genealogy of the term, see the excellent Nongbri 2013, while the issue of how religions are classified is brilliantly discussed in the influential Masuzawa 2005. There have been recent attempts to define and offer a theory of religion, such as Tweed 2006 and Riesebrodt 2010. Segal 2006 has pointed out the problem with postmodernism and its ramifications for the social scientific study of religion in general and theories of religion in particular.
11 Strenski 2015, 4–5.
12 See Winiarczyk 1991, T 1C (henceforth W.) and the discussion in Winiarczyk 2013, 5–6.
13 De Angelis and Garstad 2006. Despite the criticism their approach received by Marek Winiarczyk (2013, 6), who is skeptical toward anything that is not supported by concrete historical or textual evidence, I believe that their argumentation is solid and unlikely to be disputed in the near future.

14 Contrary to Winiarczyk 2013, 5, who makes Euhemerus's dating even broader by arguing that "at most one can say that he lived in the 4th/3rd BC," I think that based on the available sources one can narrow down that dating to the second half of the fourth and the first half of the third century BCE. Winiarczyk, however, is right to dispute an even more accurate dating, as he correctly points out in his discussion on the issue (2013, 1–5).

15 The information regarding the minimum length of the *Sacred Inscription* is mentioned by Athenaeus, *Deipnosophists* 14.658e–f (cf. W. T 77), who is also one of the authors who offer an alternative birthplace for Euhemerus as he connects him with the island of Cos.

16 Winiarczyk 2013, 109–122 has offered the best analysis of Ennius's translation and its actual title of the work in Latin.

17 Eusebius, *Preparation for the Gospel* 2.2.58–59 (W. T 49).

18 Eusebius, *Preparation for the Gospel* 2.2.53 (W. T 25).

19 The latter is argued by Clay and Purvis 1999, 99.

20 Diodorus Siculus, *Historical Library* 5.44.6 (W. T 50).

21 Diodorus Siculus, *Historical Library* 5.44.7 (W. T 34).

22 Eusebius, *Preparation for the Gospel* 2.2.58 (W. T 49): μετὰ ταῦτά φησι πρῶτον Οὐρανὸν γεγονέναι βασιλέα; Lactantius, *Divine Institutes* 1.13.14 (W. T 51A): *initio, inquit, primus in terris imperium summum Caelus habuit. is id regnum una cum fratribus suis sibi instituit atque paravit*; Lactantius, *Epitome of Divine Institutes* 14.3 (W. T 51B): *Euhemerus eundem Uranum primum in terram regnasse.*

23 Diodorus Siculus, *Historical Library* 5.44.6 (W. T 50).

24 Lactantius, *Divine Institutes* 1.11.63 (W. T 62).

25 Eusebius, *Preparation for the Gospel* 2.2.58 (W. T 8): τῶν δὲ μυθολόγων Ὅμηρος καὶ Ἡσίοδος καὶ Ὀρφεὺς καὶ ἕτεροι τοιοῦτοι τερατωδεστέρους μύθους περὶ θεῶν πεπλάκασιν.

26 Herodotus, *Histories* 2.53.1–2. The translation is here drawn from Henrichs 2010, 27.

27 Eusebius, *Preparation for the Gospel* 2.2.57 (W. T 36): ἐν τούτῳ τῷ ἱερῷ στήλην εἶναι χρυσῆν, ἐν ᾗ τοῖς Παγχαίοις γράμμασιν ὑπάρχειν γεγραμμένας τάς τε Οὐρανοῦ καὶ Κρόνου καὶ Διὸς πράξεις κεφαλαιωδῶς; Diodorus Siculus, *Historical Library* 5.46.7 (W. T 37): κατὰ μέσην δὲ τὴν κλίνην ἔστηκε στήλη χρυσῆ μεγάλη, γράμματα ἔχουσα τὰ παρ' Αἰγυπτίοις ἱερὰ καλούμενα, δι' ὧν ἦσαν αἱ πράξεις Οὐρανοῦ τε καὶ Διὸς ἀναγεγραμμέναι, καὶ μετὰ ταύτας αἱ Ἀρτέμιδος καὶ Ἀπόλλωνος ὑφ' Ἑρμοῦ προσαναγεγραμμέναι; Lactantius, *Divine Institutes* 1.11.34 (W. T 65): *ubi auream columnam positam esse ab ipso Iove titulus indicabat, in qua columna sua gesta perscripsit, ut monumentum posteris esset rerum suarum.*

28 Eusebius, *Preparation for the Gospel* 2.2.59–60 (W. T 49; T 53; T 60).

29 See Lactantius, *Divine Institutes* 1.14.1–8 (W. T 54).

30 Ibid., 1.14.11–12 (W. T 58).

31 Thus it becomes evident that it is one thing to claim that 'all' kings become gods and another that all gods were once (or still are) kings. Cronus is not depicted as a god in any of the available testimonies, which leads us to accept that euhemerism as a principle of 'all ancient gods were primarily kings' is not accurate. Obviously, Euhemerus allowed for kings—even those belonging to a 'divine' dynasty—not becoming or deemed gods.

32 Eusebius, *Preparation for the Gospel* 2.2.61 (W. T 61); Lactantius, *Divine Institutes* 1.11.63 and 65 (W. T 62; T 52).

33 Eusebius, *Preparation for the Gospel* 2.2.61 (W. T 61).

34 Lactantius, *Divine Institutes* 1.22.22–23; 26 (W. T 64A).

35 Among the modern theorists of religion, Max Weber's theory as presented in his *The Sociology of Religion* is a classic example of different stages of religion, each with its own distinct need. See Weber 1963.
36 Tylor 1883, 385–386.
37 Ibid., 252–253.
38 Ibid., 386.
39 Müller 1867, 96.
40 Segal forthcoming, citing Müller 1878, 174; emphasis in the original.

## References

Capps, Walter H. 1995. *Religious Studies: The Making of a Discipline.* Minneapolis, MN: Fortress Press.

Clarke, Peter B. and Peter Byrne. 1993. *Religion Defined and Explained.* New York: St. Martin's Press.

Clay, Diskin and Andrea Purvis. 1999. *Four Island Utopias.* Newburyport, MA: Focus.

De Angelis, Franco and Benjamin Garstad. 2006. "Euhemerus in Context." *Classical Antiquity* 25 (2): 211–242.

Deal, William E. and Timothy K. Beal. 2004. *Theory for Religious Studies.* New York and London: Routledge.

Eliade, Mircea. 1959. *The Sacred and the Profane: The Nature of Religion.* Translated by Willard R. Task. New York: Harvest Books.

Evans-Pritchard, Edward E. 1965. *Theories of Primitive Religion.* Oxford: Clarendon Press.

Henrichs, Albert. 2010. "What is a Greek God?" In *The Gods of Ancient Greece: Indentities and Transformations,* edited by Jan N. Bremmer and Andrew Erskine, 19–39. Edinburgh, UK: Edinburgh University Press.

Hick, John. 2005. *An Interpretation of Religion: Human Responses to the Transcendent.* New Haven, CT: Yale University Press.

Jensen, Jeppe S. 2014. *What Is Religion?* London and New York: Routledge.

Kippenberg, Hans G. 2002. *Discovering Religious History in the Modern Age.* Princeton, NJ and Oxford: Princeton University Press.

López-Ruiz, Carolina. 2015. "Gods: Origins." In *The Oxford Handbook of Ancient Greek Religion,* edited by Esther Eidinow and Julia Kindt, 369–382. Oxford: Oxford University Press.

Masuzawa, Tomoko. 2005. *The Invention of World Religions: Or, How European Universalism Was Preserved in the Language of Pluralism.* Chicago, IL and London: University of Chicago Press.

Masuzawa, Tomoko. 2015. "Regarding Origin: Beginnings, Foundations, and the Bicameral Formation of the Study of Religion." In *Writing Religion: The Case for the Critical Study of Religion,* edited by Steven W. Ramey, 131–148. Tuscaloosa, AL: The University of Alabama Press.

Müller, Friedrich Max. 1867. *Chips from a German Workshop.* Vol. II. London: Longmans Green.

Müller, Friedrich Max. 1878. *Lectures on the Origin and Growth of Religion.* London: Longmans Green.

Nongbri, Brent. 2013. *Before Religion: A History of a Modern Concept.* New Haven, CT and London: Yale University Press.

Pals, Daniel L. 2014. *Nine Theories of Religion*. New York and Oxford: Oxford University Press.

Preus, J. Samuel. 1987. *Explaining Religion: Criticism and Theory from Bodin to Freud*. New Haven, CT: Yale University Press.

Riesebrodt, Martin. 2010. *The Promise of Salvation: A Theory of Religion*. Translated by Steven Rendall. Chicago, IL and London: University of Chicago Press.

Segal, Robert A. 2005. "Theories of Religion." In *The Routledge Companion to the Study of Religion*, edited by John R. Hinnells, 49–60. London and New York: Routledge.

Segal, Robert A. 2006. "All Generalizations Are Bad: Postmodernism on Theories." *Journal of the American Academy of Religion* 74 (1): 157–171.

Segal, Robert A. forthcoming. "Max Müller on Religion and Myth." In *Friedrich Max Müller and the Role of Philology in Victorian Thought*, edited by John R. Davis and Angus Nicholls. Special issue of *Publications of the English Goethe Society* 85 (2–3).

Sharpe, Eric J. 2005. "The Study of Religion in Historical Perspective." In *The Routledge Companion to the Study of Religion*, edited by John R. Hinnells, 21–45. London and New York: Routledge.

Stausberg, Michael. 2009. "There Is Life in the Old Dog Yet: An Introduction to Contemporary Theories of Religion." In *Contemporary Theories of Religion: A Critical Companion*, edited by Michael Stausberg, 1–21. London and New York: Routledge.

Stausberg, Michael. 2010. "Prospects in Theories of Religion." *Method and Theory in the Study of Religion* 22 (4): 223–238.

Strenski, Ivan. 2015. *Understanding Theories of Religion: An Introduction*. Malden, MA and Oxford: Wiley-Blackwell.

Stroumsa, Guy. 2010. *A New Science: The Discovery of Religion in the Age of Reason*. Cambridge, MA and London: Harvard University Press.

Stroumsa, Guy. 2015. "The Scholarly Discovery of Religion in Early Modern Times." In *The Cambridge History of the World. Vol. 6: The Construction of a Global World 1400–1800 CE*, edited by Jerry H. Bentley, Sanjay Subrahmanyam, and Merry E. Wiesner-Hanks, 313–333. Cambridge: Cambridge University Press.

Turner, James. 2014. *Philology: The Forgotten Origins of the Modern Humanities*. Princeton, NJ and Oxford: Princeton University Press.

Tweed, Thomas. 2006. *Crossing and Dwelling: A Theory of Religion*. Cambridge, MA and London: Harvard University Press.

Tylor, Edward B. 1883. *Primitive Culture: Researches into the Development of Mythology, Philosophy, Religion, Language, Art and Custom*. Vol. I. New York: Henry Holt.

Weber, Max. 1963. *The Sociology of Religion*. Translated by Ephraim Fischoff. Boston, MA: Beacon Press.

Winiarczyk, Marek. 1991. *Euhemerus Reliquiae*. Stuttgart and Leipzig: De Gruyter.

Winiarczyk, Marek. 2013. *The Sacred History of Euhemerus of Messene*. Translated by Witold Zbirohowski-Kościa. Berlin and Boston, MA: De Gruyter.

# 2 Before Euhemerism

In *Religion: The Classical Theories* (1999), a work primarily preoccupied with modern theories of religion, that is, approaches that emerged in the seventeenth century onwards, James Thrower also included pre-modern thinkers in his survey, dealing with them as fully fledged theorists of religion.[1] The classical theorists that he listed are Xenophanes of Colophon, Democritus, Prodicus of Ceos, Critias, Euhemerus of Messene (who all lived between the sixth and the third century BCE), as well as the Stoic philosophers of the Hellenistic and Roman periods. All these thinkers, according to Thrower, were exponents of naturalistic theories of religion, that is, approaches that sought to "get behind the overt claims of religions and to uncover the true and the, more often than not, human origins of religion."[2] Contrary to religious (or theological) theories of religion, which claim that both the emergence and persistence of religious phenomena are predicated on the very existence of a supernatural source, naturalistic approaches deny such a *sui generis* approach to phenomena classified as religions.[3] Both approaches, however, seek to give explanations and answers pertaining to the pressing issue of how, when, and why religion originates and persists. The discussion that follows is triggered by the quite common, and in some cases, partly justified argument that Euhemerus was deeply influenced by some or all of the aforementioned thinkers.[4] Indeed, the Messenean author was most likely influenced by previously formulated ideas, but he did not merely copy them and presented them as his own. On the contrary, upon careful reading one encounters certain differences in both style and argumentation that do not permit us to see Euhemerus as a theorist of religion who brought nothing new in the ancient discourse on the origins of belief in gods and religion.

## Against Anthropomorphism

One rarely encounters a publication on ancient Greek religion that does not dedicate some space to Xenophanes's famous criticism of the traditional anthropomorphic religious ideas. Xenophanes attacks the stories about the gods one finds in the great epic poems of Homer and Hesiod. According to his approach, it is inconceivable, if not rather lame, to accept that the gods act just as humans do: "Both Homer and Hesiod have ascribed to the gods all deeds which among men are matters of reproach and blame: thieving, adultery, and deceiving one another."[5] Xenophanes is particularly infuriated by this equalization of gods and human beings. Anthropomorphism lies at the very core of the Greek understanding of gods: "But mortals suppose that the gods are born, have human clothing, and voice, and bodily form."[6] The anthropomorphic features found in the Greek gods are, as he famously argued, traits that any living being could have attributed to their divinities, if only they had the ability to write or draw:

> If horses had hands, or oxen or lions, or if they could draw with their hands and produce works as men do, then horses would draw figures of gods like horses, and oxen like oxen, and each would render the bodies to be of the same frame that each of them have.[7]

Xenophanes points out that the anthropomorphic characteristics of the gods are not something one encounters solely in Greek culture. For example, it is well known that according to the biblical narration, the God of the book of Genesis is portrayed as an anthropomorphic agent with flaws and is undeniably not omniscient and omnipotent, without however a detailed physical description such as the ones found in the Greek poems regarding the Greek gods.[8] Similarly, other peoples act alike, representing their gods according to their own physical traits as Xenophanes further contends: "Ethiopians say that their gods are snub-nosed and dark, Thracians, that theirs are grey-eyed and red-haired."[9] It is obvious that for the presocratic philosopher such a discourse was unacceptable. The existence of divinity is something beyond human understanding and thus irrelevant to the manner in which the Greek poets have described the popular gods of tradition. If those gods are not as Homer and Hesiod asserted, does that mean that he was an atheist?[10] The answer comes from Xenophanes himself when he claims that the divinity's existence lies beyond the poetic superficial understanding of the supernatural world. There exists "[o]ne god, greatest among gods and men, not at all like mortals in form or thought."[11] However, the human mind is incapable of conceiving both the nature and the abilities of such an entity. Xenophanes's understanding of the divine realm has led to the conclusion that he might have been one of the first monotheists, an assertion that cannot however be verified by the existing sources.[12]

Thrower's inclusion of Xenophanes among the classical naturalistic theorists of religion was based on the idea of the projection of human traits upon the traditional gods. However, the theory of projection as used by Xenophanes does not explain the origin or the function of religion; it only explains why the perceived gods are described in anthropomorphic terms. How people come to think about the gods remains unresolved. Contrary to the way Ludwig Feuerbach (1804–1872) developed the idea of projection in the nineteenth century,[13] Xenophanes seems more interested in theologizing rather than theorizing about religion. This forces us to reconsider whether his theory actually stems from a naturalistic approach to religion. By taking for granted that divinity exists, regardless of the confusion pertaining to his monotheistic or polytheistic understanding of the supernatural realm, Xenophanes is more interested in stripping away anthropomorphism of god-talk than actually providing his readers with a naturalistic theory of religion. He emphasizes the limitations of human knowledge by arguing that "nor will there be anyone who knows about the gods,"[14] which reminds us of Protagoras's famous agnostic statement about the traditional divine agents. The fifth century BCE sophist maintained that the brevity of human life, the difficulty of the subject, and the limits of human knowledge do not permit any coherent argument about the gods.[15] Any connections between Xenophanes and Euhemerus seem to dissipate when we come to think of the theory promoted by the Messenean writer which was based on a historical account of the traditional gods. However, Kees Bolle, one of the most notable scholars of euhemerism, sees 'euhemeristic' elements in Xenophanes's discussion about the gods.[16] Bolle seems to overlook or miss altogether the very fact that Xenophanes had no interest whatsoever in a historical explanation pertaining to the genealogy of gods. On the contrary, as Aristotle informs us (*Rhetoric* 2.23.18), the presocratic philosopher seems to have disregarded any such attempt as impious, since such an assertion would obviously lead to the conclusion that there was a time when gods did not exist.[17] Even if we argue that Aristotle is misrepresenting Xenophanes, based on the premise that the existence of the "one god, greatest among gods and men" does not preclude the possibility of a later creation of those lesser deities, it is apparent that the major issue that Xenophanes was addressing is not a historical account of the gods but a theological one.[18] In addition, by denuding the traditional deities of their anthropomorphic depictions, Xenophanes essentially ruled out any historical explanation given that, following his reasoning, those supernatural agents could not any longer be placed within spatial and temporal limits.

## The 'Fear Factor' Theory

In his excellent study on Democritus, Thomas Cole argued that there is a connection between Democritus and Euhemerus, taking the former as a probable source of the latter.[19] The basis for this argument is Diodorus's usage of Democritus in the first book of his *Historical Library*, with Cole however not failing to mention that the parallel here is drawn mainly based on Ennius's and Lactantius's version of Euhemerus's theory, which essentially contradicts Diodorus's version in book five and Eusebius's summary of book six.[20] This inconsistency in Cole's argumentation is resolved by contending that, in this case, the rendering offered by Ennius and Lactantius is most likely accurate. However, in order to determine whether Democritus can be deemed a source of Euhemerus's theory we need to first establish how the presocratic atomist philosopher approached the issue of the origin of gods.

Democritus is, if not the very first, among the first thinkers to promote the 'fear theory' as the way of explaining the origins of religion.[21] Belief in gods, thus, was the consequence of the feelings of awe and fear experienced by humans in the face of terrifying natural phenomena (such as thunder, lightning, the movement of celestial objects, etc.):

> For when ancient humans saw the disturbances in the heavens, such as thunder and lightning, conjunctions of stars, and eclipses of sun and moon, they were frightened, thinking that gods were responsible for these things.[22]

Democritus explains away such a religious idea by rejecting any kind of divine involvement in these natural phenomena.[23] However, the 'fear theory' was not the only one attributed to Democritus regarding the origin of the belief in gods. Another one, more sophisticated and better matching with his atomistic theory, was also promoted: the origin of religion is to be found in the contact of humans with "giant, alarming and humanlike images (εἴδωλα) that terrified people,"[24] which must not be taken as mere products of human imagination or hallucinations, but as actual existing entities composed by atoms. This, in turn, meant that those agents are natural and thereby had all the anthropomorphic features of the gods but, contrary to the traditional understanding of a deity, they were not indestructible.[25] The latter is undoubtedly problematic. The immortality of the traditional deities was, along with power and anthropomorphism, one of the three core characteristics in how the ancient Greeks conceived of their gods. By removing any one of these three traits, one was virtually denying that the agent in question was truly divine.[26]

The issue of how εἴδωλα are understood by Democritus remains a difficult one. Andrew Gregory has offered a very persuasive interpretation that could help determine whether those agents that people had contact with should be restricted to the notion of gods or could be expanded onto other categories of agency. By drawing on the usage of the term in Homer, where εἴδωλα have a "broader meaning than 'image' and can mean 'phantom' or 'ghost'"[27] usually encountered in dreams, he argues that, without restricting the Democritian adoption of the term to dreams alone, "*idôla* are not gods but they explain belief in a great deal more phenomena than simply the gods,"[28] therefore maintaining that this theory could well have had a more explicit agenda aiming at the Homeric construction of the divine world. Whatever Democritus's agenda might had been, however, what lies at the crux of both theories assigned to him is apparently related to the feelings of fear and awe that humans experience within the natural world and due to natural stimuli. Even though scholars have identified Democritus's influence in later philosophers, such as in the works of Hobbes, Vico, and Hume,[29] it comes as a surprise that no direct connections have been made between Democritus and Edward B. Tylor regarding both theories promoted by the presocratic philosopher. If in the case of the εἴδωλα Tylor himself acknowledges his debt to the philosopher from Abdera,[30] we do not find similar parallels when dealing with Democritus's 'fear theory.' Even if the feeling that urges the creation of the notion of the gods is fear, the stimulus that leads to the feeling itself is, naturally, mere observation of the natural world. Humans observe their natural world, contemplate, and reach the conclusion that there has to be an agent behind each natural phenomenon that regulates it. The control of meteorological phenomena by individual gods acts in place of the scientific explanations that humans have not yet mastered. It is exactly this scientific solution offered by Democritus and his atomistic theory that replaces the religious ideas about how the natural world functions and which essentially denies the existence of gods behind meteorological and celestial phenomena. Democritus's explanation of how thunder, lightning, hurricane, etc. occur virtually eliminates any other possibility; scientific explanation replaces religious explanation.[31] Similarly, for Tylor "gods originate out of the personification of nature" and they become "the causes—the professed literal causes—of the origin and operation of the world."[32] Once science emerges, religion is not anymore needed.

One can argue that Democritus's 'fear theory' regarding the origin of religion might have had some kind of impact on Euhemerus's thought. However, the scope and aim of Democritus's project seem broader and less interested in a historical assessment of how religion originates. By providing a naturalistic theory of religion that denies the existence of gods and takes religion to be a counterpart to science, Democritus is not so much interested in addressing the historical origin of Greek religion, that is, where and when Greek religion first arose, but rather he is focusing on the why of the origin and function of religion. It is obvious that, as for Tylor, a scientific explanation of the natural phenomena makes religion impossible, since Democritus's atomistic theory explains scientifically what humans failed to explain and, as a result, turned to the creation of religious myths. Contrary to what one would expect, Democritus was not included in ancient records of atheists, even though both of his theories in effect deny the existence of gods, but it is possible that his complicated notion of the εἴδωλα could have saved him from such accusations.[33]

## The 'Big Brother' Theory

The Sisyphus fragment, traditionally assigned to Critias, is probably the most straightforward naturalistic theory of religion coming from antiquity. The issue of authorship remains uncertain, with scholars (both ancient and modern) arguing either in favor of Critias or of Euripides.[34] As the text informs us, there was a time when gods did not exist. Humans lived in a state of anarchy, where order and ethics were completely absent. The subsequent creation of laws brought the desired order in the social and public sphere but perpetrators continued their lawless activities secretly. This was addressed by an (unnamed) man who came up with the idea of an agent who is able to screen and monitor human life even within the most clandestine and isolated contexts.[35] The fragment has received wide attention by classicists and scholars of religion, since it constitutes a classic example of religion as a human by-product rather than a *sui generis* phenomenon, that is, ahistorical, irreducible, and unique, that cannot be explained or studied using the theories and methods employed for the study of any other social phenomenon.[36]

An issue not addressed by the fragment is how we get from one god, who sees, hears, and knows everything, to many gods who act alike (lines 17–24):

> The idea that there is a deity flourishing with immortal life,
>     Hearing in *his* mind, seeing, thinking,
> Attending to these things and having a divine nature,
> Who will hear everything said among mortals,
>     And will be able to see everything that is done.
> If you plan some base act in silence,
> The *gods* will not fail to notice; for they have
> Thought.[37]

There seems to be a transition in that unknown man's thought from one god to many, without providing any further explanation however of how that transition takes place. This is an approach to the notion of the divine reminiscent of Xenophanes's theory of "one god, greatest among gods" without however any evidence that could connect the two theories. It seems that the appearance of multiple gods comes almost simultaneously, but the text is obviously summarizing rather than presenting to the audience a detailed exposition of the theory. Given that the Sisyphus fragment was part of a theatrical play, most likely a tragic rather than a satiric one as is the traditional view,[38] the issue of who speaks here and to what ends remains unclear. The authorship problem is closely related to the question of whether Critias (or Euripides) was actually an atheist who shared such views, or simply use the figure of Sisyphus who was a known "cunning rogue" to simply promote ideas that contradicted the traditional views about the gods.[39]

Whatever the case might be, the Sisyphus fragment offers a naturalistic theory of religion but does not place the origin of religion within a specific historical or, as Euhemerus's theory does, spatial context. The *why* of origin is a nonreligious need and the *how* is related to the acts of one (unnamed) man. Religion emerges to fulfill a need for social order and persists for the same reason. Resembling the theory of religion of Sigmund Freud, who also places the origin of religion deep into the dawn of human history, but who nevertheless assigns the creation of religion to a group of primordial males responding to his famous Oedipus complex,[40] the Sisyphus fragment is less interested in the *how* of origin but more in the *why*, which also gives us the function of religion. There is hardly any palpable connection that we can argue about regarding the possible influence of this theory upon Euhemerus, apart from the generalization that he could have been aware of the fragment through whatever channels. The fact that the author of the Sisyphus fragment also dedicated space to the celestial phenomena and the feelings of fear that they elicit in humans places the theory closer to Democritus than to Euhemerus.[41] The reductionist approach employed by the Sisyphus fragment and the apparent rejection of the traditional ideas about the gods is nevertheless part of an attempt to address the issue of origin of religion that seemed quite popular in antiquity.

Before proceeding, however, there is an issue that must be addressed in relation to one of the latest treatments of the Critias fragment. In Patrick O'Sullivan's article on the topic, the Critian theory is approached from another angle that, however, neglects the ongoing discussions in the field of religious studies in the last 300 years or so. As he puts it,

> [r]ather than being simply a cynical undermining of religion, the contents of Critias fr. 19 are far better understood as a paradoxical recognition of the social benefits that can flow from belief in the gods, even as it acknowledges that the basis for such belief is grounded in a fiction.[42]

The problem with O'Sullivan's approach is not only his focus on alleviating or softening the fragment's critical output, which has been rigorously and rightly so criticized by Tim Whitmarsh,[43] but also the lack of a deeper understanding of how theorizing about religion functions. As I have argued in this and the preceding chapter, naturalistic theories of religion occur when thinkers treat religion in non-religious terms, that is, when the need for which religion emerges is not a religious one. Whether the theorist is a religious person or not is virtually irrelevant to the theory promoted. As such, O'Sullivan's emphasis on the possibility of the author's religiosity, along with the concluding statement that "[i]t is true that the speaker in Critias fr. 19 presents the link between the human and the divine as an illusion. But, in this instance at least, it comes across as a grand one,"[44] sounds more like an apologetic attempt to rescue religion from a social scientific examination than actually evaluate the merits of such an approach—even more so when it comes from such an ancient text, which says much about the antiquity of theorizing about religion.

## The Benefaction Theory

Scholars have long identified Euhemerus's debt to Prodicus of Ceos and his theory of the origin of religion, although there are certain problems with this view.[45] Such claims are indeed established regardless of the source problems one faces when dealing with what ancient authors transmit about Prodicus's approach to religion. The prevailing view of Prodicus's theory is that he acknowledged two stages of religious development, both of which are related to the sentiment of gratitude that people felt. Contrary to deeming religion the result of fear as Democritus and Critias did, Prodicus adopts a more positive attitude in relation to the origin of religion. It is, he says, appreciation that leads people to religion. In the first stage, people came to acknowledge as divine all those celestial and natural phenomena that were useful to them, such as the moon, sun, stars, rivers, and springs. Within the same category, Prodicus included the various objects that aided people, such as fire, water, wine, bread, etc., which were in turn personified and worshipped as gods: Hephaestus, Dionysus, Demeter, etc.[46] In the second stage, people began to worship human benefactors who discovered foods, shelter, and other crafts, with a special attention given to agriculture as the factor par excellence that leads to the advancement of human culture.[47]

Prodicus's twofold theory has led to various interpretations due to the problems encountered in the sources containing and transmitting his view on religion. There is no conclusive agreement on whether both stages were indeed part of Prodicus's thinking or, on the contrary, later additions that altered and corrupted what the philosopher from the island of Ceos actually claimed about the origin of religion. Considering that what we do know about Prodicus comes from different sources, such as Sextus, Cicero, Philodemus, and Minucius Felix,[48] the issue of whether what has come down to us reflects Prodicus's genuine theory has been recently criticized. This scholarly debate is based on the very fact that there are strong reservations about whether the second theory is indeed an idea promoted by Prodicus himself, or simply a later addition based on what Persaeus argued about the origin of religion, which resembles Euhemerus's theory.[49] Hence, some scholars tend not to include the second stage when discussing Prodicus,[50] which in turn creates certain problems regarding his influence on Euhemerus.

If we are to accept that the second stage of religion, traditionally attributed to Prodicus, is the result of a later addition, then we are left with the first stage that none of our sources deny. The deification of natural (including celestial) phenomena and other objects does not allow for taking Prodicus as Euhemerus's basic source. On the contrary, Prodicus is here seen as a theorist of religion that takes the names of the gods to be mere personifications of objects and, thus, mere symbols. Those scholars who share such an approach connect Prodicus's theory to the fact that he was famous for his linguistic skills. Hence, as Peter Harrison has argued, Prodicus's theory practically contended that

> people named useful objects and fell into the error of using the names as proper names. The use of a proper name for an object thus led to the misconception that an object was in fact an acting being—in short, a god.[51]

Harrison's assessment coincides with what all of our sources convey, that is, the erroneous connection of things to names and the ensuing belief that the names themselves refer to real gods as the two instances of the verb νομίζειν denote in Sextus (θεοὺς ἐνόμισαν and τὸν μὲν ἄρτον Δήμητραν νομισθῆναι).[52]

Such an approach, however, generates additional problems when we try to link it to the second stage of religion, which, admittedly, seems completely out of place. We cannot reconcile the two stages as that would mean that Prodicus did not have an unambiguous theory of religion but, rather, two divergent theories that do not logically coincide. The origin of belief in gods cannot be the result of both a simultaneous linguistic misconception and deification of benefactors, since the two are mutually exclusive, and would simply make Prodicus inconsistent and eventually unreliable. However, the two stages can be seen as two distinct phases, just like the ones attributed to Democritus or Euhemerus. The insistence on the first stage of religion as the only genuine theory promoted by Prodicus does not, however, imply that the philosopher from Ceos did not influence Euhemerus. The central role played by natural phenomena in the birth of religion—but not the explanation of linguistic-misconception about the origin of the Olympian gods—is in agreement with Euhemerus, but the gods are explained historically rather than linguistically by the Messenean, whereas natural and celestial phenomena and objects also hold a key role in his theory. The claim however put forth by Albert Henrichs that "[i]t is hardly an exaggeration to say that the essential features of Euhemerism are in fact the property of Prodicus," while also arguing that "[i]t is unlikely, however, that Euhemerus had direct access to Prodicus,"[53] seems at least problematic and should be approached cautiously.

The influence of Prodicus is more apparent on Persaeus of Citium, a Stoic of the third century BCE, who wrote a book entitled Περὶ Θεῶν (*On the Gods*). Both Cicero and the Herculaneum Papyrus 1428 demonstrate the direct influence of Prodicus on Persaeus.[54] Although some have seen an influence of the *Sacred Inscription* on Persaeus (or vice versa), Marek Winiarczyk has countered such a view when he correctly claimed that "the benefactors Euhemerus had in mind were powerful kings whereas Prodicus and Persaeus referred to 'culture heroes',"[55] an element which is very often neglected or overseen by scholars of ancient euhemerism.

Hecataeus of Abdera also promoted the benefaction theory. Even though his book, conventionally known as *On Egypt*,[56] did not survive, scholars have long identified Diodorus Siculus's debt to Hecataeus in his description of Egypt as portrayed in the first book of his monumental and invaluable *Historical Library*.[57] Hecataeus's naturalistic theory acknowledges two groups of gods whose origin is profoundly different but somehow interlinked. The first, the celestial gods, were identified as such by the first humans in Egypt after observing the nature of the universe and being struck by awe and wonder (καταπλαγέντας τε καὶ θαυμάσαντας). The sun and the moon were the two most powerful deities, which those first Egyptians named Osiris and Isis, respectively. They also identified five elements of the universe and assigned names to them: spirit (πνεῦμα) was called Zeus; fire (πῦρ), Hephaestus; earth (γῆν), Demeter; wet (ὑγρὸν), Oceanê (Ὠκεάνην); while air (ἀέρα) was called Athena. All those gods visited the inhabited world in the shape of animals or humans and they are the givers of life to all living beings (οὗτοι πρὸς ἀλήθειάν εἰσιν οἱ πάντα γεννῶντες).[58] The origin of religion in this stage is related to the benefactions offered by those celestial gods, with the gift of life holding the most central role that led to their acknowledgment as gods by those first humans. The second group, the terrestrial gods, were humans; kings of ancient Egypt who were deified due to their benefactions. Hecataeus, however, complicates the narration in this second section, since he claims that some of those gods had the same names as the celestial ones, while others were also acknowledged, such as Helios, Cronus, Rhea, and Hermes. Still, Helios is related to the sun (being the Greek rendering of the English word), while Hephaestus is deemed the first king of the priests according to their own provided interpretation.[59] The benefaction theory here is related to what each of those kings offered to humanity: Hephaestus gave the fire; Osiris offered agriculture and established cities; Isis introduced wheat and barley; while Hermes developed the language, named objects, and invented the alphabet.[60]

The influence of Hecataeus upon Euhemerus is, more or less, taken for granted.[61] They both referred to two groups of gods with the why of origin being the explanation of the workings of the universe and the development of human culture. However, the criticism promoted by Marek Winiarczyk should not go unheeded nor should it be easily rejected. By comparing Hecataeus to Herodotus and Manetho, Winiarczyk claims that Hecataeus did speak about the celestial gods but he would have probably not considered the gods of Egypt as deified monarchs.[62] It is generally accepted that Manetho relied upon both Herodotus and Hecataeus, but there are considerable differences between the former two and the latter in dealing with the second group of the gods. Whereas Hecataeus, according to Diodorus, takes the terrestrial gods to be deified kings, Herodotus and Manetho agree that the first Egyptian kings were gods rather than humans that were later deified.[63] Winiarczyk's rejection of this branch of Hecataeus's theory is based on the likelihood that Diodorus modified Hecataeus's theory, which brings us back to the question of who speaks here and to what ends.

\*   \*   \*

Thinking about religion in the Classical and Hellenistic antiquity is not restricted to the aforementioned figures, but attempting to classify other authors as introducers of naturalistic theories of religion encounters certain problems. The 'centrality' of a twofold understanding of the religious realm seems quite popular in antiquity and it was natural to find its way into

Euhemerus's theory. From this perspective, all of the theorists discussed above influenced the Messenean author, as most likely did other thinkers of antiquity who, nevertheless, did not offer a naturalistic theory of religion. Seeing the celestial objects as divine and distinct from the Olympian gods was a familiar idea for the two most known philosophers of Greek antiquity, Plato and Aristotle. The founder of the Academy in Athens presents a theory similar to Prodicus's, according to which the origin of belief in the gods is to be found at the dawn of Greek history. However, and contrary to Prodicus, those first men deified the celestial objects not due to their benefaction but due to their movement and constant motion, which also provides us with the etymological root of the word *theós* (θεός, from the verb θεῖν, run). The belief in the traditional gods comes later, seemingly as the result of some kind of a revelation or contact with those entities.[64] Similarly, Aristotle acknowledges the distinction between celestial and traditional deities by invoking ancient traditions that took the former to be really divine (τὸ θεῖον):

> A tradition has been handed down by the ancient thinkers of very early times, and bequeathed to posterity in the form of a myth, to the effect that these heavenly bodies are gods [θεοί τέ εἰσιν], and that the divine pervades the whole of nature.[65]

In another context, Aristotle's famous unmoved mover is the one who puts the celestial objects into motion, thereby rejecting the idea of an (anthropomorphic) Atlas holding up the world on his shoulders.[66] However, neither Plato nor Aristotle provide us with a naturalistic theory of religion. On the contrary, and in another context, Plato condemned such theories as mere expressions of atheism and impiety. The latter, as he asserts, is the result of non-belief in the traditional gods.[67] Both philosophers, however, do embrace the distinction of celestial and traditional deities, making the idea a prevalent one in antiquity.

In a recent publication on Herodotus and religion, Scott Scullion called the historian from Halicarnassus a "religious theorist."[68] However, the known diffusionist approach of Herodotus to religion, with the Greek gods coming to Greece from Egypt, and their subsequent transformation that alienated their original truly divine character,[69] cannot be deemed a naturalistic theory of religion. The fact that Homer and Hesiod were responsible for the anthropomorphic depiction of the Greek gods does not simultaneously mean that Herodotus regarded those gods as a human by-product.[70] In addition, nowhere does he doubt the existence or the divinity of the gods—that would make his explanation a naturalistic one if followed by a theory that answers the question of a need—and it is well known that the *Histories* are full of divine interventions and references.[71] Finally, the diffusionist theory Herodotus argued for cannot be deemed a generalization about religion, as is the case with theories of religion. Herodotus does not offer a theory of the origin of religion, that is of the phenomenon in general, but a theory of the origin of Greek religion in particular anchored in Egyptian conceptualizations.[72]

It was within such an intellectual context that Euhemerus of Messene introduced his own approach to religion. But as with all other previous explanations, his interpretation of the divine world is predicated on the prevalent assumption of a twofold understanding.

## Notes

1 As far as I am aware, this is among the very few books in English on theories of religion that includes a section on antiquity. A similar but shorter section can be found in the more specialized Harrison 2002, 14–18.
2 Thrower 1999, 93. For a different view, which sees ancient (specifically presocratic) theorizing about religion through different lens, largely disagreeing with my assessment, see Broadie 1999.
3 See McCutcheon 2007, 102–103. On the *sui generis* problem in the academic study of religion, see McCutcheon 1997.
4 For example, the debt of Euhemerus to Prodicus has been extensively discussed by Henrichs 1975 and 1984; cf. Winiarczyk 2013, 48.
5 Curd 2011, 34. Cf. Kirk and Raven 1977, 168. The attack on Homer and Hesiod was better formulated later on by Plato, *Republic* 2.377d ff.
6 Curd 2011, 34. Cf. Kirk and Raven 1977, 168.
7 Curd 2011, 34. Cf. Kirk and Raven 1977, 169.
8 See Segal 2013. There is an explicit difference between the understanding of the divine of the Hebrew Bible and Greek mythology. In the latter, there is not a clear distinction between humans and gods, whereas Greek gods are more easily accessible than the God of the Bible.
9 Curd 2011, 34. Cf. Kirk and Raven 1977, 168.
10 Regarding Xenophanes's atheism, see Roubekas 2014, 232–233. A similar attack toward Homer and Hesiod is also encountered in the tenth book of Plato's *Republic*. Cf. Gladigow 1986.
11 Curd 2011, 35. Cf. Kirk and Raven 1977, 169.
12 See Gregory 2013, 107 where he explains that he takes "Xenophanes to be a monotheist, despite the phrase 'greatest among Gods and men' [. . .] This phrase is emphatic or formulaic rather than asserting many gods of which one is supreme." Gregory's interpretation of the fragment could well have some merit, since Xenophanes virtually dedicates most of his discussion on rejecting the traditional gods according to the way the poets and the people imagined them. However, nowhere does he claim that those deities do not exist; on the contrary, he criticizes the nature but not the very existence of those gods. As such, one cannot easily dismiss the possibility that, in his understanding, the traditional gods actually existed whereas the human ability to understand their nature was rejected.
13 See Guthrie 1993, 62–90; Guthrie 2000. For a nice analysis of Feuerbach's projection theory, see Harvey 1995.
14 Curd 2011, 36. Cf. Kirk and Raven 1977, 179.
15 Ibid., 146. On an interesting approach to Protagoras and his religious views, see Whitmarsh 2015, 87–91.
16 Bolle 1970, 21; for a short introduction to euhemerism, see Bolle 2005.
17 Curd 2011, 36.

18 See the excellent summary of Xenophanes's theology in Meier 1981, 221–223.

19 Cole 1967, 202–205.

20 Ibid., 202 n. 2.

21 Harrison 2002, 15. A modern version of the 'fear theory,' this time from the perspective of the cognitive study of religion, is Guthrie 1993.

22 Sextus Empiricus, *Against the Mathematicians* 9.24: ὁρῶντες γάρ, φησί, τὰ ἐν τοῖς μετεώροις παθήματα οἱ παλαιοὶ τῶν ἀνθρώπων, καθάπερ βροντὰς καὶ ἀστραπάς, κεραυνούς τε καὶ ἄστρων συνόδους ἡλίου τε καὶ σελήνης ἐκλείψεις, ἐδειματοῦντο, θεοὺς οἰόμενοι τούτων αἰτίους εἶναι. The translation is drawn from Bett 2012. Cf. Cole 1967, 202; Henrichs 1975, 103; Gregory 2013, 185.

23 Mikalson 2010, 234:

> To Democritus such fear was unjustified, because 'the gods give all the good things to humans but not what is bad, harmful, and unbeneficial' (frag. B 175), and he no doubt explained such celestial phenomena by his theory of atoms, without divine intervention.

24 Winiarczyk 2013, 47. Cf. Sextus Empiricus, *Against the Mathematicians* 9.19.

25 See Gregory 2013, 194–195; Thrower 1999, 94.

26 See Henrichs 2010.

27 Gregory 2013, 195.

28 Ibid., 196. Thrower 1999, 94 mistakenly restricts the appearance of those agents to dreams only. For an attempt to explain the nature of the εἴδωλα, see Cicero, *On the Nature of the Gods* 1.12.29; cf. Franek 2013, 63–64.

29 See Harrison 2002, 15; Gregory 2013, 194.

30 Tylor 1883, 449. On the connection between the second theory of Democritus and Tylor, also see Franek 2013, 65–66.

31 See Stobaeus 1.29.1.

32 Segal 1999, 12. Cf. Segal 2004, 13–23 for a discussion on myth, religion, and science in Tylor.

33 See Gregory 2013, 195. Democritus is not among the ancient thinkers treated in the classical study by Drachmann 1922. Harrison 2002, 15 on the contrary, maintains that Democritus did not go as far as explaining away the gods, based on the discussion on εἴδωλα. Winiarczyk 1984, 163 does list Democritus among the atheists based on Apuleius, *Apologia* 27, with the text however not being explicit whether Democritus was indeed accused of atheism or his name was simply used by Apuleius as an example of a natural philosopher (*rerum naturae patronos*).

34 See the discussions in Kerferd 1981, 171; Mikalson 2010, 232–233; Franek 2013, 66 n. 41; Winiarczyk 2013, 47 n. 135. Sutton 1981, 35 and Whitmarsh 2014, 109 present the disagreement encountered among ancient authors regarding the authorship of the Sisyphus fragment. Kahn 1997, 249 argues without any hesitation in favor of Euripides as the author of the text. A very detailed discussion is found in Davies 1989, 24–28.

35 See Sextus Empiricus, *Against the Mathematicians* 9.54. For a translation of the text, see Whitmarsh 2014, 124–125; cf. Kahn 1997, 247–248. For a modern approach to the 'big brother' theory, see Norenzayan 2013, who nevertheless deals only with the modern monotheistic religions. However, he fails to make the connection of his theory to Critias's, who introduced the very idea more than two millennia ago.

36 On this issue, see Eliade 1959 and the discussion offered by Nye 2008, 112–114. Thrower 1999 dedicates most of his treatment of ancient theories of religion on the Sisyphus fragment.

37 Emphasis added; the translation is drawn from Whitmarsh 2014, 124.

38 See Whitmarsh 2014, 112.
39 See the interpretation offered by Sutton 1981, 37–38. A more elaborate discussion is offered by Whitmarsh 2014, which I find more probable.
40 See Freud 2001.
41 See Nilsson 1940, 2; Henrichs 1975, 98; Mikalson 2010, 233.
42 O'Sullivan 2009, 170.
43 See Whitmarsh 2014, 114, where addressing O'Sullivan's approach argues that

> [t]he most recent discussion—actually a positive evaluation of the fragment —explicitly urges readers to approach it uninfluenced by 'populist, fundamentalist atheism' and its 'zealous preachers', and concludes that 'an avowedly atheistic stance need not be reducible to a facile, anti-religious one'; the play is thus (he argues) not atheistic but philosophically rich. A pungent reminder, this, that Classics is not always the secularised discipline we have been led to think it is since the nineteenth century.

44 O'Sullivan 2009, 185.
45 The best study on Euhemerus's debt to Prodicus, which employs however a rather dismissive attitude toward Euhemerus, remains Henrichs 1984; this position is more or less embraced by Whitmarsh 2015, 154. Winiarczyk 2013, 48, however, is more cautious. He talks about similarities between Euhemerus's and Prodicus's views rather than intellectual debt.
46 Sextus Empiricus, *Against the Mathematicians* 9.18. Cf. *PHerc.* 1428 fr. 19.12–19.
47 Philodemus, *On Piety* 9.7.
48 Cf. Cicero, *On the Nature of the Gods* 1.37.118 and Minucius Felix, *Octavius* 21.2.
49 For example, see the discussion in Franek 2013, 69–70. Cf. Baumgarten 1996, 97–98.
50 For example, see Drachmann 1922, 42–44; Burton 1972, 56; Harrison 2002, 16–17. Although Cole 1967, 156 n. 27 takes both stages to be part of Prodicus's thought, he is nevertheless more careful. On the contrary, Henrichs 1984, 141 takes the second stage as the basic one of Prodicus's theory, whereas Kerferd 1981, 168–169, Drozdek 2006, 62, and Winiarczyk 2013, 48 express no doubts. On the acceptance of both stages as the work of Prodicus, also see Mikalson 2010, 231 (even though he does show some kind of reluctance) and Thrower 1999, 94 (only mentioning the second stage in passing).
51 Harrison 2002, 17. Cf. Drachmann 1922, 43.
52 See above, n. 46.
53 Henrichs 1984, 151. In an earlier essay, Henrichs 1976, 20 argued that "finally Euhemerus of Messene (who wrote 'impious books' in which he took half of Prodicus' religious theory and turned it into a work of fiction)," which, again, implies that Euhemerus had direct access to Prodicus's work.
54 Cicero, *On the Nature of the Gods* 1.38; *PHerc.* 1428 2.28–3.13.
55 Winiarczyk 2013, 131; also 48, 117, 130. Cf. Whitmarsh 2015, 154–155, who accepts the relationship with Prodicus, but also adds Euhemerus in the same equation.
56 Περὶ Αἰγυπτίων. However, the exact title is unknown.
57 For example, see Murray 1970, 144–150; Henrichs 1984, 147 n. 32; Winiarczyk 2013, 64 n. 237. There are also different views, mainly as were discussed by Spoerri 1959, 164–211, who is rather skeptical toward the traditional view on Diodorus's debt to Hecataeus. Cf. the recent discussion in Muntz 2011.
58 Diodorus Siculus, *Historical Library* 1.11–12.
59 Ibid., 1.13.

60 Ibid., 1.14–16.
61 See Murray 1970, 151. Also Winiarczyk 2013, 64 n. 238 offers extended bibliography on this issue. I find the argument by Henrichs 1984, 148 that Hecataeus was drawing upon Prodicus a far-fetched statement that primary seeks to make the case of Euhemerus copying Prodicus rather than dealing with Euhemerus as an independent thinker who most likely relied on previous ideas.
62 Winiarczyk 2013, 65–66.
63 Ibid., 66; Herodotus, *Histories* 2.144.2. On Manetho, see Dillery 1999. On the influence of Herodotus on the Hellenistic historians in general and on Hecataeus in particular, which practically supports Winiarczyk's hypothesis that Hecataeus most likely followed Herodotus regarding the first Egyptian kings being gods, see Murray 1972, 207; Hornblower 2007, 313; Priestley 2014, 2.
64 Plato, *Cratylus* 397c–d. Cf. Eusebius, *Preparation for the Gospel* 3.9.14. Also Nilsson 1940, 3; Schott 2008, 155. On Plato's belief that the celestial objects were divine, see *Laws* 820e–822d. Cf. Mikalson 2010, 210 n. 7.
65 Aristotle, *Metaphysics* 12.1074b. Cf. the discussion in Bolle 1970, 21–22 and Roubekas 2011, 39–40.
66 Aristotle, *On the Heavens* 283b; 294a. Cf. French 1994, 66–67.
67 Plato, *Laws* 885a–b. For the interested reader, the phrase here translated as "non-belief" is οὐχ ἡγούμενος, whereas the phrase "believe in the gods" is θεοὺς ἡγούμενος εἶναι. Cf. the second volume of Bury's edition of the *Laws* in the LOEB library. Also Mayhew 2008.
68 Scullion 2007. I find the very characterization of Herodotus as "religious theorist" quite problematic. It can be interpreted in different ways: a) a theorist of religion who was religious. This implies that Herodotus was a devout person that decided to theorize about religion, which makes him, in this context, an apologist of religion given his non-naturalistic approach to religion; b) a theorist of religion. Here I take the characterization to mean what scholars in religious studies maintain, that is, a theorist who addresses the main questions of what is religion and how and why it originates and persists. I am assuming that Scullion means the former, which nevertheless seems like a contradiction of terms from a theoretical perspective.
69 See ibid., 198–200.
70 Herodotus, *Histories* 2.53. Kerferd 1981, 169 refers to this passage as an indication of Herodotus's search for the origin of the gods. However, it is merely the search for the origin of the anthropomorphic depiction of gods that Herodotus discusses here.
71 See Fowler 2010, 319 and n. 5 for a criticism of Scullion's argument. Whitmarsh 2015, 255 n. 11 accepts that Herodotus does indeed insert divine interventions in his work (for example, see *Histories* 1.87; 6.105; 8.36–39), but also maintains that the ancient historian used the supernatural "primarily in abstract ways," with 'god' or 'the divine' (Herodotus's favorite concepts when including the supernatural in his work) meaning "not the god of religion but an abstract, underlying system that the author claims to disclose thanks to his painstaking research" (ibid., 81).
72 For a discussion, see López-Ruiz 2015, 371–372. Similarly, Bowden 2004 deals with Xenophon as a theorist of religion or, at least, this is what the title of his paper implies ("Xenophon and the Scientific Study of Religion"). However, the paper is mainly dealing with Xenophon's religious views, his acceptance of the existence of the gods, and his position that human knowledge about the gods is very limited (245). This, in turn, is a theological rather than a social scientific approach to religion.

# References

Baumgarten, Albert I. 1996. "Euhemerus' Eternal Gods: Or, How Not To Be Embarrassed by Greek Mythology." In *Classical Studies in Honor of David Sohlberg*, edited by Ranon Katzoff, Yaakov Petroff, and David Schaps, 91–103. Ramat Gan: Bar-Ilan University Press.

Bett, Richard. 2012. *Sextus Empiricus: Against the Physicists*. New York and Cambridge: Cambridge University Press.

Bolle, Kees W. 1970. "In Defense of Euhemerus." In *Myth and Law Among the Indo-Europeans*, edited by Jaan Puhvel, 19–38. Berkeley, CA and London: University of California Press.

Bolle, Kees W. 2005. "Euhemerus and Euhemerism." In *Encyclopedia of Religion*, edited by Lindsay Jones, vol. 5, 2882–2884. New York: Macmillan.

Bowden, Hugh. 2004. "Xenophon and the Scientific Study of Religion." In *Xenophon and his World: Papers from a Conference Held in Liverpool in July 2009*, edited by Christopher Tuplin, 229–246. Stuttgart: Franz Steiner Verlag.

Broadie, Sarah. 1999. "Rational Theology." In *The Cambridge Companion to Early Greek Philosophy*, edited by Anthony A. Long, 205–224. Cambridge: Cambridge University Press.

Burton, Anne. 1972. *Diodorus Siculus, Book I: A Commentary*. Leiden: E. J. Brill.

Cole, Thomas. 1967. *Democritus and the Sources of Greek Anthropology*. Cleveland, OH: Western Reserve University Press.

Curd, Patricia. 2011. *A Presocratic Reader: Selected Fragments and Testimonia*. Indianapolis, IN and Cambridge: Hackett.

Davies, Malcolm. 1989. "Sisyphus and the Invention of Religion ('Critias' TrGF 1 (43) F 19 = B 25 DK)." *Bulletin of the Institute of Classical Studies* 36: 16–32.

Dillery, John. 1999. "The First Egyptian Narrative History: Manetho and Greek Historiography." *Zeitschrift für Papyrologie und Epigraphik* 127: 93–116.

Drachmann, Anders B. 1922. *Atheism in Pagan Antiquity*. Copenhagen: Gyldendal.

Drozdek, Adam. 2006. "Prodicus: Deifying Usefulness." *Myrtia* 21: 57–63.

Eliade, Mircea. 1959. *The Sacred and the Profane: The Nature of Religion*. Translated by Willard R. Task. New York: Harvest Books.

Fowler, Robert L. 2010. "Gods in Early Greek Historiography." In *The Gods of Ancient Greece: Identities and Transformations*, edited by Jan N. Bremmer and Andrew Erskine, 318–334. Edinburgh, UK: Edinburgh University Press.

Franek, Juraj. 2013. "Presocratic Philosophy and the Origins of Religion." *Graeco-Latina Brunensia* 18 (1): 57–74.

French, Roger. 1994. *Ancient Natural History*. London and New York: Routledge.

Freud, Sigmund. 2001. *Totem and Taboo*. Translated by James Strachey. London and New York: Routledge.

Gladigow, Burkhard. 1986. "Mythologie und Theologie: Aussagestufen im griechischen Mythos." In *Theologen und Theologien in verschiedenen Kulturkreisen*, edited by Heinrich von Stietencron, 70–80. Düsseldorf: Patmos.

Gregory, Andrew. 2013. *The Presocratics and the Supernatural: Magic, Philosophy and Science in Early Greece*. London and New York: Bloomsbury.

Guthrie, Stewart. 1993. *Faces in the Clouds: A New Theory of Religion*. New York and Oxford: Oxford University Press.

Guthrie, Stewart. 2000. "Projection." In *Guide to the Study of Religion*, edited by Willi Braun and Russell T. McCutcheon, 225–238. London: Cassell.

Harrison, Peter. 2002. *'Religion' and the Religions in the English Enlightenment.* Cambridge: Cambridge University Press.

Harvey, Van A. 1995. *Feuerbach and the Interpretation of Religion.* Cambridge: Cambridge University Press.

Henrichs, Albert. 1975. "Two Doxographical Notes: Democritus and Prodicus on Religion." *Harvard Studies in Classical Philology* 79: 93–123.

Henrichs, Albert. 1976. "The Atheism of Prodicus." *Chronache Ercolanesi* 6: 15–21.

Henrichs, Albert. 1984. "The Sophists and Hellenistic Religion: Prodicus as the Spiritual Father of the ISIS Aretalogies." *Harvard Studies in Classical Philology* 88: 139–158.

Henrichs, Albert. 2010. "What Is a Greek God?" In *The Gods of Ancient Greece: Indentities and Transformations*, edited by Jan N. Bremmer and Andrew Erskine, 19–39. Edinburgh, UK: Edinburgh University Press.

Hornblower, Simon. 2007. "Herodotus' Influence in Antiquity." In *The Cambridge Companion to Herodotus*, edited by Carolyn Dewald and John Marincola, 306–318. Cambridge: Cambridge University Press.

Kahn, Charles H. 1997. "Greek Religion and Philosophy in the Sisyphus Fragment." *Phronesis* 42 (3): 247–262.

Kerferd, George B. 1981. *The Sophistic Movement.* Cambridge: Cambridge University Press.

Kirk, Geoffrey S. and John E. Raven 1977. *The Presocratic Philosophers: A Critical History with a Selection of Texts.* Cambridge: Cambridge University Press.

López-Ruiz, Carolina. 2015. "Gods: Origins." In *The Oxford Handbook of Ancient Greek Religion*, edited by Esther Eidinow and Julia Kindt, 369–382. Oxford: Oxford University Press.

McCutcheon, Russell T. 1997. *Manufacturing Religion: The Discourse on Sui Generis Religion and the Politics of Nostalgia.* New York and Oxford: Oxford University Press.

McCutcheon, Russell T. 2007. *Studying Religion: An Introduction.* London and Oakville: Equinox.

Mayhew, Robert. 2008. *Plato: Laws 10.* Oxford: Clarendon Press.

Meier, P. A. 1981. "Philosophers, Intellectuals and Religion in Hellas." In *Faith, Hope and Worship: Aspects of Religious Mentality in the Ancient World*, edited by Henk S. Versnel, 216–263. Leiden: E. J. Brill.

Mikalson, Jon D. 2010. *Greek Popular Religion in Greek Philosophy.* Oxford: Oxford University Press.

Muntz, Charles E. 2011. "The Sources of Diodorus Siculus, Book 1." *Classical Quarterly* 61 (2): 574–594.

Murray, Oswyn. 1970. "Hecataeus of Abdera and Pharaonic Kingship." *Journal of Egyptian Archaeology* 56: 141–171.

Murray, Oswyn. 1972. "Herodotus and Hellenistic Culture." *Classical Quarterly* 22 (2): 200–213.

Nilsson, Martin P. 1940. "The Origin of Belief Among the Greeks in the Divinity of the Heavenly Bodies." *Harvard Theological Review* 33 (1): 1–8.

Norenzayan, Ara. 2013. *Big Gods: How Religion Transformed Cooperation and Conflict.* Princeton, NJ and Oxford: Princeton University Press.

Nye, Malory. 2008. *Religion: The Basics.* London and New York: Routledge.

O'Sullivan, Patrick. 2012. "Sophist Ethics, Old Atheism, and 'Critias' on Religion." *Classical World* 105 (2): 165–185.

Priestley, Jessica. 2014. *Herodotus and Hellenistic Culture: Literary Studies in the Reception of the Histories*. Oxford: Oxford University Press.

Roubekas, Nickolas P. 2011. Αναζητώντας τους Θεούς: Θρησκεία, Μύθος, και Ουτοπία στον Ευήμερο τον Μεσσήνιο. Thessaloniki: Vanias.

Roubekas, Nickolas P. 2014. "Ancient Greek Atheism: A Note on Terminological Anachronisms in the Study of Ancient Greek Religion." *Ciências da Religião* 12 (2): 224–241.

Schott, Jeremy M. 2008. *Christianity, Empire, and the Making of Religion in Late Antiquity*. Philadelphia, PA: University of Pennsylvania Press.

Scullion, Scott. 2007. "Herodotus and Greek Religion." In *The Cambridge Companion to Herodotus*, edited by Carolyn Dewald and John Marincola, 192–208. Cambridge: Cambridge University Press.

Segal, Robert A. 1999. *Theorizing About Myth*. Amherst, MA: University of Massachusetts Press.

Segal, Robert A. 2004. *Myth: A Very Short Introduction*. Oxford: Oxford University Press.

Segal, Robert A. 2013. "The Blurry Line Between Humans and Gods." *Numen* 60 (1): 39–53.

Spoerri, Walter. 1959. *Spälhellenistische Berichte über Welt, Kultur und Götter: Untersuchungen zu Diodor von Sizilien*. Basel: F. Reinhardt.

Sutton, Dana. 1981. "Critias and Atheism." *Classical Quarterly* 31 (1): 33–38 Cambridge: Cambridge University Press.

Thrower, James. 1999. *Religion: The Classical Theories*. Edinburgh: Edinburgh University Press.

Tylor, Edward B. 1883. *Primitive Culture: Researches into the Development of Mythology, Philosophy, Religion, Language, Art and Custom*. Vol. I. New York: Henry Holt.

Whitmarsh, Tim. 2014. "Atheistic Aesthetics: The Sisyphus Fragment, Poetics and the Creativity of Drama." *Proceedings of the Cambridge Philological Society* 60: 109–126.

Whitmarsh, Tim. 2015. *Battling the Gods: Atheism in the Ancient World*. New York: Alfred A. Knopf.

Winiarczyk, Marek. 1984. "Wer galt im Altertum als Atheist?" *Philologus* 128 (2): 157–183.

Winiarczyk, Marek. 2013. *The Sacred History of Euhemerus of Messene*. Translated by Witold Zbirohowski-Kościa. Berlin and Boston, MA: De Gruyter.

# 3   Returning to the Sources

It is only due to later authors that we get a glimpse of the *Sacred Inscription* and Euhemerus's theory of the origins of the gods and religion. Marek Winiarczyk has correctly pointed out that "we do not actually possess any fragments" of the text "in the strict sense of the word."[1] Such an assertion derives from the peculiar channels through which Euhemerus's work managed to find its way to both ancient and modern readers. Virtually everything we know—and admittedly, it is very little—about Euhemerus's work and theory is via the writings of two 'pagan' and two Christian authors: Diodorus Siculus, Ennius, Eusebius of Caesarea, and Lactantius. It is due to Winiarczyk's valuable work, which includes a publication of all available testimonies along with his monograph on the *Sacred Inscription*, that we can now confidently claim that none of the authors who incorporated (or translated) the original work into their own did so verbatim. This, of course, has various implications in how we, later readers, deal with the *Sacred Inscription* and the theory that Euhemerus promoted. In this chapter, however, I am not so interested in whether the available sources actually correspond to the original work, but why, how, and what those authors chose to utilize and incorporate from the lost original text according to their own agendas. In addition to this, I am interested in who those authors were and what we may learn from their choice to provide their readers with extensive summaries (and a translation) of the *Sacred Inscription*, fortuitously rescuing it from oblivion.

Given that I have dealt with the *Sacred Inscription* as a work of theorizing about religion, these questions become more critical when we consider how scholars of religion have approached such texts (and still do)—be it religious texts or works on religion(s). In the fourth of his now famous "Theses on Method," Bruce Lincoln posited that, when we deal with any speech act related to religious discourse, a series of questions needs to be posed and addressed:

> Who speaks here?—that is, what person, group, or institution is responsible for a text, whatever its putative or apparent author. Beyond that, To what audience? In what immediate and broader context?

Through what system of meditations? With what interests? And further, Of what would the speaker(s) persuade the audience? What are the consequences if this project of persuasion should happen to succeed? Who wins what, and how much? Who, conversely, loses?[2]

Undoubtedly, Lincoln's methodological concerns apply to the study of both the *Sacred Inscription* and its emerging theory of euhemerism when we turn our gaze upon the 'middlemen' to whom we owe our very knowledge of the work and theory. I am here concerned with the ancient authors who claimed authority about Euhemerus's work, rather than the ones from antiquity who utilized the theory either partially or mistakenly (deliberately or involuntarily) without having read the original text—these will be discussed later on in the book (see especially Chapter 6).

It is indeed a misfortune that Euhemerus's original work is now lost and we have to cope with certain barriers that must be removed in deciding how one can evaluate the theory itself and its place in those secondary sources. But, on the other hand, this should not be a formidable problem for students of euhemerism, even if it considerably alters our focus and interpretational stance. The incorporation of texts into other sources has been a com-mon practice that can be found in the study of both the modern and the ancient world. A text can indeed have too many authors, to para-phrase Samuel Wheerer III, who has demonstrated how an incorporated text within an incorporating text "whose authors make inconsistent claims can both be incorporated into a story making one claim," due to the domi-nation of the intended meaning conveyed by the incorporating text.[3] Thus, Euhemerus's euhemerism is by and large (or, indeed, predominantly) Diodorus's, Ennius's, Eusebius's, and Lactantius's euhemerism as well. Whatever Euhemerus's original text and its intended meaning was, it is shaped and (re)formed accordingly by the authors whose works happened to incorporate his ideas and managed to survive to the modern era.

When incorporating a text, however, a particular process is at work. The author of the incorporating text initially acts as a reader, making judgments and evaluations of the incorporated text according to his or her aims, ideology, social and political realities, religious beliefs, etc. before actually deciding to exploit it. The third level, that of the reader of the incorporating text's author, therefore, has no direct or clear knowledge of the incorp-orated text—especially so if the latter is lost, as in the case of the *Sacred Inscription*. This has been the crux of the exegetical problem in the study of the texts of the New Testament as well, as discussed by Bart Ehrman, who has argued that "scholars have recognized that it is important to know not only what an author wrote (i.e., in the autograph), but also what a reader read (i.e., in its later transcriptions)."[4] Although 'transcription' is hardly the case with the *Sacred Inscription*, Ehrman's point is valuable when one studies the sources we have at hand and their relation to the lost original. If the modern reader of the available testimonies is interested in Euhemerus's intention, there is hardly any concrete evidence from our ancient texts that will incontestably make a solid case. We are only left with speculations, which, surprisingly enough, often neglect the fact that what we do read is some readers' views. It is the latter that will preoccupy us in the next sections of this chapter.[5]

## Diodorus

It is an enduring issue whether Diodorus in his monumental *Historical Library* should be considered a mere copyist and compiler of texts, or if he must be taken as an original author who not only promoted his own views, but considerably pitched his sources to fulfill his own agenda. Recent scholarship has championed the latter, without however lacking voices supporting the former.[6] This turn in scholarship has significant consequences in addressing the validity of Diodorus's testimony when he presumably cites Euhemerus's *Sacred Inscription* verbatim. To further stress this issue, it is indeed surprising, albeit true, that recent studies on Diodorus have shown that the traditional view supporting a direct influence by Hecataeus of Abdera on the first book of the *Historical Library*—the discussion on the so-called Egyptian *theologoumena*—is contested and virtually denied.[7] This has serious repercussions to the overall understanding of Euhemerus's work and place in the *Historical Library*. Some thirty years ago, Kenneth Sacks promoted an interesting, but often overlooked, idea worthy of repeating here:

> Among Diodorus's sources for the first six books are several Hellenistic authors credited with the tradition of the deified mortal, especially Hecataeus of Abdera, Euhemerus, Megasthenes, and Dionysius Scytobrachion. But so little of their work exists outside of the *Bibliotheke* that the integrity of their ideas apart from Diodoran intrusion cannot be established with certainty. Indeed, there is substantial reason to believe that Diodorus played a significant role in designing the image of culture hero often attributed to his sources.[8]

It is this 'designing of the image of culture hero' that plays a significant role in Diodorus's work that needs to be addressed in order to see why and how Diodorus chose the *Sacred Inscription* among his sources and toward what end. There are considerable differences between Diodorus's concept of culture hero and what he transmits about Euhemerus's story. However, for the accuracy of the discussion here, I will only concentrate on what we learn from the fifth book alone, since the sixth book—that essentially contains Euhemerus's theory of religion in more detail—will be assessed below when dealing with Eusebius, which constitutes another important problem in itself as we will see.

Diodorus's culture hero and benefactor model (ἥρως εὑρετής) is linked to the known idea in antiquity of the relationship between civilization and agriculture.[9] The very birth of civilization, according to the Sicilian historian, was the result of certain actions—for example, in Egypt by Osiris and Isis—that demarcate the barbaric and animal-like from the civilized way of life. Those actions included the establishment of laws, the offering of the secrets of agriculture, and the foundation of cities, resulting in the negation and elimination of cannibalism as a clear indication of the transition from the prior to the new advanced stage. The gifts endowed by Isis and Osiris to the people led to their deification.[10] The list of benefactors is not exhausted to the most important Egyptian deities par excellence during the Hellenistic period. Sesostris, Semiramis, Dionysus, and Herakles all received immortal honors due to the benefactions that were primarily related to the gift of agriculture (for example, new techniques, new plants, prevention of floods) and secondarily to the advancement of the newly-born civilization (such as construction work, establishment of festivals, erection of temples, replacement of wicked rulers).[11] As a matter of fact, the theme of the 'cultural hero being deified' emerges numerous times in the *Historical Library* and it is founded on a reciprocal pattern exemplified by the scheme of 'necessity ($\chi\rho\epsilon i\alpha$) and benefaction ($\epsilon\dot{\nu}\epsilon\rho\gamma\epsilon\sigma i\alpha$)': the progress from the uncivilized to the civilized stage was based on the necessities humans had that were fulfilled by the individual benefactors, who themselves were members of those emerging societies.[12] Iris Sulimani has schematically represented the process as a motif that pervades the *Historical Library*: "gods were previously human; a man can become immortal on account of his benefactions; a hero sets his mind on gaining divine honours and thus calculates his actions accordingly; a hero goes through hardships in order to gain immortality."[13] Thus, for Sulimani, deification is the result of a well-organized plan, occurring a short time after those particular individuals realized the power of their benefactions that corresponded to the needs of the emerging societies. What she fails to explain, however, is how these individuals came up with the idea of godhead. Although she takes Osiris, Sesostris, and Herakles as having a political agenda, she adds that "[t]his is not to say that these mythical leaders did not care for religion as such [. . .] they used religion as a means to establish and to strengthen their rule both inside and outside their kingdoms."[14] If there was no traditional religion prior to the emergence of these individuals—as one can discern in Diodorus, given that they are the ones who become the first gods—how could they "care for religion as such"? In this scheme, Diodorus's Herodotian understanding of the origins of religion provides the (pre)historical context but not the need for the emergence of religion, since it places it in the mind of certain individuals as a preconceived or accidental idea, differing greatly from the deification by the people as an expression of gratitude, which in turn does provide us with a need being fulfilled.

Diodorus's intrusion into the sources he used, as argued by Sacks, can be seen on various occasions.[15] One related to Dionysus in India, as part of his civilizing journeys, is of particular interest. In 2.38.5, Diodorus claims that

Dionysus received divine honors in return for his various benefactions in India. However, in Arrian's *Indica* (7.8), it is Dionysus who teaches the inhabitants to worship him as a god, a status that he already held prior to his visit to India.[16] These two versions are incompatible although they come from the same source, that is, Megasthenes. Sacks has correctly argued that Diodorus here intervened in his sources in order to fit the tradition into his own principle of deification (θεὸν νομισθῆναι) as a result of benefactions. The obvious alteration and adaptation of the story by Diodorus signifies his consistent need to demonstrate how benefactions lead to deification, a palpable indication of his own belief and worldview stemming from the very cultural milieu in which he found himself. The centrality of Caesar's case in his work denotes Diodorus's admiration for the Roman leading figure and the retrospective application of the political and religious developments that occurred during his own lifetime onto the distant past of humanity. Caesar is praised in the *Historical Library* in many instances, from the very beginning of the work to the end, being called a god five times, while also deemed the epitome of the deification paradigm that is employed throughout the work.[17]

In book five of the *Historical Library*, however, Diodorus seems to follow another path, seemingly inconsistent to his own agenda which, it appears, he alters and adapts in his lost sixth book found in Eusebius. Although Diodorus provides information pertaining to some gifts bestowed by Zeus to the Cretans, his ancestors, and successors, in addition to other unnamed deeds performed by him, there is no clear indication of a deification as a result of those deeds:

ἐδείκνυον δὲ καὶ ἀναγραφάς τούτων, ἃς ἔφασαν τὸν Δία πεποιῆσθαι καθ' ὃν καιρὸν ἔτι κατ' ἀνθρώπους ὢν ἱδρύσατο τὸ ἱερόν [. . .] κατὰ μέσην δὲ τὴν κλίνην ἔστηκε στήλη χρυσῆ μεγάλη, γράμματα ἔχουσα τὰ παρ' Αἰγυπτίοις ἱερὰ καλούμενα, δι' ὧν ἦσαν αἱ πράξεις Οὐρανοῦ τε καὶ Διὸς ἀναγεγραμμέναι, καὶ μετὰ ταύτας αἱ Ἀρτέμιδος καὶ Ἀπόλλωνος ὑφ' Ἑρμοῦ προσαναγεγραμμέναι.

And they [Cretan priests] used to point to records, which they say Zeus made up the time when he was still dwelling among men and constructed the sacred precinct [of Zeus Triphyllius] [. . .] At the middle of the couch there stood a tall stele, inscribed with letters known in Egypt as hieroglyphs. These represented the deeds of Uranus and Zeus. And after these inscriptions Hermes added a sequel recording the deeds of Artemis and Apollo.[18]

Nowhere does Diodorus explicitly mention whether Zeus was deemed or proclaimed a god by the inhabitants. Additionally, the advancement from a lower to a higher stage of civilization is utterly dismissed throughout the parts of the fifth book that draw upon Euhemerus's *Sacred Inscription*, both of which are highlighted in Lactantius's Ennian version of the story.

A similar problem is encountered when dealing with Uranus. Euhemerus seems to be indifferent in relation to Uranus's deification, although Zeus's grandfather plays a central role in both Eusebius and Lactantius (that is, Ennius) as we will see:

μυθολογοῦσι γὰρ τὸ παλαιὸν Οὐρανὸν βασιλεύοντα τῆς οἰκουμένης προσηνῶς ἐνδιατρίβειν ἐν τῷδε τῷ τόπῳ, καὶ ἀπὸ τοῦ ὕψους ἐφορᾶν τόν τε οὐρανὸν καὶ τὰ κατ' αὐτὸν ἄστρα.

Legend is that in ancient times, when Uranus was king of the inhabited world, he spent a lot of his time there [The Throne of Uranus or Triphyllian Olympus]. From its height he observed the heaven and its array of stars.[19]

Not only Diodorus here does not provide us with the information pertaining to Uranus's deification, but also omits the discussion—or even a brief remark—about the distinction between heavenly (or celestial) and earthly (or human) gods.

Given Diodorus's consistency in repeating several times in his work any information that fits his agenda, it comes as a surprise that in book five he somehow neglects such important information, only to return to it in book six. By comparison, he is quite consistent when referring to the stele and the hieroglyphs (in both books), which is more or less identical with his account in 1.27.3, when he discusses the existence of Isis's and Osiris's tombs in the city of Nysa in Arabia, where a stele for each god is standing, bearing inscriptions in hieroglyphs (εἶναι δὲ καὶ στήλην ἑκατέρου τῶν θεῶν ἐπιγεγραμμένην τοῖς ἱεροῖς γράμμασιν), narrating Isis's numerous benefactions to humankind (cf. 1.27.4 ff.).[20] It seems highly unlikely that Diodorus chose not to incorporate in book five the result of Zeus's and Uranus's deeds, that is, their deification—unless Euhemerus treated this effect as something erroneous, which would contradict Diodorus's view of the origins of religion. Furthermore, the complete absence of the distinction between the two groups of gods seems equally bizarre, given the centrality of this classification in Euhemerus's thought as survived in Eusebius. These issues, of course, cannot be resolved without arguing, for example, that either Diodorus chose certain details from the *Sacred Inscription* to be added in his description of Panchaea in his fifth book, or that Eusebius was essentially intervening or altering the Diodorian text in book six. Whatever the case might be—which I will try to answer in the next section—it must be claimed that Diodorus's pattern of modifying or adapting his sources is not something restricted to his treatment of Euhemerus's work and theory. Rather, the Sicilian historian, following his own agenda and being influenced by his cultural, political, and historical environment, throughout his work is deliberately manipulating his data to serve his own purposes, which in turn needs to be taken into consideration when dealing with the *Sacred Inscription*.

## Eusebius

Although Diodorus's fifth book barely informs us about the process of Uranus's and Zeus's deification—and even more importantly, whether there was one—the lost sixth book, survived by Eusebius, provides us with essentially everything we know about the theory. It is here that we learn from Eusebius that Uranus not only observed the movement of the celestial objects but also "was the first one to honor with sacrifices the gods of the heaven."[21] Additionally, we get a clear picture of how Zeus was deified by the various peoples: by travelling and conquering many nations, he was "shown honors and was declared god."[22] Thus, in Eusebius's summary of the *Historical Library*'s sixth book we do encounter the familiar motif found in the rest of the first five books, yet with some significant additions, omissions, and innovations.

In addition to the distinction between heavenly and earthly gods, there are three basic elements in Eusebius's summary that require our attention. First, apart from a vague allusion to Uranus's character, being a clement and moderate man, and his good deeds (ἐπιεικῆ τινα ἄνδρα καὶ εὐεργετικὸν; W. T 49), Eusebius does not mention what those actions were that eventually led to Uranus's deification. The choice of words, however, indicates here that Eusebius is perhaps citing verbatim some of the original Diodorian text. Clemency, merciful behavior, and benefactions are the three pivots around which Diodorus unfolds his history of mythical figures receiving divine honors.[23] From the prehistoric past to the contemporary era of the Roman empire, Diodorus follows the same pattern, which is epitomized by Caesar.[24] Second, we find the addition of Zeus deifying Uranus, which was completely muted in book five: "and afterwards he arrived at Panchaea, an island near the Ocean, and established an altar for his grandfather Uranus."[25] Considering that Diodorus takes deification as a result of benefactions acknowledged by many (if not all) people, Uranus's exaltation by his grandson somehow interrupts Diodorus's pattern. This development is closer to the Hellenistic tradition of the ruler and dynastic cults (mainly in the kingdoms of the Seleucids and the Ptolemies—and later on in the Roman empire) than to Diodorus's transition from a lower to a more advanced culture/society. Third, nowhere does Eusebius mention any benefactions on behalf of Zeus that would justify the Diodorian understanding of the dipole benefaction/deification. Seemingly, Zeus is travelling the world, conquering new lands, and defeating rival kings, which results in his deification by all nations[26]—apparently due to his power rather than to his benefactions.

After establishing the main differences of the theory between books five (Diodorus) and six (Diodorus-via-Eusebius), we need to examine the nature of the *Preparation for the Gospel* (where the summary of book six is found) as well as Eusebius's own agenda. These two issues may shed further light on the motive(s) behind the employment of the *Sacred Inscription* by the Christian author and help us determine whether the summary of book six was altered by Eusebius, thereby further complicating the soundness of an ancient euhemeristic theory.

The *Preparation for the Gospel* is an astounding work in and of itself. It constitutes a library of ancient knowledge, carefully assembled in order to demonstrate the supremacy of the Christian doctrine against the 'pagan' beliefs and traditions. However, Eusebius is mainly writing against the Greek culture, rather than in opposition to all 'pagans,' in an attempt to show that culture's inferiority that has been mistakenly deemed innovative and great.[27] This is affirmed by a careful reconstruction of the prehistory of the Greek *ethnos*, which Eusebius sees as a mere copy of the Phoenician and Egyptian ones, via Cadmus and Orpheus respectively. Both figures are related to religion, literacy, and customs, forming a hybrid Greek culture that must be considered inferior to both the Phoenician and Egyptian.[28] Naturally, the most prominent element in Eusebius's discussion is that of religion, but it is swiftly expanded to include ethnicity and how Christians can justifiably claim a place in the world. After all, the very beginning of the *Preparation* (1.2.1) denotes the aim of the work at large:

> Someone might reasonably ask who we are who have come forward to write, whether we are Greeks or barbarians—or what can be between these? And who do we claim to be, not in regard to name, because this is manifest to all, but in our character and way of life? For they see that we neither think like the Greeks nor pursue the ways of the barbarians.[29]

Eusebius was obviously replying to certain questions posed to the early Christians by various outsiders. However, as the work reveals, the bishop of Caesarea has a specific opponent in mind, that is, Porphyry. It is the Neoplatonic philosopher from Tyre, whose accusations against the Christians—mainly, that they have abandoned and rejected their ancestral traditions—as well as his demand for their adherence to Judaism or Hellenism instead, that preoccupies the first six books of the *Preparation*.[30]

Eusebius employs a well-thought out and structured argumentation, unfolding around the beginnings of religion, in order to demonstrate that Christians have reasonably rejected the ancestral traditions since the latter were erroneous.[31] This is argued about through the two different channels that led ancient peoples to deviate from the true religion of the ancient Jews, finding themselves among the dead-ends of idolatry and polytheism. The first channel was the result of an adoration of the natural world, which led to the transformation of natural phenomena into gods and their subsequent worshipping. The second began with the eventual deification of heroes and rulers due to their inventions, benefactions, and wisdom. Both developments appeared among the Phoenicians and the Egyptians before spreading to the rest of the known world, including to the Greeks. The latter only employed, adopted, and slightly modified those mythologies, offering nothing new to this Eusebean history of religion.[32] These two stages have been nicely summarized by Aryeh Kofsky:

> Primitive men first lived as savages without urban settlements or social organization, and without the knowledge of God. However, they had an idea of natural religion and formulated principles that led them to the conclusion that there was a divine authority, whom they called God and regarded as a beneficent power. But since they did not possess a proper understanding of the deity, their concept of a transcendent God deteriorated into a cult of images of dead kings and rulers, to whom they attributed divine power.[33]

Eusebius's basic source for this prehistory of religion is Philo of Byblos and his *Phoenician History*, a now lost work, fragments of which can only be found in Eusebius's work. Philo has been deemed a euhemerist by many scholars, although I am reluctant to employ this characterization.[34] Kofsky's summary of the two stages of religion in the *Preparation* demands some further reflection. First, Eusebius—resting upon Philo and Porphyry—does not explain the need for which religion arises, or what the concept of god actually offers to people. The 'idea of natural religion' as a preexisting notion is perhaps one of the most ancient renderings of the *sui generis* argument, promoted here by Eusebius to denote that the very concept of god lies within all human beings implanted by (the Christian) God himself—even if it was profoundly distorted in the process. Second, the depiction of early societies as savage and barbarian that eventually and due to the concept of god developed into a more organized and humane society reminds us more of the Sisyphus view of religion than Euhemerus's (see Chapter 2). Third, Eusebius's take on 'pagan' religion perceives the deification of heroes and kings as a reflection of ancient people's inability to conceive the notion of a superhuman, transcendental deity. This, in turn, denotes that this second stage of religion replaces the first stage not because people become more advanced cognitively but due to their illogicality. Thus, by "[s]etting Christian truth in opposition not to falsehood but to inhuman irrationality and animality, Eusebius fixes Christianity as the mark of civilization,"[35] which consequently emphasizes the uniqueness of the Christians that not only deserve to be placed between the Jews and the Greeks, but also must be deemed the authoritative group (or, *ethnos*) which holds the keys of (the genuine) religion's truth.

This brings us to the nature of the *Preparation* as a work that is interested in religious history but with a specific end: establishing a distinctive identity for the Christians, which will place them above the cultures traditionally deemed 'superior' at the time. To accomplish this, Eusebius resorts selectively to sources that he himself had probably never read, with the exception of Porphyry and Diodorus, in which he finds Euhemerus's and Philo's interpretations of religion.[36] Further proof in favor of keeping a rather reticent stance is evident in Eusebius's insistence on taking the *Sacred Inscription* not as a utopian novel—which introduced a theory articulated within a specific historical period and with possibly particular motives—but rather as a testimony based on historical facts and figures, hence taking myth (of whatever coloring) as history, and rejecting any allegorical explanation.[37]

However, the most serious problem we run into when dealing with Eusebius's summary is related to the nature of the citation used by the Christian author: does Eusebius summarize Diodorus's sixth book with or without additions, alterations, or omissions? Sabrina Inowlocki has persuasively shown that to talk about exact reproductions by Eusebius in the *Preparation*, which constituted the traditional view, is contested and must be approached in a tentative fashion. Eusebius uses expressions that aim to convince his readers that he is citing from his sources verbatim, such as πρὸς λέξιν, κατὰ λέξιν, πρὸς ῥῆμα, and ῥήμασιν αὐτοῖς.[38] Nevertheless, as Inowlocki argues, the impression created here does not necessarily correspond to the actual process of composition. For Inowlocki, Eusebius

> theatralized acts of reading and writing, turning them into cultural statements supporting his construction of a Christian literary culture. [. . .] Whether or not Eusebius really had the books from which he quotes at his disposal is not a relevant question here. What matters is the impression he tries to create: that his citations are the "real" text excerpted as if taken up from a book and read to the reader.[39]

This is further supported by the citation process in antiquity as a literary technique, which hardly imitated its modern scholarly counterpart. In her *Eusebius and the Jewish Authors: His Citation Technique in an Apologetic Context* (2006), Inowlocki addresses this issue which plays a decisive role in our overall assessment and reconstruction of Euhemerus's theory—and is not only related to Eusebius's rendition. In her discussion, Inowlocki refers to various changes employed by the author of an incorporating text, such as omission or addition of words, grammatical changes, combination of citations, and modification of the primary meaning of a quotation—changes that were either deliberate or accidental.[40] Additionally, prose texts were more easily modified compared to poetic texts, given the flexibility prose texts allow for. This flexibility could lead to summarizations, paraphrasing, or even radical makeovers.[41] Last but not least, "the meaning of the text was not seen as a projection of the phrasing," which in turn implies that any modifications "could constitute, as it were, the explicitation of a certain truth."[42] Yet, making deliberately the meaning of a text more explicit does not simultaneously mean that the modification corresponds to the original author's intended emphasis, and we should also allow for the possibility of an initial misinterpretation, or even intentional alteration, of the original intended meaning in order to serve new agendas.

In his discussion of Euhemerus's theory as given in Diodorus's sixth book, Eusebius indeed follows his favorite style of persuading his readers that he is faithful to the original work. He is allegedly citing Diodorus verbatim by introducing the latter's text as follows:

ταῦτα ὁ Διόδωρος ἐν τῇ τρίτῃ τῶν ἱστοριῶν. ὁ δ' καὶ ἐν τῇ ἕκτῃ ἀπὸ τῆς Εὐημέρου τοῦ Μεσσηνίου γραφῆς ἐπικυροῖ τὴν αὐτὴν θεολογίαν, ὧδε κατὰ λέξιν φάσκων.

This is Diodorus's account in the third book of his Histories. This same author confirms the same theology in his sixth book, taking his argument from Euhemerus of Messene, using the *following exact words*.[43]

However, when it comes to citing Euhemerus's words (as survived by Diodorus), Eusebius chooses a summarization of the theory rather than a verbatim citation. This is how he introduces the topic:

καὶ τῶν μὲν ἱστορικῶν Εὐήμερος, ὁ τὴν Ἱερὰν Ἀναγραφὴν ποιησάμενος, ἰδίως ἀναγέγραφεν, τῶν δὲ μυθολόγων Ὅμηρος καὶ Ἡσίοδος καὶ Ὀρφεύς καὶ ἕτεροι τοιοῦτοι τερατωδεστέρους μύθους περὶ θεῶν πεπλάκασιν· ἡμεῖς δὲ τὰ παρ' ἀμφοτέροις ἀναγεγραμμένα πειρασόμεθα συντόμως ἐπιδραμεῖν, στοχαζόμενοι τῆς συμμετρίας.

Among the historians, Euhemerus, the author of the *Sacred Inscription*, wrote a monograph on this question, while, of the mythographers, Homer and Hesiod and Orpheus and the others of their kind have invented monstrous stories about the gods. For our part, we will try to provide *a brief summary* of the accounts which both groups of writers have given, aiming at due proportion in our exposition.[44]

First, Eusebius makes clear that he will take Euhemerus as a historian who provides facts and figures, contrary to the 'creators of monstrous tales,' that is, the quintessential introducers of traditional Greek religion: the poets. From the outset thus Euhemerus is perceived as an exponent of truth, which indicates Eusebius's opposition to any allegorical explanation, but also shows his preferred interpretation of the euhemeristic theory: as historical truth extracted, however, from its context; that is, the utopian genre and travelogue that lacks any historical credibility in this case. Second, Eusebius will not cite verbatim Diodorus's alleged verbatim citation of Euhemerus's ideas; rather, he will summarize what the Sicilian author mentions in his sixth book, which in turn raises the issue of how much interference is at work in what follows. Third, it becomes evident that Eusebius will use Euhemerus's work to demonstrate the superiority of Christianity vis-à-vis traditional 'pagan' religion, which of course fits into the larger agenda of the *Preparation*'s structure. That agenda included the appropriation and subsequent subordination of Greek literature to Eusebius's cause, that is, to establish Christianity as the most elaborate and advanced religious and cultural development worthy of his readers' attention and acceptance. This, in turn, prompts us to consider to whom this work was addressed, becoming obvious that Eusebius was writing for educated people, who either had previously converted to Christianity or were about to do so. The apologetic nature of the text is not here so much given as a reply to specific accusations, but as a handbook to interested readers who wish to expand their knowledge and attain further argumentation against the 'pagan' attitudes and rhetoric toward the Christians.[45] It is within such a context that Eusebius chooses to incorporate what Diodorus says about Euhemerus's theory of religion, which allows for considerable skepticism when we take his delivery of the theory at face value.

## Ennius and Lactantius

Much of Euhemerus's theory of the origin of the gods (and, thus, religion) comes from Ennius, who translated the *Sacred Inscription* into Latin. However, the translation did not manage to survive and we only get excerpts of the text in Lactantius, the third-century Christian author. Various information about the theory, absent in both Diodorus and Eusebius, appear only in the Ennian version. This in itself prompts us to further question our premises regarding the actual content of the lost Greek original.

Thus, it is in Lactantius's *Divine Institutes* where we learn for the first time that Euhemerus (via Ennius's translation) included further aspects in his theory. First, we encounter a detailed narration of the genealogy of the Olympians, which does not concentrate on Uranus but on Saturn (Cronus) (1.14.1–8; W. T 54. Also 1.14.10; W. T 10 and 1.14.11–12; W. T 58). Second, Jupiter (Zeus), the protagonist of the work, is portrayed in a completely different manner. He initially resides on Olympus, where people come and visit to present him with new discoveries that were useful to human life (1.11.35; W. T 67). It is due to Jupiter that a transition from cannibalism to civilization is marked by the constitution of laws and customs. Until his time, all people ate human flesh, including Saturn and his wife Ops (Rhea) (1.13.2; W. T 66)—not excluding, of course, Uranus, the clement and moderate man of Diodorus and Eusebius, who established the religion of the celestial objects. In Lactantius, on the contrary, it is Jupiter who observes the heaven and establishes an altar on the Triphyllian Olympus, accompanied by the initiation of the first sacrifice in honor of his grandfather, rather than as an acknowledgment of the existence of celestial or heavenly gods (1.11.63; W. T 62 and 1.11.65; W. T 52).[46] Third, Jupiter's deification is not merely the result of his victories promoted by the peoples themselves, but a well-conceived and executed plan by Jupiter himself, who ordered each of his (defeated) hosts to build altars commemorating their friendship. This resulted in an annual festival and ritual organized and celebrated by the various kings (1.22.21–27; W. T 64A).[47] Fourth, it is only in the Ennian version that we learn of Jupiter's death. After travelling the world five times and giving laws, customs, food, and performing various good deeds for the peoples he visited, he returned to Crete—his birthplace—where, in old age, he passed away. It is on this island, in the town of Cnossus, that his tomb is found bearing the inscription 'ZAN KRONOY,' Jupiter son of Saturn (1.11.44–48; W. T 69A. Cf. *Epitome of Divine Institutes* 13.4–5; W. T 68B).

The differences between the Diodorian and Ennian versions are striking to say the least. Why did Diodorus omit so many important details? Or, if he did not, why did Eusebius choose not to include further proof of Greek religion's 'monstrous stories'? These questions, however, presuppose that Ennius did translate the *Sacred Inscription* to the letter and Lactantius incorporated the Ennian text verbatim in his *Institutes*. Such an assertion, nevertheless, has absolutely no grounds, and both Ennius and Lactantius need to be approached with equal sedulity as Diodorus and Eusebius.

Ennius's translation, entitled *Euhemerus sive sacra historia*,[48] cannot be treated as a word-for-word translation. Marek Winiarczyk has argued extensively about this issue by indicating the probable additions by Ennius in the Latin text, which include matters of Latium etymology (see W. T 58), references to Aeneas (W. T 64A), and explanations for some of the Greek names (W. T 54; 69A; 69B).[49] In his conclusion on the issue of the translation's nature he argues that "one cannot rule out that Euhemerus's style was different to that of Ennius" and that it was rather "a free prose translation" which allowed Ennius to make additions or amendments according to his own agenda and style.[50] This, however, must be considered self-evident given the very nature of translation as a literary exercise. By definition, a translation from one language to another seeks to convey the intended meaning but does not necessarily do so by using the exact same words. As Umberto Eco argued in his *Experiences in Translation* (2001) on an excerpt of his *Foucault's Pendulum* and its English translation, the latter is "snappier than the Italian" which, in case he would proceed with a revised edition, he would probably "use the English formula." However, as he goes on to argue, "[w]ould we then say that I have changed my text? We certainly would." The English version, for Eco, is not an exact translation but, nonetheless, "says exactly what I wanted to say."[51] Here, however, we are also faced with another problem. Does Ennius's translation (as presented by Lactantius) say exactly what Euhemerus's wanted to say? Or did Ennius add to the text in order for it to say what he himself wanted to convey?

These questions are fundamentally related to Ennius's reasons for assuming such a wearisome task. Marek Winiarczyk has argued that Ennius went on with the translation in order to "prepare the way for the possible deification of Publius Cornelius Scipio Africanus" and thereby places the translation between the years 200 and 194 BCE.[52] Winiarczyk's hypothesis can be further supported by the absence of Caelus as a deified king in the Lactantian text, given that for Ennius this was virtually irrelevant to Scipio's apotheosis. On the other hand, however, we can learn more about Ennius's agenda through Cicero and his usage of *Euhemerus sive sacra historia*. The *de Re Publica*, as Spencer Cole has contended, constitutes Cicero's "native template for apotheosis" that could be based on Romulus as the quintessential example of deification in Roman history.[53] In doing so, Cicero draws on Ennius and his approach to Romulus. It could well be the case that this was ultimately Ennius's aim behind the translation of the *Sacred Inscription*: to apply the theory on Romulus and, thus, create a precedent that could then be applied to Scipio, Caesar, Pompey, or whoever would be worthy of being apotheosized. Cicero's utilization of Ennius is not accidental. Given that times had changed and Roman institutions, such as the concept of apotheosis, were now at the center of the contemporary political scene, Ennius functioned as a convenient tool for bringing together tradition and modernization[54] and, in connection with what Marek Winiarczyk argues about Scipio, we also encounter examples of such a practice in *de Re Publica* that Cicero presents to us as told by Scipio:[55]

> As Ennius said after the death of a great king; and at the same time they speak this way to one another: "Romulus, divine Romulus, what a guardian of the country the gods brought forth in you! Oh father, oh life-giver, oh blood sprung from the gods." They did not call those whom they justly obeyed "lords" or "masters," and not even "kings," but "guardians of the country," "fathers," "gods"—and not without reason. (1.64)
>
> We should allow this much to tradition, because it is not only ancient but wisely passed down by our ancestors that men who have deserved well of the community should be thought to be divine by birth as well as by talent. (2.4)
>
> Could anything display divine ability more than Romulus's embrace of the benefits of the coast while avoiding its vices by placing his city on the bank of a large river that flows strongly into the sea throughout the year? (2.10)
>
> When Romulus had ruled for thirty-seven years and had created these two excellent foundations for the common-wealth, the auspices and the senate, he was so successful that when he did not reappear after a sudden darkening of the sun, he was thought to have become a god; no mortal could ever have achieved that without an extraordinary reputation for virtue. (2.17)

Cicero's usage of Ennius in his works, and not merely in *de Re Publica*, is further exemplified by the very fact that we owe him the survival of the balkier fragments of Ennius's works. This has led James Zetzel to argue that the Roman politician and philosopher has influenced so much our (modern) understanding of Ennius that one could talk about, as his article's title demonstrates, Cicero's influence on Ennius—rather than the other way round, as one would naturally anticipate.[56] Parallel to what I have already argued about euhemerism as a theory that has been also shaped by the authors who chose to incorporate the whole or parts of the *Sacred Inscription* in their own works, Cicero "read, quoted, and used different works of Ennius for different reasons in different contexts and at different times of his life,"[57] which demonstrates the need to separate Ennius from Cicero's Ennius. Given that the Roman world came into contact with Euhemerus mainly through Ennius's translation,[58] one should similarly contend that the student of ancient euhemerism needs to separate Euhemerus from Ennius's Euhemerus.

Lactantius, on the other hand, is a different case. He is ostensibly citing from Ennius, similar to Eusebius claiming to be quoting from Diodorus. This is hardly surprising, since both Lactantius and Eusebius are essentially using the same method in compiling their massive works. Those projects were not treatises of defense or persuasion but, rather, serious instructions that— contrary to the aim of the earlier apologetic works—sought to establish Christianity's truth in an elaborate and sophisticated way.[59] The *Divine Institutes*, in which the only surviving fragments of Ennius's translation are found, is thereby in many respects similar to the *Preparation for the Gospel*. The issue of whether Lactantius is here citing verbatim from Ennius has been mainly repudiated. Marek Winiarczyk reckons that it is almost impossible for Lactantius to have had access to Ennius's original when writing in Asia Minor in the beginning of the fourth century. Rather, as he maintains, the Christian author utilized an intermediary work, thereby further adding to the problem of alterations and changes that the original text most likely underwent.[60] Furthermore, Alan Cameron has expressed his doubts pertaining to Lactantius's access to his sources, arguing that he probably got his quotations from Cicero or other authors.[61]

The *Divine Institutes* aims at exposing the failures of 'pagan' traditions, the false religions, in comparison to true religion, that is, Christianity. The motivation, similar to what also prompted Eusebius to compose his *Preparation*, was Porphyry's attacks on Christianity, in addition to the role played by the Diocletian persecution.[62] However, Lactantius employs an interesting method in exposing the inferiority of those false religions, which is based on the principle of a link between "ethnogenesis and the origins of religion," which sequentially means that "to write a history of religions is simultaneously to conduct an ethnographic survey."[63] It is not altogether difficult to fathom Lactantius's final goal: Christians deserve to be a distinct group (*gente*), since their religion is the true (*vera*) one when compared to the fallacies of the traditional religions. It is thus anticipated that the major enemy in Lactantius's eyes is Greek culture, given Porphyry's sophisticated argumentation against the Christians. Contrary to how Eusebius approaches the origins and diffusion of those 'false' religious ideas, Lactantius sees the Greeks as the introducers of those erroneous ideas and customs that they subsequently offered to other peoples.[64] Lactantius assigns to the Egyptians the worshipping of stars, planets, and other natural elements and phenomena (2.13.12), which was then replaced by animal iconography and, afterwards, gave way to the deification of dead kings (2.16.1–3). What is problematic here, however, is the disassociation between Lactantius's exposition of euhemerism in book one and Euhemerus's first stage of his theory, that is, the deification of the celestial or heavenly bodies. Lactantius treats euhemerism only as a theory of deification of (primarily dead) kings, which implies also that Ennius focused only on that aspect of the theory. It is therefore inferred that the Ennian-Lactantian euhemerism claims that Euhemerus was only interested in posthumous deification of powerful kings, neglecting altogether or even suggesting that Euhemerus did not deal with the first stage, that of the heavenly gods, or with ante mortem deification.

Lactantius's attempt to make Christianity the only true religion[65] prompted him to address the very etymology of the term *religio*, which constitutes the first candid presentation of the *sui generis* argument. Contrary to Cicero's derivation of the term from the verb *relegere* (to reread; go over again), Lactantius argues that the term stems from the verb *religare* (to tie back), which brings people back to the original true religion, linking them with the genuine God of Christianity (4.28.3). Such a definition of *religio* makes religion an ahistorical and a-cultural phenomenon, interconnected with the perceived transcendent and ahistorical divine agent of Christianity.[66] Obviously, such an understanding seeks to overcome Porphyry's allegations that the Christians do not follow or respect the ancestral traditions; on the contrary, those traditions, that were historically established, do not correspond to the linkage Lactantius here attempts to initiate between *religio* and ahistoricity. Christianity, in this view, is over and above those mistaken *religiones* of the various peoples.

\*   \*   \*

I have endeavored in this chapter to unveil the various layers found on top of the lost original text we now call *Sacred Inscription*. Euhemerus's theory pertaining to the origin of belief in gods (and, thus, religion) can only be assessed if we are prepared to accept that his work's validity stands as long as we recognize that from the outset we are dealing with its reception. When one chooses to read Euhemerus through Diodorus then s/he must be willing to acknowledge that the theory's focus differs greatly from what Ennius makes of it. Equally, Eusebius's and Lactantius's presentations of euhemerism have considerable differences that deviate from their 'pagan' counterparts. The question here is not who conveys the original text—this is probably lost forever—but what one can discern from the different versions and contexts within which the theory is presented. All four authors to whom we owe the survival of the *Sacred Inscription* claim to be either accurately summarizing, verbatim citing, or truthfully translating the original text or their sources that purportedly contain that original text. Yet none of these authors is resorting to the theory in order to merely rescue it; on the contrary, they all chose it after appraising its value for their own literary compositions that had specific agendas anchored to the historical context and the cultural and ideological questions and issues they needed to address. In this regard, the *Sacred Inscription* and its theory is as much Euhemerus's as it is that of Diodorus, Ennius, Eusebius, and Lactantius. A main problem often neglected by contemporary utilizations of the theory is that by using the Lactantian or the Eusebian versions scholars eventually ignore the Diodorian or the Ennian ones, thus reaching assessments and conclusions that do not necessarily correspond with what we actually have at our disposal about the theory of ancient euhemerism. Obvious differences and varied contexts notwithstanding, Brennan Breed has recently also argued about this problem in connection to the biblical reception history:

> When one chooses to read a particular form of a text in reference to a particular historical context, one chooses to draw the lines in a particular way. By choosing to read the *BHS* version of the book of Amos with reference to eighth-century BCE Israelite language, culture and history, for example, one creates a particular bounded space within which the text has a certain potential to mean. Yet part of Amos was written much later, and thus one could read it in reference to its sixth-century Judean redactors. Which context is the right one? If I am correct that biblical texts are processes, then this question is absurd.[67]

Euhemerus's ideas obviously have different connotations when set against the authors who included them in their works and their milieus. This, however, does not necessarily mean that we cannot proceed further with euhemerism; but it does indicate that we need to be conscious of whose euhemerism we are employing and hence whose euhemerism we leave behind.

## Notes

1  Winiarczyk 2013, 13.
2  Lincoln 2012, 1.
3  Wheeler III 2012, n. p.
4  Ehrman 1995, 361 n. 1.
5  This has been nicely articulated by Walter Benn Michaels, who argued that

> if you think the intention of the author is what counts, then you don't think the subject position of the reader matters, but if you don't think the intention of the author is what counts, then the subject position of the reader will be the only thing that matters.
>
> (Michaels 2004, 11)

6  In past decades, it was the idea of Diodorus as a mere epitomizer that prevailed. For bibliography, old and new, still supporting this view, see Muntz 2011.
7  For example, see Winiarczyk 2013, 135 and mainly Muntz 2011, whereas Pachis 2014, 313; 321 follows a more traditional view although he is primarily interested in Diodorus's first book rather than in Euhemerus per se.
8  Sacks 1990, 70–71.

9  See Pachis 2003.

10 On the offering of laws, see Diodorus Siculus, *Historical Library* 1.14.4; foundation of cities, 1.15.1–5; agriculture and grains, 1.14; 1.15.6; 1.17.1; end of cannibalism, 1.14.1; deification as a result of these gifts (εὐεργεσία) 1.17.2: οὐ μόνον γὰρ τοὺς κατ᾽ ἐκείνους τοὺς χρόνους τυχόντας τῆς δωρεᾶς ταύτης, ἀλλὰ καὶ πάντας τοὺς μετὰ ταῦτα ἐπιγενομένους διὰ τὴν ἐν ταῖς εὑρεθείσαις τροφαῖς χάριτα τοὺς εἰσηγησαμένους ὡς ἐπιφανεστάτους θεοὺς τετιμηκέναι; advancement from a lower to an advanced stage 1.6–8. Cf. Pachis 2014, 311–313; Sacks 1990, 69.

11 On Sesostris, 1.55.7; Semiramis, 2.13.2; 2.13.6–8; 2.14.3; Dionysus, 2.38.5; 3.64.2; 3.70.8; 3.72.3; 3.74.2; 4.3.2; Herakles, 1.2.3; 3.30.4; 4.18.2; 4.18.4; 4.24.1; 4.38–39. Cf. Sulimani 2011, 64–65; 83–89; 229; 280–295; Pachis 2014, 319–321; Winiarczyk 2013, 136.

12 See Sacks 1990, 68–71.

13 Sulimani 2011, 65.

14 Ibid., 296.

15 Ibid., 83–89.

16 Diodorus Siculus, *Historical Library* 2.38.5: μετὰ δὲ ταῦτα τῆς παραθέσεως τῶν καρπῶν ἐπιμεληθέντα μεταδιδόναι τοῖς Ἰνδοῖς, καὶ τὴν εὕρεσιν τοῦ οἴνου καὶ τῶν ἄλλων τῶν εἰς τὸν βίον χρησίμων παραδοῦναι. πρὸς δὲ τούτοις πόλεών τε ἀξιολόγων γενηθῆναι κτίστην, μεταγαγόντα τὰς κώμας εἰς τοὺς εὐθέτους τόπους, τιμᾶν τε καταδεῖξαι τὸ θεῖον καὶ νόμους εἰσηγήσασθαι καὶ δικαστήρια, καθόλου δὲ πολλῶν καὶ καλῶν ἔργων εἰσηγητὴν γενόμενον θεὸν νομισθῆναι καὶ τυχεῖν ἀθανάτων τιμῶν. Cf. Sacks 1990, 72. Also see Vernière 1990 and Seaford 2006.

17 Diodorus Siculus, *Historical Library* 1.4.7; 4.19.2; 5.21.2; 5.25.4; 32.27.1; 32.27.3. Cf. Sulimani 2011, 70–73; Sacks 1990, 73–74.

18 Diodorus Siculus, *Historical Library* 5.46.3; 5.46.7 (W. T 35; 37).

19 Ibid., 5.44.6 (W. T 50).

20 Cf. Pachis 2014, 317.

21 ὃν καὶ πρῶτον θυσίαις τιμῆσαι τοὺς οὐρανίους θεούς (W. T 49).

22 παρὰ πᾶσιν τιμηθῆναι καὶ θεὸν ἀναγορευθῆναι (W. T 63).

23 See above, n. 13.

24 See Sulimani 2011, 102; cf. 57. Sacks 1990, 74 adds "noble birth, military and oratorical skills, and indifference to money."

25 καὶ μετὰ ταῦτα εἰς τὴν Παγχαίαν νῆσον πρὸς τῷ ὠκεανῷ κειμένην παραγενόμενον Οὐρανοῦ τοῦ ἰδίου προπάτορος βωμὸν ἱδρύσασθαι (W. T 61).

26 See Eusebius, *Preparation for the Gospel* 2.2.60–61 (W. T 61; 63).

27 See Kofsky 2000, 80, who calls the work an "anti-Greek apology and a positive presentation of Christian doctrine."

28 See the excellent discussions in Johnson 2004, 39–43; 2006a, 77–80.

29 Translation drawn from Johnson 2004, 26.

30 See Schott 2008, 138. Cf. Wilken 1979, 120.

31 See *Preparation for the Gospel* 1.6.7; cf. 1.5.13.

32 On nature worship, see ibid. 1.9.5–6; on deified heroes and kings, 1.9.29 along with the excerpt from Diodorus on Euhemerus; on the influence of the Phoenician and Egyptian theologies on the Greeks, 1.6; 1.9; 2.1.54–55; 2.2.52.

33 Kofsky 2000, 135.

34 See Baumgarten 1981, especially 242–243; Winiarczyk 2013, 138–139. My reluctance to take Philo as a euhemerist—in the strict sense of the term—is his insistence on benefactions and, more importantly, post mortem deification (see *Preparation for the Gospel* 1.9.29). When compared to the absence of tangible benefactions on behalf of Zeus and his ante mortem deification, it is only the central idea of euhemerism, that is, the deification of kings, that could potentially be applied to the *Phoenician History*. Philo speaks of the discoveries of fire,

sea navigation, arts of hunting and fishing, iron, oratory, magic, whereas he additionally engages with the etymology of the ancient deities, as Johnson 2006a, 69–70 has rightly pointed out. The secondary role of the celestial stage of religion, as portrayed in Philo, does not necessarily correspond to Euhemerus's view. Cf. *Preparation for the Gospel* 1.9.16; 1.10.9–12.

35 Schott 2008, 138.
36 See ibid., 140.
37 See *Preparation for the Gospel* 1.10.55; cf. Johnson 2004, 43–47; 2006a, 86; Schott 2008, 143.
38 Inowlocki 2011, 203.
39 Ibid., 199, 203–204.
40 Inowlocki 2006, 40.
41 Ibid., 42–43.
42 Ibid., 47.
43 Eusebius, *Preparation for the Gospel* 2.2.52 (W. T 25), emphasis added.
44 Ibid. 2.2.54 (W. T 8), emphasis added.
45 See the discussion in Inowlocki 2011, 215; 221. Johnston 2006b, 86 refers to a combination of "elementary Christian instruction" and "the creation and maintenance of a master narrative to shape the late antique Christian mind" as the aims of the *Preparation*; the former, as he argues, could well indicate that the text was meant as a manual "for teachers rather than students" (81).
46 On this issue, see Winiarczyk 2013, 119.
47 Further on this issue, see Sulimani 2011, 64.
48 I here follow Marek Winiarczyk's title (2013, 109), who has convincingly shown that the other titles mentioned in Lactantius (*Sacra historia* and *Historia sacra*, and also *Euhemerus sive Sacra scriptio*, see 114–115) were not the original ones.
49 Ibid., 118–119.
50 Ibid., 116–117; 122.
51 Eco 2001, 8.
52 Winiarczyk 2013, 109; cf. 114 and 122.
53 Cole 2006, 540.
54 See ibid., 547–548; cf. Cole 2013, 6; 155–156.
55 All excerpts and translations are drawn from Cole 2006.
56 See Zetzel 2007.
57 Ibid., 16.
58 Winiarczyk 2013, 119–122 has shown that the work was known to and read by Cicero and Varro.
59 See DePalma Digeser 2000, 9–11. The similarities between Lactantius's and Eusebius's works are many. The *Institutes* was probably addressed to an educated audience as well, familiar with ancient traditions and modern Christian teachings. Cf. Schott 2008, 80.
60 See Winiarczyk 2013, 118 as well as his discussion in 117 and conclusion in 122.
61 See Cameron 2011, 402.
62 See Schott 2008, 80–81.
63 Ibid., 97. Cf. Lactantius, *Divine Institutes* 1.15.7–10.
64 Schott 2008, 98.
65 The dipole true religion/false religions is also linked to the opposition between one and many gods. Cf. Lactantius, *Divine Institutes* 1.20.21; 1.23.6–7.
66 Schott 2008, 105–106. Cf. the discussion of the term *religio* in Latin authors in Nongbri 2013 (especially chapter two).
67 Breed 2014, 12.

## References

Baumgarten, Albert I. 1981. *The Phoenician History of Philo of Byblos: A Commentary*. Leiden: E. J. Brill.

Breed, Brennan W. 2014. *Nomadic Text: A Theory of Biblical Reception History*. Bloomington, IN and Indianapolis, IN: Indiana University Press.

Cameron, Alan. 2011. *The Last Pagans of Rome*. Oxford: Oxford University Press.

Cole, Spencer. 2006. "Cicero, Ennius, and the Concept of Apotheosis at Rome." *Arethusa* 39 (3): 531–548.

Cole, Spencer. 2013. *Cicero and the Rise of Deification at Rome*. New York and Cambridge: Cambridge University Press.

DePalma Digeser, Elizabeth. 2000. *The Making of a Christian Empire: Lactantius and Rome*. Ithaca, NY and London: Cornell University Press.

Eco, Umberto. 2001. *Experiences in Translation*. Translated by Alastair McEwan. Toronto and London: University of Toronto Press.

Ehrman, Bart D. 1995. "The Text as Window: New Testament Manuscripts and the Social History of Early Christianity." In *The Text of the New Testament in Contemporary Research: Essays on the Status Quaestionis*, edited by Bart D. Ehrman and Michael W. Holmes, 361–379. Grand Rapids, MI: Eerdmans.

Inowlocki, Sabrina. 2006. *Eusebius and the Jewish Authors: His Citation Technique in an Apologetic Context*. Leiden and Boston, MA: Brill.

Inowlocki, Sabrina. 2011. "Eusebius' Construction of a Christian Culture in an Apologetic Context: Rereading the *Praeparatio Evangelica* as a Library." In *Reconsidering Eusebius: Collected Papers on Literary, Historical, and Theological Issues*, edited by Sabrina Inowlocki and Claudio Zamagni, 199–223. Leiden and Boston, MA: Brill.

Johnson, Aaron P. 2004. "Identity, Descent, and Polemic: Ethnic Argumentation in Eusebius' *Praeparatio Evangelica*." *Journal of Early Christian Studies* 12 (1): 23–56.

Johnson, Aaron P. 2006a. *Ethnicity and Argument in Eusebius' Praeparatio Evangelica*. New York and Oxford: Oxford University Press.

Johnson, Aaron P. 2006b. "Eusebius' *Praeparatio Evangelica* as Literary Experiment." In *Greek Literature in Late Antiquity: Dynamism, Didacticism, Classicism*, edited by Scott Fitzgerald Johnson, 67–89. Aldershot, UK and Burlington, VT: Ashgate.

Kofsky, Aryeh. 2000. *Eusebius of Caesarea Against Paganism*. Leiden and Boston, MA: Brill.

Lincoln, Bruce. 2012. "Theses on Method." In *Gods and Demons, Priests and Scholars: Critical Explorations in the History of Religions*, 1–3. Chicago, IL and London: University of Chicago Press.

Michaels, Walter Benn. 2004. *The Shape of the Signifier: 1967 to the End of History*. Princeton, NJ: Princeton University Press.

Muntz, Charles E. 2011. "The Sources of Diodorus Siculus, Book 1." *Classical Quarterly* 61 (2): 574–594.

Nongbri, Brent. 2013. *Before Religion: A History of a Modern Concept*. New Haven, CT and London: Yale University Press.

Pachis, Panayotis. 2003. Ἥρως Εὑρετής: Γεωργία καὶ Πολιτισμός στον Ἀρχαιοελληνικό Κόσμο. Thessaloniki: Vanias.

Pachis, Panayotis. 2014. "The Discourse of a Myth: Diodorus Siculus and the Egyptian *Theologoumena* During the Hellenistic Age." In *Chasing Down Religion:*

*In the Sights of History and the Cognitive Sciences: Essays in Honor of Luther H. Martin*, edited by Panayotis Pachis and Donald Wiebe, 303–336. Sheffield, UK: Equinox.

Sacks, Kenneth S. 1990. *Diodorus Siculus and the First Century*. Princeton, NJ: Princeton University Press.

Schott, Jeremy M. 2008. *Christianity, Empire, and the Making of Religion in Late Antiquity*. Philadelphia, PA: University of Pennsylvania Press.

Seaford, Richard. 2006. *Dionysos*. London and New York: Routledge.

Sulimani, Iris. 2011. *Diodorus' Mythistory and the Pagan Mission: Historiography and Culture-Heroes in the First Pentad of the Bibliotheke*. Leiden and Boston, MA: Brill.

Vernière, Yves. 1990. "L' expédition mythique d'Osiris-Dionysos en Asie et ses prolongements politiques." In *Mythe et Politique: Actes du Colloque de Liège, 14–16 septembre 1989 organisé par le Centre de recherches Mythologiques de l' Univertè de Liège*, edited by André Motte and François Jouan, 279–285. Paris: Les Belles Lettres.

Wheeler III, Samuel. 2012. "Intentionalism and Texts with Too Many Authors." *Nonsite 6*. Online: http://nonsite.org/article/intentionalism-and-texts-with-too-many-authors (accessed December 4, 2015).

Wilken, Robert L. 1979. "Pagan Criticism of Christianity: Greek Religion and Christian Faith." In *Early Christian Literature and the Classical Intellectual Tradition: In Honorem Robert M. Grant*, edited by William R. Schoedel and Robert L. Wilken, 117–134. Paris: Beauchesne.

Winiarczyk, Marek. 2013. *The Sacred History of Euhemerus of Messene*. Translated by Witold Zbirohowski-Kościa. Berlin and Boston, MA: De Gruyter.

Zetzel, James E. G. 2007. "The Influence of Cicero on Ennius." In *Ennius Perennis: The Annals and Beyond*, edited by William Fitzgerald and Emily Gowers, 1–16. Cambridge: Cambridge Philological Society.

# 4 Euhemerism and Atheism

I concluded the first chapter by arguing that although the earthly or human gods are to be seen as mere humans, Euhemerus's view of the heavenly or celestial gods radiates a sense of acceptance of their divinity regardless of the lack of sources that would clarify this issue beyond any doubt. This position, embraced also by Marek Winiarczyk,[1] virtually denies the traditional—already from antiquity—observation of Euhemerus's atheism; by taking the celestial gods qua gods, the Messenean is easily exonerated from the longstanding accusation of atheism.[2] Still, the sources themselves are not so much help on this matter. The possibility that Euhemerus merely informs us of what Uranus himself thought about those deities after observing the movement of the heavenly bodies, forces us to keep the issue open to the likelihood of a straightforward atheism. There is no strong textual indication that Euhemerus himself shared Uranus's understanding of the heavenly realms and, given his total deconstruction of the traditional beliefs pertaining to the earthly or human gods, we must at least examine whether classifying him as an atheist has any merit whatsoever.

Yet, the mere examination of Euhemerus's potential atheism seems somehow doomed by the very classification itself. The question of atheism in antiquity (as well as the adjective *atheos*, ἄθεος) has for many years bedeviled scholars—and still does to a large extent. Most attempts to classify individuals of antiquity as atheists have been dealt with skepticism and, typically, outright rejection. However, Tim Whitmarsh's latest book, entitled *Battling the Gods: Atheism in the Ancient World* (2015), is a breath of fresh air to the whole debate in relation to whether one can talk about atheism in antiquity and, more importantly, what is meant by the term. The former question is confidently—and quite rigorously—accepted by Whitmarsh when he argues that

> [a]theism, we are so often told, is a modern invention, a product of the European Enlightenment: it would be inconceivable without the twin ideas of a secular state and of science as a rival to religious truth. This is a myth nurtured by both sides of the "new atheism" debate: adherents wish to present skepticism toward the supernatural as the

result of science's progressive eclipse of religion, and the religious wish to see it as a pathological symptom of a decadent Western world consumed by capitalism. Both are guilty of modernist vanity. Disbelief in the supernatural is as old as the hills.[3]

Although there is hardly any scholar who would disagree with the final sentence in the above excerpt, lately there has been a well-established trend among classicists to see downright atheism as something that constitutes a pure case of anachronism that has no place in ancient discourses on religious criticism. Hence, before addressing the question of Euhemerus's atheism, I will tackle the complicated and rather problematic issue of 'atheism in antiquity' before proceeding to a brief examination of the main figures who dealt with and classified Euhemerus as atheist, namely Cicero, Plutarch, and Sextus Empiricus.

## Atheism in Antiquity

Whitmarsh's thesis cannot be easily overlooked or dismissed. The traditional trend of seeing the ancient Greek world as a religious locale par excellence has undoubtedly influenced and, in many cases, manipulated the study of ancient atheism. However, what most scholars seem to neglect is the peculiar case of atheism as a common descriptor that is somehow applicable, in whatever chosen form, throughout both antiquity and modernity. There is hardly any objection when, say, one argues that atheism did not exist in antiquity, if by the term it is the modern notion of atheism within a monotheistic religious worldview that is being employed. After all, even the understanding of theism is vastly different when examined within, as it were, an Abrahamic appreciation of 'God' when compared to any similar notion in antiquity. As such, contrary to what an ancient Greek *theós* was, the modern biblically-based notion of *God* has its own complicated history that, in turn, shifts the meaning of both theism and, of interest here, atheism when we examine its existence or not in antiquity.[4]

Furthermore, there is no evidence that atheism in antiquity had a concrete form, thereby being easily identifiable and classifiable as a phenomenon wherever and whenever it was encountered. This is mainly due to the different understanding of what atheism means to us compared to whatever notion the Greeks had in antiquity. As such, it comes as a surprise that the famous opening of Protagoras's lost work *On the Gods*—"Concerning the gods, I cannot know whether they exist or whether they do not, or what form they have, for there are many impediments to knowledge, including obscurity and the brevity of human life"—gave him a place on the list of atheists considering that his view, in modern standards, is straightforwardly agnostic.[5] Yet, this assertion is, once again, anchored to what such terms (theism, atheism, agnosticism, etc.) mean today. The problem with atheism, however, seems different; the mere fact that, as a term, it comes from the ancient Greek (or, at least its derivative *atheos* does),[6] somehow allows its anachronism-free adoption and application to individuals of antiquity. In and of itself, this creates fewer setbacks than theism does, as it were. The problem, however, lies in the content rather than the actual lexical usage of the term. This is further exemplified from a definition-centered point of view, with scholars having literally struggled to provide an acceptable definition—a problem somehow similar to the one of defining religion—that is applicable through time and space.[7] Ethan Quillen's distinction between historical (or lexical) and theoretical (or essential) definitions has indicated the root of the problem, at least from a religious studies point of view. As he puts it in the beginning of his article,

> the former consists of definitions based upon first-order examples, wherein the Atheism being described is based upon the ways in which Atheists have either been defined by others, or have defined them-selves, within particular historical contexts. The latter, then, consists of attempts at combining these historically different definitions into something more general, and thus applicable across a much larger contextual field.[8]

It is undoubtedly this 'essential or general' definition being sought that creates this semantic and classificatory unbridged gap when talking about atheism in antiquity. In the case of the ancient Greek world, there is hardly any example of a self-proclaimed atheist but numerous individuals classified as ἄθεος by others. The list is long, including famous figures, such as Socrates, Diagoras, Hippon, Theorodus of Cyrene, Prodicus, Democritus, Critias, and Euhemerus among others.[9]

Last but not least, an additional issue that is hooked on disciplinary nails that go deep into the ways scholars approach ancient religion and religiosity is at play here. The traditional, and largely still dominant, approach to Greek religion is almost always dictated by the notion of embeddedness. Simply put, religion in ancient Greece "was totally embedded in society—no sphere of life lacked a religious aspect."[10] There are two main objections to such an artificial classification of ancient societies, each tangling with different issues although they are essentially interconnected. The first is related to the issue of what 'religious' means in such statements. As it has been recently argued, religion cannot qualify as a category applicable to antiquity given its recent creation as a Western (Protestant) Christian-biased descriptor. This view claims that it is by definition anachronistic to talk about religion in antiquity, and that the term is not an indigenous but a modern category that scholars employ. Brent Nongbri has successfully presented this issue, arguing against an unexamined utilization of the term when studying ancient cultures. Such uninformed adoption, as the argument goes, virtually transforms the term from a redescriptive (outsider) into a descriptive (insider) one.[11] If religion is an outsider term, then the embeddedness argument collapses, as it is merely a scholarly creation that inserts certain elements deemed religious in the modern sense into cultures that did not categorize those elements as such, nor did they see themselves as living in societies in which religion was, as it were, embedded. By the same token, if religion is in this way utilized, then atheism is equally problematic, although via alternative routes as well—for example, when its presence within ancient societies is mostly denied by scholars who are ready to acknowledge the existence of 'religion' in antiquity.

This brings us to the second objection. Explicit or implicit denial of the existence of atheism in antiquity has been recently promoted, even in cases where religious belief is plainly rejected(!). The problem here lies beyond the one related to the available sources and the, often justifiable, reservations ancient historians have when characterizing individuals from antiquity as atheists. Tim Whitmarsh has eloquently argued that

> [s]o keen have classicists been to avoid "Christianizing" the Greeks (a cardinal offense in the academy!) that the standard textbooks have tended to describe Greek polytheism as in effect a straightforward inversion of modern Christianity (particularly in its Protestant guise): focused on collective ritual rather than individual contemplation, the public sphere rather than the private self, outward performance rather than inner belief, conformity to past practice rather than scripture. There is much in this portrait that is true, but rigid, schematic oppositions can be deeply misleading. It is demonstrably wrong to suggest that Greek religion was unproblematically "embedded" (to use the scholarly parlance) in society, fully naturalized in all of the day-to-day rhythms of the ancient city, to the extent that no ancient could imagine a world without religion.[12]

The advocated ritual-based, collective nature of Greek religion has so much penetrated the study of the field that it has even reached to the other extreme, that of denying the existence of belief in the ancient gods.[13] Normally revolving around the semantics of verbs such as *nomizein*, as in the known indictment against Socrates and the phrase *oude theous nomizein* (οὐδὲ θεοὺς νομίζειν),[14] such a Christian-centric view of belief virtually denudes ancient Greek religion of any kind of belief in the existence of the Greek gods.[15] As Henk Versnel has rightly put it,

> how does one communicate with divine beings through prayer, gift-giving, and attributing them a full scale of anthropomorphic (and allomorphic) features [. . .] *without* believing (that is taking as true) that these beings exist (in whatever sense of the word 'exist')?[16]

Consequently, and if taken at face value, such an approach transforms the ancients into quintessential atheists, in whatever manner one wishes to define the term; which, in turn, contradicts the trend of refusing the existence of atheism in antiquity.

Taking belief in the existence of the Greek gods as an unconditional parameter in any discussion of atheism in antiquity, one needs to also address the problem of embeddedness before proceeding. In addition to Whitmarsh's argumentation, Bruce Lincoln's position is, from a religious studies point of view, appealing and methodologically difficult to be denied, since he manages to reply to both the anachronistic usage of religion when studying ancient cultures and the problem of embeddedness. Without denying the problem in question, and addressing both issues succinctly, he points out that

> [t]o say that nothing in antiquity was free of religion—not war, disease, erotic love, science, the arts, poetry, or the state; not the landscape, the family, the meat on the table, or the fire on the hearth—is to say not that everything "was" religious, only that religious concerns were a part of all else, and a part that remains—to us, at least—analytically recognizable.[17]

This opens up the way for dealing with ancient atheism as the opposite of belief in the existence of Greek gods, without denying the Greeks their religious ideas and practices, nor seeing them as cognitively incapable individuals who did things labeled as religious (from a modern perspective) without knowing why they did so.

## Was Euhemerus an Atheist?

There are two sub-questions that must be taken into consideration before addressing the core question. First and foremost, who in antiquity asked the question and why, and, subsequently, what was the verdict. This is closely related to the doxographical tradition. The inclusion of Euhemerus among the atheists of antiquity was the result of the creative works by authors such as Cicero, Philodemus, Plutarch, Diogenes Laertius, Sextus Empiricus and others, who connected their contemporary readers with the immense repository of earlier thought through, as Tim Whitmarsh calls it, 'virtual networks.'[18] I choose three of those doxographers (Cicero, Plutarch, and Sextus) in order to see how and why Euhemerus ended up in their works as an atheist as well as to examine the purposes served by such a classification. Second, what do the remaining sources claim and what can one make out of them pertaining to Euhemerus's atheism or lack thereof?

### Cicero

One of the main sources from antiquity that deals with Euhemerus as an atheist is Cicero's *On the Nature of the Gods*. The oft-cited passage referring to Euhemerus is the following:

*Quid qui aut fortis aut claros aut potentis viros tradunt post mortem ad deos pervenisse, eosque esse ipsos quos nos colere precari venerarique soleamus, nonne expertes sunt religionum omnium? Quae ratio maxime tractata ab Euhemero est, quem noster et interpretatus et secutus est praeter ceteros Ennius; ab Euhemero autem et mortes et sepulturae demonstrantur deorum; utrum igitur hic confirmasse videtur religionem an penitus totam sustulisse?*

Or those who teach that brave or famous or powerful men have been deified after death, and that it is these who are the real objects of the worship, prayers and adoration which we are accustomed to offer—are not they entirely devoid of all sense of religion? This theory was chiefly developed by Euhemerus, who was translated and imitated especially by our poet Ennius. Yet Euhemerus describes the death and burial of certain gods; are we then to think of him as upholding religion, or rather as utterly and entirely destroying it?[19]

Who is speaking here? *On the Nature of the Gods* is structured around three characters: Gaius Velleius, the exponent of Epicurean theology; Lucilius Balbus, who represents the Stoics; and Aurelius Cotta, the Academic skeptic, who replies to the argumentation of both Velleius and Balbus and rejects their views. A fourth character, the young Marcus Cicero, is associated with the author himself. The aforementioned words belong to Cotta and, although they have been seen on occasions as representing Cicero's own views, this is hardly acceptable considering young Cicero's words with which the work concludes (3.95): "After the discussion we went our different ways. Cotta's argument seemed to Velleius more truthful, but to me Balbus's argument seemed to be closer to a semblance of the truth."[20] It is striking, however, that Cicero is siding with Balbus's Stoic position considering his own Academic background. Nevertheless, this can be accepted if we take into consideration the centrality of providentialism in the work, which Cicero takes to be more suitable than any other alternative, for the simple reason that it is the concept that preoccupies the author throughout the work.[21] The Stoic view of the myths about the gods, as Albert Baumgarten has shown, are in direct opposition to Euhemerus's explanation. The former argued in favor of "a physiologizing interpretation of myth which turned the poets into exponents of their philosophy" whereas the latter promoted the "transformation of the gods of myth into mortals."[22] This, however, cannot be taken as the golden rule in this case, since Balbus does accept the long-established practice of deification of human benefactors when he argues that "[h]uman experience and widespread custom have it that men providing outstanding benefits were raised to the sky by their reputation and our gratitude" (2.62).[23] Given that Cicero did himself adopt such a stance when discussing Romulus's deification, it cannot be argued that his appreciation of Balbus's argumentation comes as a surprise.[24]

The acceptance of the Ennian version of Euhemerus's work on behalf of Cicero provides us with a straightforward answer to the question of who speaks here. Cicero presents Euhemerus's (through Ennius) theory but makes sure to include the suspicion with which it was viewed by the Academic skeptics in order to allow the dialogue to flow. The importance of Ennius here is essential. It is obvious that Cicero did know Ennius's translation of the *Sacred Inscription*. What remains doubtful, however, is his knowledge of the Greek original.[25] If we accept that Diodorus did include the exact summary of the *Sacred Inscription* in his *Historical Library*, and Eusebius was copying correctly, then the problematic description of Euhemerus's theory here suggests the knowledge of the theory solely through the Ennian version. The phrase '*post mortem ad deos pervenisse*' indicates partial familiarity with the Greek text, since this practice applies only to the deification of Uranus by Zeus and not to Zeus's ante mortem deification, according to Diodorus's testimony (6.1.10).[26] Additionally, nowhere does Cotta (and, subsequently, Cicero) mention the celestial or heavenly gods, encountered in Diodorus (6.1.8–9).[27]

Further indication of Cicero's acceptance of the Ennian euhemeristic theory can be traced in the discussion found in 3.53–60, pertaining to the list of divine names. Although the text here has been traditionally viewed as an attack on Euhemerus and the author of the list as being a euhemerist(!),[28] Marek Winiarczyk has rightly pointed out the problem that emerges with such a contradictory approach. Given that Cicero assigns the authorship to the 'theologians' (*theologi*; 3.53), it is rather problematic to assume that he meant Euhemerus, considering that the particular adjective was not a characterization of the Sicilian author in any of our sources.[29]

If Euhemerus here is seen as an atheist, then the classification should be ascribed not to Cicero but to Cotta, or more accurately, to the group of Academic skeptics that he represents in *On the Nature of the Gods*. Cicero's agreement with Balbus's position cannot be reconciled with the statement in 1.199 that takes Euhemerus as a destroyer of religion (*an penitus totam sustulisse?*). The question posed here by Cotta is perhaps Cicero's way of keeping the issue open until he willingly demonstrates his agreement with Balbus in the end of the work, which coincides with his utilization of Ennius's adoption of Euhemerus's theory pertaining to Romulus's deification. A rejection of the Ennian euhemeristic theory would simultaneously mean the rejection of Romulus's divinity, which would contradict both Ennius's and Cicero's promotion of the deification of the founder of Rome.[30]

## Plutarch

The most known ancient author who attacked Euhemerus calling him an outright atheist was Plutarch. The Messenean author receives Plutarch's severe attack in *On Isis and Osiris* 360a–b, where we read:

μεγάλας μὲν τῷ ἀθέῳ Λέοντι κλισιάδας ἀνοίγοντας καὶ ἐξανθρωπίζοντι τὰ θεῖα, λαμπρὰν δὲ τοῖς Εὐημέρου τοῦ Μεσσηνίου φενακισμοῖς παρρησίαν διδόντας, ὃς αὐτός ἀντίγραφα συνθεὶς ἀπίστου καὶ ἀνυπάρκτου μυθολογίας πᾶσαν ἀθεότητα κατασκεδάννυσι τῆς οἰκουμένης, τοὺς νομιζομένους θεοὺς πάντας ὁμαλῶς διαγράφων εἰς ὀνόματα στρατηγῶν καὶ ναυάρχων καὶ βασιλέων ὡς δὴ πάλαι γεγονότων, ἐν δὲ Παγχοντι γράμμασι χρυσοῖς ἀναγεγραμμένων, οἷς οὔτε βάρβαρος οὐδεὶς οὔθ᾽ Ἕλλην, ἀλλὰ μόνος Εὐήμερος, ὡς ἔοικε, πλεύσας εἰς τοὺς μηδαμόθι γῆς γεγονότας μηδ᾽ ὄντας Παγχῴους καὶ Τριφύλλους ἐντετυχήκε.

[O]pening wide the great doors to the godless throng, degrading things divine to the human level, and giving a splendid license to the deceitful utterances of Euhemerus of Messene, who of himself drew up copies of an incredible and non-existent mythology, and spread atheism over the whole inhabited earth by obliterating the gods of our belief and converting them all alike into names of generals, admirals, and kings, who, forsooth, lived in very ancient times and are recorded in inscriptions written in golden letters at Panchaea, which no foreigner and no Greek had ever happened to meet with, save only Euhemerus. He, it seems, made a voyage to the Panchaeans and Triphyllians, who never existed anywhere on earth and do not exist.[31]

If Euhemerus's atheism remains open for further discussion in Cicero, Plutarch is explicit: not only is Euhemerus an outright atheist, but his testimony is a downright lie. However, in order to understand Plutarch's classification of the Messenean author as an atheist, we need to succinctly examine his own take on religion.

There are three elements that play a central role in Plutarch's attack on Euhemerus: his priestly role, his (Middle) Platonism, and his flirting with Stoic allegory. It is known that the historian and biographer from Chaeronea was a member of the Delphi priesthood and served as one of the two priests of Apollo at the sanctuary, while his travels in Asia Minor, Egypt, and Rome also led to his initiation in the mysteries of Dionysus and Isis.[32] Hence, right from the outset, we are dealing with a devout religious person who offered great respect and honor to the traditional deities, an aspect of his character that could not possibly be reconciled with Euhemerus's work and theory. However, it is the other two elements that truly determine the motivation and ferocity of his criticism toward the euhemeristic theory.

Plutarch's take on the traditional stories about the gods was not homogeneous, but his theology followed a more or less consistent trajectory. Being a (Middle) Platonist, he adopts the notion of the first principle: a male god who is "eternal, unchanging, non-composite, uncontaminated by matter."[33] Similar to Cicero's concept of providentialism, Plutarch maintained that the world is governed by this benevolent and eternal divinity, and humans receive god's goodness and philanthropy as well as punishment.[34] This Platonic notion of the divine realm must be harmonized, however, with the traditional gods and their place in the world. Plutarch subsumes deities like Apollo, Dionysus, and Osiris under this single divinity and treats them not as false or non-divine agents but as expressions or aspects of divinity. Contrary to, say, the Epicureans, Plutarch is not willing to eradicate the traditional gods; rather, he approaches the ancient wisdom with great respect, acknowledging the value and significance of ancient theologies.[35]

It is exactly this combination of respect for ancient wisdom and the Platonic notion of a single and benevolent deity that encourages Plutarch to accept, even with certain restrictions, a Stoic approach to mythology that adopts an allegorical interpretation when assessing the stories pertaining to the divine world. Nevertheless, even when he does integrate Stoic ideas, it is always within the Platonic context which guides his overall approach to religion.[36] This, however, does not mean that his approach to mythology follows a consistent path. As Philip Hardie has put it, "Plutarch's approach to myth varies according to the hat that he chooses to wear at any particular time," ranging from a strict Platonic view to a hybrid form of Platonism and Stoicism.[37] The latter is mostly apparent in *On Isis and Osiris*, the very work in which he attacks Euhemerus and his theory. The treatise deals with how to interpret religion and, in particular, the far-fetched and dishonorable stories of the poets. Similar to Xenophanes's opposition to the Homeric and Hesiodic anthropomorphic depiction of the Olympian gods and their immoral nature, *On Isis and Osiris* is a forthright attack against the poets, who create their fabricated accounts like spiders make their webs.[38] Plutarch's own interpretation of the Isis and Osiris myth is of course Platonic, although he does give credit to the Stoic allegorical approach: Osiris is "the intelligence and reason of the universe" while Isis "the female principle and receptacle."[39]

Before offering his own interpretation, Plutarch reviews other interpretational attempts, which he readily dismisses—among them Euhemerus's approach. For Plutarch, Euhemerus simply obliterates the gods by turning the traditional myths into historical narratives, which in his view denotes outright atheism. There are two problems with Plutarch's classification of Euhemerus as an atheist. First, he refers not only to deified kings—as Diodorus (and Eusebius) and Lactantius (and Ennius) do—but adds "generals and admirals" in the list of Euhemerus's deified individuals. Just as in the criticism on Cicero, the problem here is one related to access to the original text or the sources that were used. Whether Plutarch had access to more information is something that cannot be verified by his very brief summary of Euhemerus's theory. It seems highly unlikely that such important information, which alters significantly the main ideas of the *Sacred Inscription*, are omitted or simply not mentioned by Diodorus, Ennius, and all the Christian authors who utilized Euhemerus's theory, as we will see (Chapter 6). Plutarch's chronological proximity to Euhemerus does not automatically mean that he had more access to the *Sacred Inscription* than we do. Given his severe opposition to the euhemeristic interpretation,[40] Plutarch's additions could be interpreted as a form of trivializing Euhemerus' ideas and not simply as an indication of a better knowledge of Euhemerus' now lost work. If Euhemerus was not talking only about kings, I believe that both Eusebius and Lactantius would not have consciously rejected such additional elements from their summaries—after all, deified admirals and generals in Euhemerus's theory could only work in Christianity's favor as further proof of the falsity of the traditional beliefs about the 'pagan' gods. Second, there is no solid reason for Plutarch to classify Euhemerus as an atheist given the Messenean's acceptance of the celestial or heavenly gods. However, and this adds to Plutarch's possible partial knowledge of Euhemerus's theory, he seems unfamiliar with such an aspect in the *Sacred Inscription*. Although he does reject the transformation of natural phenomena (e.g., winds, streams, and the changes of the seasons) into divine beings, thus demonstrating his awareness of such ideas existing in other contexts, he does not however connect them with Euhemerus.[41]

Plutarch's possible unfamiliarity or lack of direct contact with the actual text, as well as his classification of Euhemerus as an atheist based on partial knowledge of the theory, should not come as a surprise or be dismissed without some further reflection. Dana Sutton has made a similar argument in her examination of Critias's atheism. Although Plutarch does classify Critias as an atheist (*On Superstition* 171b–c), Sutton maintains that he probably "did so on the basis of fr. 19,"[42] which as we have seen (cf. Chapter 2) was attributed to either Critias or Euripides. Sutton is cautious enough to allow for the possibility that Plutarch had more information at his disposal that we are unaware of—a possibility argued about pertaining to Plutarch's classification of Euhemerus as an atheist, but one that is simply too far-fetched to account for Plutarch's attack on Euhemerus. However, as she goes on to argue, the lack of any contemporary of Critias that styled him as an atheist is indeed problematic when one takes Plutarch's characterization at face value.[43]

This leaves us with one final remark. If, according to Plutarch and regardless of how he came across euhemerism, Euhemerus should be deemed an atheist for degrading the gods to the level of men, how was Plutarch himself supposed to be treated by his peers and contemporaries when he "reduces the divine to one God, identified with the Good and Being, and demotes the traditional gods to subordinate powers"?[44] By both rejecting any worship of the heavenly or earthly gods and demoting the traditional gods, his approach to religion should not be seen as less atheistic than Euhemerus's historicizing of the Olympian gods. After all, taking away any of the three main characteristics that distinguished a Greek god from humans (that is, anthropomorphism, immortality, and—of importance here—power),[45] meant committing the offence of impiety, which was often punishable by death. Ultimately, given the lack of a specific law against impiety, "it would always be up to someone to try to convince his peers that the offence in question was an impiety" as Delli Pizzi has succinctly put it.[46] If Socrates did not manage to elude the accusation of impiety, regardless of his belief in his 'famous' *daimonion*,[47] Plutarch could have also easily faced a similar charge, but obviously his inconsistent approach to religion and his ties with Delphi by default excluded him from such considerations. Hence, the styling of Euhemerus as an atheist by Plutarch was not based, as I see it, on a complete rejection of any divine being on behalf of the Messenean author, but on the clash of two different interpretative systems (that is, traditionalist versus theoretical) and on purely personal opinion and assessment.

## Sextus

The third and last case is the second-century CE skeptic Sextus Empiricus. A prominent member of the doxographic tradition, he engaged in lengthy examinations of theological reflection. Sextus represents a skeptic approach according to which nothing is a given and one must "generate suspension of judgement from the conflicting arguments and opinions on any given topic" including, of course, the existence and nature of god(s).[48] The discussion on the existence of the gods is encountered in the *Outlines of Pyrrhonism* (3.2–12) and *Against the Mathematicians* (9.13–134). It is in the latter where he references Euhemerus's name twice.

Euhemerus is briefly mentioned within a list of other thinkers from antiquity who are all classified as atheists (Protagoras, Diagoras of Melos, Prodicus, Theodorus, Critias, Epicurus). This list is matched against the opinions held by the believers, without favoring any of the two groups, with the ultimate goal of demonstrating the inability of the skeptic to opine that the gods do or do not exist—thus, holding his principle of suspension of judgment throughout the work.[49]

In both instances Sextus calls Euhemerus an atheist but, contrary to how the Messenean author is dealt with by other doxographers, he makes clear—although indirectly as the texts portray—that he is disseminating a classification coming from others:

Εὐήμερος δὲ ὁ ἐπικληθεὶς ἄθεος φησιν· ὅτ᾽ ἦν ἄτακτος ἀνθρώπων βίος, οἱ περιγενόμενοι τῶν ἄλλων ἰσχύι τε καὶ συνέσει ὥστε πρὸς τὰ ὑπ᾽ αὐτῶν κελευόμενα πάντας βιοῦν, σπουδάζοντες μείζονος θαυμασμοῦ καὶ σεμνότητος τυχεῖν, ἀνέπλασαν περὶ αὑτοὺς ὑπερβάλλουσάν τινα καὶ θείαν δύναμιν, ἔνθεν καὶ τοῖς πολλοῖς ἐνομίσθησαν θεοί.

And Euhemerus, nicknamed Atheist, says "When the life of humans was without order, those who exceeded the others in strength and clever-ness, to the point that everyone lived in response to their orders, in their eagerness to achieve more admiration and esteem made up a sort of superlative divine authority belonging to themselves, and thus were thought of by the many as gods."

τῶν οὖν περὶ ὑπάρξεως θεοῦ σκεψαμένων οἱ μὲν εἶναι φασι θεόν, οἱ δὲ μὴ εἶναι, οἱ δὲ μὴ μᾶλλον εἶναι ἢ μὴ εἶναι. καὶ εἶναι μὲν οἱ πλείους τῶν δογματικῶν καὶ ἡ κοινὴ τοῦ βίου πρόληψις, μὴ εἶναι δὲ οἱ ἐπικληθέντες ἄθεοι, καθάπερ Εὐήμερος γέρων ἀλαζών, ἄδικα βιβλία ψήχων

καὶ Διαγόρας ὁ Μήλιος καὶ Πρόδικος ὁ Κεῖος καὶ Θεόδωρος καὶ ἄλλοι
παμπληθεῖς· ὧν Εὐήμερος μὲν ἔλεγε τοὺς νομιζομένους θεοὺς δυνατούς
τινας γεγονέναι ἀνθρώπους καὶ διὰ τοῦτο ὑπὸ τῶν ἄλλων θεοποιηθέντας
δόξαι θεούς, Πρόδικος δὲ τὸ ὠφελοῦν τὸν βίον ὑπειλῆφθαι θεόν, ὡς ἥλιον
καὶ σελήνην καὶ ποταμοὺς καὶ λίμνας καὶ λειμῶνας καὶ καρποὺς καὶ πᾶν
τὸ τοιουτῶδες.

Of those who have inquired into the reality of god, then, some say that
there is a god, some that there is not, and some that there no more is
than is not. Most of the dogmatists, and the common preconception of
ordinary life, say that there is; those labeled atheists say that there is
not, such as Euhemerus

*An old charlatan, scribbling unjust books*

and Diagoras of Melos, Prodicus of Ceos, Theodorus and a whole
lot of others. Of these, Euhemerus said that those considered gods were
certain powerful humans, and that they were deified by the others for
that reason and thought to be gods; while Prodicus said that what
benefits life was assumed to be a god, like the sun and moon and rivers
and pools and meadows and crops and everything of this sort.[50]

There are two elements that insinuate Sextus's indirect knowledge of the
*Sacred Inscription*. First, Sextus does not portray here his own opinion;
rather, he is utilizing previous classifications without, at least on the surface,
expressing any personal appraisal about Euhemerus, as is evident in the
phrases "[a]nd Euhemerus, nicknamed Atheist" and "those labeled atheists
say that there is not, such as Euhemerus." Furthermore, the latter is accompanied by the famous phrase by Callimachus (cf. Chapter 5), one of the most
notable despisers of Euhemerus's theory in antiquity. Consistent with his
skeptic method, it is almost certain that Sextus is here using the most popular
fashion with which certain people referred to Euhemerus rather than copying
from or summarizing the *Sacred Inscription* itself.

This is further amplified by Sextus's mistakenly confusing Critias's
famous theory of the origin of belief in gods with Euhemerus's golden stele
and its explanation. The 'Big Brother' theory assigned to Critias (or Euripides),
takes as its starting point the existence of a period in early prehistory in which
humans lived in a state of anarchy (cf. Chapter 2). Contrary to what the
Critias fragment maintained thereafter, Sextus here alters the story, adding
a version of euhemerism that does not correspond to Diodorus's or
Eusebius's testimonies. Rather, he is employing the Lactantian narration that
is based on Ennius's Latin translation of the *Sacred Inscription*. It is only in
the *Divine Institutes* (1.13.2; cf. W. T 66 and 1.22.21–27; cf. W. T 64A)
that one encounters an explanation as the one found in Sextus, albeit not
verbatim. If Ennius did indeed utilize such wording, it is then most likely
that Sextus relied on his rendition rather than on Diodorus's text.

Finally, both excerpts seem to ignore the existence of the first level of deification, related to Uranus's observance and acknowledgement of the celestial objects as divine, as well as to Uranus's own deification by Zeus. None of the two actually fit into what Sextus mentions about Euhemerus and his approach to religion. It cannot be claimed that Uranus sacrifices to the celestial objects in order to "achieve more admiration and esteem" nor his case fit into the "certain powerful human beings [. . .] that they were deified by the others." The latter, of course, can be argued considering that this is what applies to Zeus according to Euhemerus; Sextus, however, is here obviously alluding to the king of the gods, Zeus, rather than to his grandfather, Uranus. Thus, it is the second level of deification the skeptic thinker refers to, which was the popular view of Euhemerus and his theory. It is therefore possible that Sextus did not have direct contact with the *Sacred Inscription* but rather via the authors whose interest in Euhemerus's work prompted them to include it in their own works. This is not only related to Euhemerus however; as Richard Bett argues, when discussing Sextus's knowledge of Theodorus's work and its inclusion in the *Against the Mathematicians*: "perhaps Sextus is simply repeating what his source says about Theodorus' book, without having read it himself."[51] Thus, it could be claimed that Sextus's inclusion of Euhemerus in his list of 'non-believers' was most likely based on earlier lists of 'atheists.'[52] After all, the skeptic suspension of judgment is at the core of the treatise and preoccupies Sextus in order to indicate that the existence of gods remains an open-ended question that cannot be permanently resolved, which is demonstrated by the falsity of the argumentation employed by both the religious and the non-believers.

## Euhemerus

The brief examination of the aforementioned authors also included aspects of Euhemerus's work on which certain individuals based their classification of the Messenean author as an atheist. What remains is contrasting what Euhemerus said to the notion of atheism, how and why it has been applied to his theory, and whether it is an accurate designation.

In his influential *Atheism in Pagan Antiquity*, Anders Drachmann defined atheism as "the point of view which *denies the existence of the ancient gods.*"[53] Although Drachmann's work is now dated, his definition remains the best one when dealing with Euhemerus—and, indeed, Drachmann claims that Euhemerus's theory was "the last attempt in the old pagan world to give an explanation of the popular faith which may be called genuine atheism."[54] But it is genuine atheism based on his definition. This is a distinction that is usually not taken into consideration when addressing Euhemerus's atheism. From within the ancient milieu, as discussed above, Euhemerus is and must be dealt with as an atheist: he indeed denies the existence of the ancient gods, as he strips them of their preeminent characteristic, that is, their immortality. The issue becomes more complicated, however, when scholars adopt a blurred notion of atheism, which incorporates modern conceptions accompanied by ancient discussions of unbelief and/or denial of the existence of the gods.

As such, Euhemerus is included among the atheists in modern scholarly and popular books such as, for example, Nick Harding's *How to Be a Good Atheist*. However, the definition of atheism employed by this author is the denial of the existence of gods in general.[55] Whether Harding—or any other author for that matter—is right to include Euhemerus in his book depends on how one is to interpret the Messenean's view of the heavenly or celestial gods. This issue has three possible interpretational paths, each one changing the verdict in relation to Euhemerus's alleged atheism.

The first one leads to irrefutable atheism. Although Euhemerus did mention the heavenly and indestructible gods in relation to Uranus, he nevertheless did not proceed with a clear-cut distinction between the two groups of gods[56] as 'true-versus-false' and, thus, did not share Uranus's belief in those celestial gods—he merely informs us of what Uranus believed. This is a speculative reading of Euhemerus's work, given that nowhere in the available testimonies can one justify such a position. If Euhemerus is to be seen as an atheist in modern terms, then we must infer that the *Sacred Inscription* acted as a means to an atheistic end, in which both groups of gods are not directly refuted by the author himself but by the way the work unfolds, as a 'true' testimony based on concrete evidence rather than a personal estimation—one, however, that the author then perhaps accepted and embraced. Contrary to other 'atheistic' statements, such as the Critias fragment or Prodicus's theory, in which the author himself speaks, in the *Sacred Inscription* it is history speaking, that is, the testimonies—both material and discursive—that Euhemerus presumably encountered in the Panchaean land.

The second one—albeit equally speculative and theoretically similar to the first—leads to the reverse verdict, that of (possible) theism. Following the above reasoning, Euhemerus simply offers to his readers an alternative view encountered in a remote place of the world, without simultaneously sharing that view himself. It is not the author but the reality of Panchaea and the testimonies of its inhabitants, according to Euhemerus's interpretation, that claim the non-divine nature of the traditional gods and promote the distinction between the two groups. Throughout the testimonies it is clear that Euhemerus conveys what he was told and what he witnessed rather than offering his own ideas: "Here he [Euhemerus] observed [τεθεᾶσθαι] the Panchaeans [. . .]"; "They say [φασὶν εἶναι] that the width of the island is about [. . .]"; "The traditional account which the priestly class gives [μυθολογοῦσι] of their origin [. . .]."[57] Like that of a contemporary anthropologist or historian,[58] this interpretation advocates that Euhemerus merely disseminates the information to his readers; it does not necessarily mean that he espoused these ideas, or that he was not a religious and devout person like the vast majority of his contemporaries.

The third and final path promotes a hybrid interpretation that takes Euhemerus as an atheist, according to the ancient view, and a theist according to the modern one. The feeling one gets when reading the available testimonies—and this probably applies to how the work was seen in antiquity as well, which led to Euhemerus's inclusion in the list of atheists— is that Euhemerus wrote in order to argue against the divinity of the traditional gods. If this is the case, then Euhemerus is a genuine atheist, since he does indeed deny the existence of the ancient traditional gods by historicizing and humanizing them.[59] However, his discussion of the heavenly and indestructible gods implies that he took those to be real divinities. In this case, Euhemerus cannot be taken as an atheist in the modern understanding of the term, since he holds a belief in the existence of a divine realm, although not the traditional one. A similar criticism, as we have seen (cf. Chapter 2), was made by Xenophanes almost three centuries before Euhemerus, which nevertheless did not secure for the presocratic philosopher a place in a list of atheists, both ancient and modern.[60] If Xenophanes should be deemed a critic "of specific forms" of religion and not a critic "of religion as such,"[61] then, by the same token, Euhemerus belongs to the same pool of individuals when seen from a modern perspective.

Euhemerus's atheism, thus, as I see it, remains open to different interpretations. The classification or its denial must be seen within contexts that take into consideration various elements: who categorized him as an atheist; why such a classification persists in some instances today; how and why authors saw an atheistic agenda in the theory; and what the surviving testimonies maintain. The ancient authors, of whom three important figures were briefly examined, had certain predispositions toward religion and myth and were exponents of certain philosophical teachings, which determined and directed their criticisms. Modern authors, on the other hand, often apply the post-Enlightenment understanding of theism and atheism to Euhemerus, which creates further problems at the semantic level. Since we do not know the actual motive behind the writing of the *Sacred Inscription*, Euhemerus's atheism, or lack thereof, must be approached taking into account the plausibility of these diverse and often contradictory interpretations.

## Notes

1 Winiarczyk 2013, 99–100.
2 See Winiarczyk 1984, 171, where fourteen testimonies from antiquity are given dealing with Euhemerus as an atheist (ἄθεος).
3 Whitmarsh 2015, 4. Whitmarsh's claim is supported by various publications on the subject. For example, see Baggini 2003 and Hyman 2010.
4 For a discussion on the English language word 'God' and its biblical background, see Schüssler Fiorenza and Kaufman 1998.
5 The translation is drawn from Whitmarsh 2015, 87, who nevertheless argues that Protagoras was indeed an atheist rather than an agnostic (87–91).
6 Atheism is often taken as coming directly from the Greek term ἀθεότης, whereas atheist from the adjective ἄθεος. In modern Greek the former corresponds to αθεϊσμός, with the latter remaining unchanged.

7  See the excellent discussion in Quillen 2015.
8  Ibid., 26. There is hardly any work on atheism that does not—even in passing—adopt a linear manner of continuity, thus subscribing (even implicitly) to what Quillen calls an "essential or general" definition of atheism. This is apparent in the introductory chapters of the two most recent major publications on the topic, which present such a linearity that, in turn, sees atheism from within that essential scope. See Martin 2007; Bullivant 2013.
9  For a more detailed list of and discussion on ancient atheists, see Winiarczyk 1976 and 1984.
10  Bremmer 1994, 2. For an indicative list of works adopting the 'embeddedness' trope, see Nongbri 2008, 441 n. 4. For a criticism also see Kindt 2012, 16–19.
11  See Nongbri 2008 and 2013. For an overview of the argument and the related bibliography, see the discussion in Roubekas 2014, 226–228. On the importance of the insider versus outsider discourse in the academic study of religion, see McCutcheon 1999.
12  Whitmarsh 2015, 9. A similar but more severe criticism is given in Whitmarsh 2014, 114–115.
13  See, for example, Giordano-Zecharya 2005 and the acute criticism of her argumentation by Versnel 2011, 548–559.
14  See Plato, *Apology* 18b–c. Cf. Roubekas 2014, 231–232.
15  For a discussion, see Roubekas 2015, 3–5.
16  Versnel 2011, 552, emphasis in the original.
17  Lincoln 2007, 242.
18  See Whitmarsh 2015, 207–208. Cf. Winiarczyk 2013, 99.
19  Cicero, *On the Nature of the Gods* 1.119 (W. T 14); the translation is from LOEB's twenty-ninth volume of Cicero's works (translated by H. Rackman).
20  *haec cum essent dicta, ita discessimus, ut Velleio Cottae disputatio verior, mihi Balbi ad veritatis similitudinem videretur esse propensior.* I employ here the translation by Cole 2013, 162. I also agree with his rejection of Cotta's words as representing Cicero's skepticism (163).
21  See the discussion in Graver 2014, 127–128. Cf. Whitmarsh 2015, 212 on Cicero's theistic stance as epitomized in the end of the *On the Nature of the Gods*.
22  Baumgarten 1996, 98.
23  *suscepit autem vita hominum consuetudoque communis ut beneficiis excellentis viros in caelum fama ac voluntate tollerent.* The translation is drawn from Cole 2013, 155.
24  This is discussed in detail in Cole 2006 and 2013, 155–156.
25  Winiarczyk 2013, 120; 122 argues that Cicero knew both texts.
26  καὶ ἄλλα δὲ πλεῖστα ἔθνη ἐπελθόντα παρὰ πᾶσιν τιμηθῆναι καὶ θεὸν ἀναγορευθῆναι (Eusebius, *Preparation for the Gospel* 2.2.61; W. T 63).
27  μετὰ ταῦτά φησι πρῶτον Οὐρανὸν γεγονέναι βασιλέα, ἐπιεικῆ τινα ἄνδρα καὶ εὐεργετικὸν καὶ τῆς τῶν ἄστρων κινήσεως ἐπιστήμονα, ὃν καὶ πρῶτον θυσίαις τιμῆσαι τοὺς οὐρανίους θεούς (Eusebius, *Preparation for the Gospel* 2.2.58–59; W. T 49).
28  For example, see Solmsen 1944. A major problem with his assessment, however, is his insistence of referring to Euhemerus's theory as the deification of not only kings but also army leaders and warriors. Such a view is reminiscent of Plutarch's description of Euhemerus's theory when attacking him in *On Isis and Osiris*, 360a–b (see below).
29  Winiarczyk 2013, 142–143, with whom I absolutely agree here, does not address whether the adjective was used to refer to Euhemerus, although he does mention how Euhemerus was known in antiquity in 8–11 (that is, geographer, historian, atheist philosopher, and poet).

30 For example, see Cole 2006, 537–541; 2013, 154.
31 The translation is from LOEB's fifth volume of Plutarch's *Moralia*, translated by Frank Cole Babbitt with some small interventions of my own.
32 See Hirsch-Luipold 2014, 164; Dillon 2014, 159.
33 Dillon 2014, 161.
34 For a comprehensive examination of Plutarch's Platonic notion of god, see Hirsch-Luipold 2014, 168–169; Opsomer 2014, 88–91.
35 *On Isis and Osiris* 369b. Cf. Van Nuffelen 2011, 62–63; Hardie 1992, 4752.
36 Opsomer 2014, 88.
37 Hardie 1992, 4761. Cf. Opsomer 2014, 91.
38 ὅτι δ᾽ οὐκ ἔοικε ταῦτα κομιδῇ μυθεύμασιν ἀραιοῖς καὶ διακένοις πλάσμασιν, οἷα ποιηταὶ καὶ λογογράφοι καθάπερ οἱ ἀράχναι γεννῶντες ἀφ᾽ ἑαυτῶν ἀπ᾽ ἀρχῆς ἀνυποθέτου ὑφαίνουσι καὶ ἀποτείνουσιν (*On Isis and Osiris* 358f).
39 Frederick 2012, 79–79, where he gives a concise description of Plutarch's interpretation of the myth. Van Nuffelen 2011, 61 offers a summary of Plutarch's interpretation, which he breaks down into two parts: as expressing Plutarch's metaphysical dualism, as well as the idea that the Isis cult portrays ancient knowledge. On the partial acceptance of the Stoic allegorical method, see *On Isis and Osiris* 369a.
40 Baumgarten 1996 remains the best assessment of the methodological tensions between Plutarch and Euhemerus.
41 δεύτερον, ὃ μεῖζόν ἐστιν, ὅπως σφόδρα προσέξουσι καὶ φοβήσονται, μὴ λάθωσιν εἰς πνεύματα καὶ ῥεύματα καὶ σπόρους καὶ ἀρότους καὶ πάθη γῆς καὶ μεταβολὰς ὡρῶν διαγράφοντες τὰ θεῖα καὶ διαλύοντες· ὥσπερ οἱ Διόνυσον τὸν οἶνον, Ἥφαιστον δὲ τὴν φλόγα· Φερσεφόνην δέ φησί που Κλεάνθης τὸ διὰ τῶν καρπῶν φερόμενον καὶ φονευόμενον πνεῦμα (*On Isis and Osiris* 377d). Apart from Cleanthes, the allusion to Prodicus here is almost certain.
42 Sutton 1981, 35.
43 Ibid., 36 n. 23. Plutarch is known, when he is using extensive quotations, not to hesitate to change or alter the given passage by either omitting, adding, or even modifying what it was found in the original quotation, as Inowlocki 2006, 41 has shown. Additionally, as she argues, "[i]t is worth noting that the faithfulness to the text also depends on the feelings of the quoting author toward the quoted authors" (43); given that Plutarch (along with Callimachus; see Chapter 5) is probably the most known despiser of Euhemerus's theory, it comes as no surprise that he could have well altered the original text—if he had access to it—or his secondary source(s) in order to demonstrate Euhemerus's mistakes.
44 Frederick 2012, 79.
45 See the persuasive Henrichs 2010.
46 Pizzi 2011, 74.
47 For a discussion on Socrates's accusation of atheism, see Whitmarsh 2015, 127–133; McPherran 2011.
48 Bett 2014, 174; cf. Sextus, *Outlines of Pyrrhonism* 1.196; 3.29. On the attitude of skeptics toward the gods, see Long 2006, who demonstrates the non-consistent attitude of the skeptics on the topic. Sextus is not a representative of traditional skepticism; rather, he belongs to what Pellegrin 2010, 122 calls "the end of a movement of sceptical renaissance, a movement that drew its inspiration and took its name from Pyrrho." This suspension of judgment and assent is *mutatis mutandis* similar to the phenomenological approach to religion that dominated the field of religious studies for decades. I do not, of course, imply here that Sextus's skepticism is identical to the phenomenological approach to religion. Given that the latter unfolded around the notion and existence of 'the sacred'

and saw religion as an ahistorical and autonomous essence, the two systems are radically different, as Sextus does not take the existence of the gods as a given. However, both his skeptic approach and that of the phenomenologists adopt the position of suspension of judgment, with the latter drawing from Husserl's notion of bracketing. For a nice overview, see Blum 2012, who nevertheless attempts to place anew the phenomenological method within the field of religious studies.

49  For an overview, see Whitmarsh 2015, 166–167.

50  Sextus, *Against the Mathematicians* 9.17; 9.50–52 (W. T 27; 23). The translation is drawn from Bett 2012.

51  Bett 2015, 50.

52  Whitmarsh 2015, 167 mentions the list of Clitomachus as the possible source of ancient atheists adopted by Sextus.

53  Drachmann 1922, 41, emphasis in the original.

54  Ibid., 113.

55  See, Harding 2007, 23–24 (what is atheism); 50 (Euhemerus).

56  See, Winiarczyk 2013, 28.

57  Eusebius, *Preparation for the Gospel* 2.2.55 (W. T 3); Diodorus Siculus, *Historical Library* 5.42.1 (W. T 30); 5.46.3 (W. T 35).

58  Honigman 2009 has argued that Euhemerus must have conceived his work as historiography rather than fiction, whereas on the same matter Winiarczyk 2013, 10; 20–21 emphasizes the utopian novel character of the work and disagrees with Honigman's assessment.

59  'Historization' and 'humanization' are the terms used by Bolle 1970, 20, which I employ here although my utilization of the terminology serves different purposes and diverts from Bolle's interpretation of Euhemerus.

60  Contrary to the fourteen ancient testimonies of Euhemerus's atheism and his characterization as an ἄθεος, Xenophanes is only mentioned twice in antiquity in a somehow similar fashion (see Winiarczyk 1984, 181). Cf. Drachmann 1922, 19: "no one placed Xenophanes amongst *atheoi*." Whitmarsh 2015, 61 does not include him among the atheists "in any straightforward sense" but he does point out that his view was "the most devastating assault on traditional religion." Xenophanes's name is not mentioned at all in *The Oxford Handbook of Atheism* (2015), whereas Bremmer 2007, 13 does not call him an atheist.

61  See, Lincoln 2007, 242.

## References

Baggini, Julian. 2003. *Atheism: A Very Short Introduction*. Oxford: Oxford University Press.

Baumgarten, Albert I. 1996. "Euhemerus' Eternal Gods: Or, How Not To Be Embarrassed by Greek Mythology." In *Classical Studies in Honor of David Sohlberg*, edited by Ranon Katzoff, Yaakov Petroff, and David Schaps, 91–103. Ramat Gan: Bar-Ilan University Press.

Bett, Richard. 2012. *Sextus Empiricus: Against the Physicists*. New York and Cambridge: Cambridge University Press.

Bett, Richard. 2014. "Sextus Empiricus." In *Ancient Philosophy of Religion. Vol. 1: The History of Western Philosophy of Religion*, edited by Graham Oppy and N. N. Trakakis, 173–185. London and New York: Routledge.

Bett, Richard. 2015. "*God: M 9.13–194.*" In *Sextus Empiricus and Ancient Physics*, edited by Keimpe Algra and Katerina Ierodiakonou, 33–73. Cambridge: Cambridge University Press.

Blum, Jason N. 2012. "Retrieving Phenomenology of Religion as a Method for Religious Studies." *Journal of the American Academy of Religion* 80 (4): 1025–1048.

Bolle, Kees W. 1970. "In Defense of Euhemerus." In *Myth and Law Among the Indo-Europeans*, edited by Jaan Puhvel, 19–38. Berkeley, CA and London: University of California Press.

Bremmer, Jan N. 1994. *Greek Religion*. Oxford: Oxford University Press.

Bremmer, Jan N. 2007. "Atheism in Antiquity." In *The Cambridge Companion to Atheism*, edited by Michael Martin, 11–26. Cambridge: Cambridge University Press.

Bullivant, Stephen. 2013. "Defining 'Atheism'." In *The Oxford Handbook of Atheism*, edited by Stephen Bullivant and Michael Ruse, 11–21. Oxford: Oxford University Press.

Cole, Spencer. 2006. "Cicero, Ennius, and the Concept of Apotheosis at Rome." *Arethusa* 39 (3): 531–548.

Cole, Spencer. 2013. *Cicero and the Rise of Deification at Rome*. New York and Cambridge: Cambridge University Press.

Dillon, John. 2014. "Plutarch of Chaeroneia." In *Ancient Philosophy of Religion. Vol. 1: The History of Western Philosophy of Religion*, edited by Graham Oppy and N. N. Trakakis, 159–171. London and New York: Routledge.

Drachmann, Anders B. 1922. *Atheism in Pagan Antiquity*. Copenhagen: Gyldendal.

Frederick, Brenk E. 2012. "Plutarch and 'Pagan Monotheism'." In *Plutarch in the Religious and Philosophical Discourse of Late Antiquity*, edited by Lautaro R. Lanzillotta and Israel M. Gallarte, 73–84. Leiden and Boston, MA: Brill.

Giordano-Zecharya, Manuela. 2005. "As Socrates Shows, the Athenians Did Not Believe in Gods." *Numen* 52 (3): 325–355.

Graver, Margaret. 2014. "Cicero." In *Ancient Philosophy of Religion. Vol. 1: The History of Western Philosophy of Religion*, edited by Graham Oppy and N. N. Trakakis, 119–131. London and New York: Routledge.

Hardie, Philip R. 1992. "Plutarch and the Interpretation of Myth." *Aufstieg und Niedergang der Römischen Welt* II.33.6: 4743–4787.

Harding, Nick. 2007. *How to Be a Good Atheist*. Harpenden, UK: Oldcastle Books.

Henrichs, Albert. 2010. "What is a Greek God?" In *The Gods of Ancient Greece: Identities and Transformations*, edited by Jan N. Bremmer and Andrew Erskine, 19–39. Edinburgh, UK: Edinburgh University Press.

Hirsch-Luipold, Rainer. 2014. "Religion and Myth." In *A Companion to Plutarch*, edited by Mark Beck, 163–176. Malden, MA and Oxford: Wiley Blackwell.

Honigman, Sylvie. 2009. "Euhemerus of Messene and Plato's Atlantis." *Historia* 58 (1): 1–35.

Hyman, Gavin. 2010. *A Short History of Atheism*. London and New York: I. B. Tauris.

Inowlocki, Sabrina. 2006. *Eusebius and the Jewish Authors: His Citation Technique in an Apologetic Context*. Leiden and Boston, MA: Brill.

Kindt, Julia. 2012. *Rethinking Greek Religion*. Cambridge: Cambridge University Press.

Lincoln, Bruce. 2007. "Epilogue." In *Ancient Religions*, edited by Sarah Iles Johnston, 241–251. Cambridge, MA and London: The Belknap Press of Harvard University Press.

McCutcheon, Russell T. (Ed.) 1999. *The Insider/Outsider Problem in the Study of Religion: A Reader*. London and New York: Continuum.

McPherran, Mark L. 2011. "Socratic Religion." In *The Cambridge Companion to Socrates*, edited by Donald R. Morrison, 111–137. Cambridge: Cambridge University Press.

Martin, Michael. 2007. "General Introduction." In *The Cambridge Companion to Atheism*, edited by Michael Martin, 1–7. Cambridge: Cambridge University Press.

Nongbri, Brent. 2008. "Dislodging 'Embedded' Religion: A Brief Note on a Scholarly Trope." *Numen* 55 (4): 440–460.

Nongbri, Brent. 2013. *Before Religion: A History of a Modern Concept*. New Haven, CT and London: Yale University Press.

Opsomer, Jan. 2014. "Plutarch and the Stoics." In *A Companion to Plutarch*, edited by Mark Beck, 88–103. Malden, MA and Oxford: Wiley Blackwell.

Pellegrin, Pierre. 2010. "Sextus Empiricus." In *The Cambridge Companion to Ancient Scepticism*, edited by Richard Bett, 120–141. Cambridge: Cambridge University Press.

Pizzi, Aurian D. 2011. "Impiety in Epigraphic Evidence." *Kernos* 24: 59–76.

Quillen, Ethan G. 2015. "Discourse Analysis and the Definition of Atheism." *Science, Religion and Culture* 2 (3): 25–35.

Roubekas, Nickolas P. 2014. "Ancient Greek Atheism: A Note on Terminological Anachronisms in the Study of Ancient Greek Religion." *Ciências da Religião* 12 (2): 224–241.

Roubekas, Nickolas P. 2015. "Belief in Belief and Divine Kingship in Early Ptolemaic Egypt: The Case of Ptolemy II Philadelphus and Arsinoe II." *Religio: Revue pro religionistiku* 23 (1): 3–23.

Schüssler Fiorenza, Francis and Gordon D. Kaufman. 1998. "God." In *Critical Terms for Religious Studies*, edited by Mark C. Taylor, 136–159. Chicago, IL: University of Chicago Press.

Solmsen, Friedrich. 1944. "Cicero *De Natura Deorum* iii. 53 ff." *Classical Philology* 39 (1): 44–47.

Sutton, Dana. 1981. "Critias and Atheism." *Classical Quarterly* 31 (1): 33–38.

Van Nuffelen, Peter. 2011. *Rethinking the Gods: Philosophical Readings of Religion in the Post-Hellenic Period*. Cambridge: Cambridge University Press.

Versnel, Henk S. 2011. *Coping with the Gods: Wayward Readings in Greek Theology*. Leiden and Boston, MA: Brill.

Whitmarsh, Tim. 2014. "Atheistic Aesthetics: The Sisyphus Fragment, Poetics and the Creativity of Drama." *Proceedings of the Cambridge Philological Society* 60: 109–126.

Whitmarsh, Tim. 2015. *Battling the Gods: Atheism in the Ancient World*. New York: Alfred A. Knopf.

Winiarczyk, Marek. 1976. "Der erste Atheistenkatalog des Kleitomachos." *Philologus* 120: 32–46.

Winiarczyk, Marek. 1984. "Wer galt im Altertum als Atheist?" *Philologus* 128 (2): 157–183.

Winiarczyk, Marek. 2013. *The Sacred History of Euhemerus of Messene*. Translated by Witold Zbirohowski-Kościa. Berlin and Boston, MA: De Gruyter.

# 5  Euhemerism, Divine Kingship, and Irony

In her book *Mesoamerican Writing Systems: Propaganda, Myth, and History in Four Ancient Civilizations* (1992), Joyce Marcus opens chapter nine, entitled "Euhemerism and Royal Ancestors," with the following words:

> Sometimes around 300 B.C., intrigued by the pantheon of gods his people worshipped, a Greek writer named Euhemerus presented an interesting explanation for the emergence of polytheistic mythology in general and Greek mythology in particular. He argued that the multitude of gods had arisen from the deification of *dead* heroes. This concept, named for its originator, is today known as euhemerism.

Drawing on examples from the Aztec, Mixtec, Zapotec, and Maya cultures, she goes on to add:

> The divinity of one's royal ancestors was an important source of authority for the living Mesoamerican ruler. [. . .] Through the process of euhemerism, *dead* kings became heroes and eventually deities whose kin ties, real or imagined, to the living ruler were exploited to justify his actions.[1]

Although Marcus's authority on Mesoamerican civilizations is irrefutable— my knowledge about the history and the form of the religious practices of the great cultures that evolved, developed, and finally declined in Central and South America is quite poor—she is nevertheless using the notion of 'euhemerism' in a way that has many times been utilized and has led the study of the theory to the place it is today. The emphasis on the word *dead* in both citations is not incidental; on the contrary, it denotes the fashionable way of treating Euhemerus and his theory of the origins of the traditional gods as a *port mortem* phenomenon, which partly contorts what Euhemerus claimed in his *Sacred Inscription*. In addition, and more importantly, Marcus's choice to connect euhemerism with ideas pertaining to the notion of divine kingship is also in line with a long tradition that sees Euhemerus as a straightforward exponent of the deification of the monarchs during the so-called Hellenistic period, especially in Ptolemaic Egypt, where it is sup-posed that he compiled his narrative.[2] It is not an exaggeration to say that the idea that Euhemerus was writing to justify these practices is somehow embedded in the tradition that deals with euhemerism.[3]

It has been argued, and rightly so, that it is very likely that those practices were indeed what influenced or even nudged Euhemerus to address the issue in his *Sacred Inscription*—which is also probably the reason why scholars have mistakenly identified this with the aim of the work—without however maintaining that his ideas actually had any significant impact on those political aspirations and practices.[4] Two of the most convincing arguments are related to the very nature of the monarch deification practices, which were the result of both a top-down and bottom-up process along with the long tradition of those proclaimed divine rulers who saw themselves as descendants of gods. The former indicates that the tradition did not really need any ideological justification, especially after the first instances of the phenomenon and its successful implementation, whereas the latter sees Euhemerus's approach as essentially uncalled-for, considering the various other examples the rulers could and did invoke to justify their deification, such as the cases of the revered Asclepius, Dionysus, and Herakles.[5] I would also like to supplement this interpretation with three additional reasons, stemming from both the *Sacred Inscription* itself and from an external source, that accompany the aforementioned argumentation and, as I believe, settle the issue of seeing Euhemerus's work as an attempt to support and justify the deification of rulers during the Hellenistic period. The first one is the often-neglected single testimony pertaining to Euhemerus's biography, namely his relationship with Cassander of Macedonia. The second is the response to Euhemerus's work by Callimachus (c. 310–240) in regards to the entombment of Zeus in Crete. Although the Cyrenean author and poet is among the first sources that scholars resort to in discussing Euhemerus's atheism, he is rarely seen as further proof of Euhemerus's anti-ruler cult nature of his *Sacred Inscription*. Perhaps such a claim could turn some heads, but as I will argue in what follows, Euhemerus's response to the phenomenon of deification during the post-Alexander era was one of a non-conformist, who rejected and argued against such practices. Lastly, the issue of the political reality encountered in Panchaea should be seen as further proof of Euhemerus's objection to the deification of kings.

## "... who was a friend of King Cassander ..."

Even though Euhemerus was a member of the royal court of King Cassander, this information has always been treated as of secondary importance. According to the preserved text, the voyage to the Indian Ocean was obviously conceived by Cassander himself who gave the order to Euhemerus.[6] Marek Winiarczyk, surprisingly one must say, argues that "this statement could very well be mere literary fiction" in order to make "his account to appear as authentic as possible."[7] Although Winiarczyk presents both the favorable and critical arguments regarding the validity of this statement, his subscription to the latter essentially contradicts his acceptance that Euhemerus lived in the fourth/third century BCE, which he then merely bases on Callimachus's criticism of Euhemerus. There is no valid reason nor explicit proof that would compel us to reject the former testimony and accept the latter. This becomes even more evident when considering that Callimachus's criticism does not name Euhemerus at all, something that Winiarczyk himself acknowledges, making his discussion on the life of Euhemerus merely speculative. Although Winiarczyk hardly draws any conclusions that are not justified by the available testimonies,[8] he nevertheless adopts a skeptical stance toward the most straightforward testimony available regarding Euhemerus's life.

I believe that Peter Fraser's position is more convincing and logically situated within the context of the available sources:

> [I]t seems unlikely that if [Euhemerus] was living outside the realm of Cassander, either before or after the death of that monarch, he would fabricate so uninteresting and unlikely a falsehood, and if he was living inside it, common sense is likely to have restrained him from an obvious invention.[9]

Euhemerus's position among the friends of Cassander and his subsequent writing of the *Sacred Inscription* most likely in Ptolemaic Egypt, given the strong Egyptian influences found in the text,[10] must be seen as portraying the most possible chronological sequence of facts regarding Euhemerus's life. Furthermore, accepting that Euhemerus was influenced by the ruler cult and wrote in response to but not in favor of it, allows for accepting his experience of both Macedonian and Egyptian practices during this period.

I contend that if Euhemerus had wanted to write something in favor of divine kingship, then his work would have corresponded not to Cassander's political ideas and aspirations but to those of the Ptolemaic court (or of any other Hellenistic dynasty for that matter). If Euhemerus was indeed writing in favor of this practice, it comes as a surprise that he chose one of the most known kings of this period who did *not* claim to be a god in order to promote such an ideology. In Winthrop Lindsay Adams's excellent study, Cassander is portrayed as a connoisseur of diplomacy in his attempts to become ruler of Macedonia and Greece after the death of Alexander the Great. Having to deal with very capable and powerful enemies claiming power over the same territories, like Antigonus and his son Demetrius Poliorketes (the Besieger), he embarked on constant—mainly diplomatic—wars that lasted from 319 until 301 BCE. His whole political career was a continuous struggle to establish himself as the legitimate ruler of Macedonia, always through the arts of political captation: rewarding his friends and allies of his cause;

offering royal honors to Philip II; marrying Thessalonike, half-sister of Alexander the Great, in order to connect himself with the Argead dynasty; founding cities named after himself and his wife (Cassandreia and Thessalonike).[11] It is clear that the ongoing wars, diplomatic attempts, and coalitions that took place during this hectic period did not allow for Cassander to use the title King (βασιλεύς), at least not before "the death of Alexander IV in 310 BCE and the assumption of the title by Antigonos and his son Demetrius in 306."[12] Cassander's establishment as a King of Macedonia was finalized in 301, after the battle of Ipsus. With his death placed between 298 and 297 BCE, Cassander only managed to hold power over Macedonia for four to five years without having to deal with rivals and alleged or legitimate heirs to the Macedonia throne.

There are two incidents mentioned by Plutarch regarding Cassander that are of great importance here. In the *Life of Alexander* (74.1), we learn that when Cassander went to Babylon and "saw some Barbarians doing obeisance to Alexander, since he had been reared as a Greek and had never seen such a sight as this before, he laughed boisterously"; Alexander reacted violently, "clutching him fiercely by the hair with both hands dashed his head against the wall" (74.2). It was probably this episode that made Cassander a sworn despiser of Alexander and his policies.[13] In addition, in the *Life of Demetrius* (18.2), Plutarch informs us that "Cassander, however, although the others gave him the royal title in their letters and addresses, wrote his letters in his own untitled name, as he had been wont to do." Even if this testimony by Plutarch has now been challenged by the archaeological findings, according to which Cassander apparently did use the title in 305 BCE,[14] nowhere do we find personal portraits struck by Cassander on coins portraying him as a god, or any testimony regarding his deification or divine honors paid to him by the Macedonians or the Greeks. Helen Lund has argued that from all of Alexander's successors, only Ptolemy and Demetrius issued such personal portraits while they were alive, and she explicitly excludes Antigonus, Cassander, and Lysimachus from such a practice due to "their ephemeral power [that] precluded a posthumous issue."[15] This practice flourished in kingdoms where royal dynasties would be perdurable and their subjects would be ready to accept such ideas; usually, people that were already familiar with such phenomena as, for example, in Egypt, with its long history of deified pharaohs.

A last point that must be mentioned here that further supports the argument that Cassander (or his court) never projected himself as something more than the ruler of Macedonia comes from Demetrius Poliorketes and the well-known hymn with which the Athenians greeted and welcomed him when he freed Athens from Demetrius of Phaleron, whom Cassander had placed as the Macedonian ruler of Athens.[16] Once Demetrius Poliorketes managed to enter into the city of Athens, he was welcomed not only as a liberator from the Macedonian rule but also as a god. In the hymn, composed by Hermokles of Kyzikos and preserved by Athenaeus, we read:

Now, know that other gods are far away
or have no ears or
don't exist or do not care about us.
But thee, we see here present,
Not wood, nor stone, but real to the bone.
To thee we send our prayer:
So first of all make peace, o most beloved,
For thou has the power.[17]

Athens would have most likely paid its tribute to Cassander earlier as well if
he was (or demanded) to be seen as a god or as *isotheos*, *soter*, or any other
kind of adjective that would prove his actual or intended self-projection as a
divine figure. The fact that, among the Greeks, the Athenians were the first
to proclaim Demetrius a *king*[18] further supports the claim that Cassander not
only did not have aspirations to be seen as something more than the King of
Macedonia but was not even acknowledged as such by his Greek subjects; a
point that further attests to the fact that he indeed did not use the royal title
for the biggest part of his political career. For someone who barely used that
title during this restless period, it was inconceivable to be proclaimed a god
or receive any kind of honors surpassing his human nature.[19]

Being a member of the court of Cassander and among his friends also
signifies that Euhemerus must had been aware of Cassander's ideas about
divine kingship—ideas that would probably correspond to his spontaneous
reaction to the *proskynesis* before Alexander back in Babylon in 328 BCE—
as well as of the complete absence of any kind of propaganda leading
toward Cassander's deification, both in Macedonia and in mainland Greece.
If Cassander had something more in his mind than simple royal pretensions,
we would expect his brother, Alexarchus, to incorporate the notion of a
divine king into the utopian community he created along with the establishment of the city he named Uranopolis (City of Heaven) at the Chalkedike
peninsula. Even though Alexarchus did transform himself into the sun,
there is no indication that he demanded to be worshipped or claimed to be
a god himself. The coins the archaeological record contains depict the
sun as well as Aphrodite Urania as the dominant figures of Uranopolis. From
the extremely scarce sources we have available, Alexarchus was far more
interested in linguistic issues than divine kingship propaganda.[20] There is
the likelihood, however, that Euhemerus was influenced by Alexarchus's
Uranopolis if we accept that the latter precedes the writing of the *Sacred
Inscription*. The central role of heaven (οὐρανός) in Alexarchus's community, as portrayed by the name of the city, the citizens being called Children
of Heaven, and the figure of Aphrodite Urania certainly echoes the significance of king/god Uranus in the *Sacred Inscription*.[21] This could imply
that Cassander as well shared his brother's prioritization of heaven, of which
Euhemerus could have been aware, and which could have led to its adoption
in his own work.

With Cassander not establishing a dynasty as powerful as other Hellenistic dynasties, none of the two cases of deification found in the *Sacred Inscription* (that is, *living* and *dead* deified kings) would fit in Cassander's case. With no evidence to support Cassander's possible attempts to present himself as something more than the King of Macedonia, and given his previous negative position against such claims made by kings, it is doubtful whether among Euhemerus's orders was the production of a work that would act as a justification of the deification of the Hellenistic rulers.[22] If, however, Euhemerus decided this topic to be the aim of his work, then we must contend that not only should he not be counted among the friends of the Macedonian King, which contradicts our sources, but also that he compiled a work that actually depreciated Cassander and elevated other potentates, such as the Ptolemies in Egypt. However, the negative, and even hostile, response to Euhemerus's work by Callimachus, one of the most known advocates of the Ptolemaic divine assertions, rejects such a hypothesis.

## Zeus and the Lying Cretans: The Response by Callimachus

Zeus is undeniably the protagonist and most important figure of the *Sacred Inscription*. The strong relationship between the island of Panchaea and Crete, with Zeus acting as the link between the two locales, is unambiguous. We know that Cretans were among the inhabitants of Panchaea, and Zeus was born in Crete and led the priests from the Greek island to Panchaea while he was still a living king, something that is affirmed in the text by their language and their names of Cretan origin.[23] This tradition that spoke of a Cretan Zeus, and upon which Euhemerus was basing his narration, was not something novel. Both Arcadia and Crete claimed to be Zeus's birthplace, with both stories having their own problems. The Arcadia version has Rhea located at Mt. Thaumasion ready to give birth to Zeus, but she eventually does so at Mt. Lykaion.[24] The Cretan version has Rhea being taken to Crete, on Mt. Dikte, where she delivers the baby and is then taken to Mt. Ida,[25] where Zeus is brought up by the goat Amaltheia while the Curetes protect the baby by clanging their shields to muffle its cries. However, these stories corresponded to the Hesiodic genealogy of the gods, that is, the traditional and normative version that was dominant in Greek mythology. Euhemerus was not drawing solely from that pool of myths. The entombment of Zeus in Crete is related to an older known story in antiquity, that of a local Cretan deity of vegetation.[26] Recently, however, Nanno Marinatos rejected the prevalent idea of a vegetation deity, arguing that according to the archaeological record this old Cretan god should be seen as a "powerful warrior deity [. . .] equivalent to the storm-/warrior-gods of the Near East: Baal, Hadad, Marduk, Seth, and Horus, all of which combat enemies and establish order over chaos" and, thus, "the Minoan god embodies the ideal king."[27] This view of the Minoan Zeus could well have been the source of Euhemerus's Panchaean Zeus. The warrior nature of the king of Panchaea is evident in both Diodorus and Eusebius, in which Zeus is being deified due to his power, whereas the idea of *euergesia* as the decisive factor of Zeus's deification is only found in Lactantius (as portrayed in the excerpt below). Euhemeristic deification, as Benjamin Garstad has argued, is based on "kingly power, not *euergesia*,"[28] which denotes the relevance of the Cretan warrior deity to Euhemerus's narration. Such an approach, of course, challenges the traditional understanding of euhemeristic deification based on the benefactions of the characters in the *Sacred Inscription*, which simultaneously creates further problems when dealing with the work as a justification of the deification practices in the Hellenistic world.

Crete was not only the birthplace of Zeus; it was also where he was entombed. Although the fragments from Diodorus and Eusebius 'surprisingly' omit this information, we have the testimony of Lactantius who, citing Ennius, presents a detailed description of Zeus's interment in Crete:

> *Ennius in Sacra Historia descriptis omnibus quae in vita sua gessit ad ultimum sic ait: deinde Iuppiter postquam quinquies terras circuivit omnibusque amicis atque cognatis suis imperia divisit reliquitque hominibus leges mores frumentaque paravit multaque alia bona fecit, inmortali gloria memoriaque adfectus sempiterna monumenta sui reliquit. aetate pessum acta in Creta vitam commutavit et ad deos abiit eumque Curetes filii sui curaverunt decoraveruntque eum; et sepulchrum eius est in Creta in oppido Gnosso et dicitur Vesta hanc urbem creavisse; inque sepulchro eius est inscriptum antiquis litteris Graecis ZAN KRONOY id est Latine Iuppiter Saturni.*

> Ennius in his Sacred History described all that he did in his life and finally said: "After Jupiter had gone five times round the earth and had divided and willed his powers among all his friends and relations, while for men he prepared laws, customs and food and did many other good things, then stirred by the undying glamour of his record he left memorials to his people that would last forever. As his life went into decline, he removed to Crete and departed to the gods, and his sons the Curetes looked after him and did him honour. His tomb is in Crete, in the town of Cnossos, which Vesta is said to have founded; on the tomb is an inscription in ancient Greek lettering, 'Zan Kronou,' which means in Latin Jupiter son of Saturn."[29]

The entombment of Zeus in Crete raises some difficult questions. The first one is related to the reaction by Callimachus, roughly a contemporary of Euhemerus. In his *Hymn to Zeus* Callimachus rejects the idea of Zeus's entombment, not only in Crete but anywhere else: "'Cretans always lie.' For the Cretans even built a tomb, Lord, for you. But you did not die, for you are eternal."[30] This reaction by Callimachus could be associated with the well-known saying of Epimenides that the Cretans are always liars.[31] It is known that in *Hymn 1*, dedicated to Zeus,[32] Callimachus deals with the problem of Zeus's birthplace and opts for Arcadia, a decision that could well have been a result of his objection to both the ancient Minoan tradition and Euhemerus's recent theory. But Callimachus did not stop there. He made a direct attack on Euhemerus when he described him as "the old man who fashioned the ancient Panchaean Zeus" and who dwells "to the shrine before the wall, where [. . .] [he] chatters and scratches out his unrighteous books."[33] Callimachus's attitude is decisive when one reads Euhemerus's theory as an encouragement to the rise of ruler and dynastic cults during the Graeco-Roman era. It is known that Callimachus enjoyed the patronage of Ptolemy II Philadelphus and was resident in Alexandria, the capital of the Ptolemaic kingdom. He never expressed any interest in travelling abroad and his intellectual work in Alexandria (even though he never held, as it is often argued, the position of the librarian at the famous Library) was celebrated.[34] Callimachus's attack on Euhemerus implies that he could have personally known the Messenean author while he was resident there. Through Callimachus's survived work we see that not only was he attached to the Ptolemaic court but he also praised his patrons and was in favor of their deification. We know that he wrote on Arsinoe's death (around 270 BCE) and her subsequent apotheosis, and that in his *Hymn to Delos* he has god Apollo predicting the coming of Philadelphus (that is, Callimachus's own patron) and raising him to his own level.[35] Ludwig Koenen has rightly argued that Callimachus not only was familiar with the ideas connected to the Egyptian ideology of kingship but he was actually propagating them.[36] If Euhemerus's work is to be seen as a clear example of encouraging these practices of apotheosis and deification, how can we explain Callimachus's direct attack on him? We would expect from an adherent of divine kingship such as Callimachus to encounter in Euhemerus an ally; someone who shared the same opinions as he did. But Callimachus's attitude can only indicate that the text and the spirit of the *Sacred Inscription*, as well as what was known about Euhemerus in Alexandria and in the Ptolemaic court at that period, were not in favor of such practices but against them.[37]

## Panara's Political System

The story itself that Euhemerus presented regarding the society at the Panchaean archipelago cannot be overlooked by simply concentrating on the story about the gods in order to justify (or not) the deification practices during the Hellenistic era. Marek Winiarczyk has persuasively shown that the literary form of the *Sacred Inscription* belongs to the utopian travel narratives genre in the broad sense, with the utopian themes however playing a secondary role compared to the theory of religion that interested Euhemerus.[38] A common mistake, however, made by classicists who study the *Sacred Inscription* is a need to explain Euhemerus's motive for writing his work by taking religion to be a distinct, somehow *sui generis* phenomenon. As such, one encounters arguments such as those made by Roland Müller, Marianne Zumschlinge, Reinhold Bichler, and others, who contend that Euhemerus was not interested in political theory, or only cared about religious ideas rather than political or social ones.[39] In a world where politics, religion, and social life were not that much distinct—which is also the reason after all why so many scholars have supported the idea that Euhemerus's goal was the justification of divine monarchy—I find it quite paradoxical to claim that dealing with religious ideas in the *Sacred Inscription* meant excluding the political or the social from the discussion. The very presence, in a detailed form, of Panchaea's political and social stratification and organization encountered in the work can only be seen as closely related to the theory of the origins of gods. Thus, I find any attempt to distinguish between those elements in order to claim that the utopian aspect stood as the frame-story of the theory or vice versa as deeply problematic when it comes to the theoretical discussion of Euhemerus's approach to religion. Perhaps such classifications of the work do matter for the sake of our own categorizations and tools we employ when studying antiquity, but isolating the constituent elements of the *Sacred Inscription* when debating about its literary genre implicitly opens up the door to the *sui generis* argument, according to which religion is distinct from politics and other societal and generally cultural systems.

The information pertaining to the political regime in Panara, the capital of Panchaea, provides further support to Euhemerus's anti-ruler cult ideology. The city's residents are described as "the suppliants of Triphyllian Zeus" and are "independent and not ruled by a king" (αὐτόνομοι καὶ ἀβασίλευτοι).[40] The adjective ἀβασίλευτοι has initiated debates regarding how it is used here by Euhemerus. Despite whether the term is operating here in the same sense it was employed in the Hellenistic world in describing the privileges granted to the Greek cities by the kings, or in the broader sense of freedom from authority,[41] I find the recent argument made by Marianne Schiebe more focused and relative to the overall spirit of the *Sacred Inscription*. As she puts it, "it would be a strange feature to emphasize in a description meant to sketch a model for a society governed by an autocratic sovereign with pretensions to divine honours from his subjects."[42] Even if, due to the scarcity of our sources, we are more or less obliged to think of the possibility that the king of Panchaea did have power over the rest of the inhabitants, we must not neglect how the king is presented in the text. He is not named and his role within the society is rather ancillary, with the priests holding a more decisive role in how social cohesion is maintained.[43] Following Schiebe, it is indeed problematic how one can reconcile this presentation of the king in Panchaea with the prevalent position of seeing the *Sacred Inscription* as inspired by and, more importantly, aiming to boost the deification of kings. The counter-argument that the people in Panchaea were not always without a king but had Zeus and the others who followed after him and were deified, implying not the rejection but the confirmation of deified kings, does not coincide with the very fact that monarchy was still present but now merely denoting an honorary title. As in modern states that have retained the monarchic regime but have stripped it of any actual political power (let alone any religious one), the reality in Panchaea can only indicate Euhemerus's acceptable form of government, which obviously did not include deified monarchs. If the very practice of the deification of kings in Panchaea was discontinued at some point in history, as Sylvie Honigman has argued,[44] this does not mean that the political regime was transformed into a theocracy, which itself is an overstatement and an anachronism that barely fits into any political regime in antiquity. The fact that the ἀβασίλευτοι citizens of Panara appoint annually three archons, who make all decisions but "the most weighty [ones] they refer to the priests,"[45] does not allow for such an assertion. It can only indicate a rejection of both monarchy and the old deification practices that came with it.

Whether Euhemerus wanted to see the Panchaean society being reenacted in Egypt—or elsewhere in the Hellenistic world—remains an open issue. This would place him in the same category with other utopians, but I think that the whole reality in Panchaea is seen by Euhemerus as merely an archaic, different system, the applicability of which is not at the heart of his work.[46] The explanation of the origin of the gods, however, and its relationship to kingship is what one must take from this story. If absolute monarchy was now rejected or held a mere honorary status, deification was ceased, and religion was related to ancient practices that were not active anymore, it is almost impossible to reconcile the social and political reality of Panchaea with the claim that the *Sacred Inscription* aimed at justifying the deification of rulers.

## Euhemerus's Irony

Related to the conclusions I drew in the previous pages, what remains to be examined is how can one relate the *Sacred Inscription* to the deification of the Hellenistic potentates. It is perhaps irrefutable that the phenomenon itself inspired Euhemerus. But the centrality of his theory of religion compels the reader to reexamine the text's relationship with that popular phenomenon of the Hellenistic period. If Euhemerus was indeed influenced by such practices and got his stimulus for promoting his theory from them,[47] then his eventual rejection of deified kingship in Panara begs for a reevaluation of the phenomenon's place in his thought and work. One can deduce that the Messenean author was essentially attacking the practice, which, in turn, leads to the discussion of an old and yet readily dismissed idea by most scholars: Euhemerus's irony toward, and satirization of, such practices.

The view of the *Sacred Inscription* as a work that did not intend to justify but, on the contrary, to satirize the divine pretensions of the rulers was already argued in the late nineteenth century, most lucidly by Rudolf

Hitzel.[48] Despite the various criticisms, the same idea was promoted more recently by Niklas Holzberg, which I think still has some merit but needs to be approached from another angle.[49] The traditional view was based on the work *Deipnosophists* of the third century CE Greek grammarian and author Athenaeus, who in the fourteenth book mentions that Euhemerus had called Cadmus a cook in a royal house, and his wife, Harmonia, a flute girl.[50] Contrary to the criticism in relation to Plutarch's generalization when referring to Euhemerus (see Chapter 4), Athenaeus's testimony is too detailed and precise to be dismissed as a sheer expression of trivializing Euhemerus's work. Given that in the same excerpt Athenaeus apprises his audience that the information comes from the third book of the *Sacred Inscription* (ἐν τῷ τρίτῳ τῆς Ἱερᾶς Ἀναγραφῆς τοῦθ' ἱστορεῖ), we should take his testimony as a direct citation or, at least, a slightly modified version of what was found in Euhemerus's work. If Euhemerus was indeed satirizing the royal cults by humanizing all traditionally deemed gods, this satire should be seen through the lens of irony in relation to such practices rather than as a straightforward case of satirization.

In the introduction of his edited volume *A Companion to Satire*, Ruben Quintero allows for the satirization of the "immutably divine or demonic" only "through a humanizing or a thoroughly iconoclastic perspective."[51] One could argue, of course, that such an assertion perfectly fits into the idea of promotion rather than rejection of deification proclamations; by humanizing the Olympian gods, Euhemerus opens up the way for the Hellenistic rulers to claim divinization themselves: contemporary rulers, just as at the dawn of history with Zeus, can be elevated to the divine realm. However, this interpretative path essentially neglects what Euhemerus' iconoclasm actually creates. The humanization of Zeus and his predecessors and successors denudes them of the divine kirtle, which in turn clearly conveys an explicit new message: Zeus and the rest of the Panchaean alleged divinities were mere humans and so are the Hellenistic potentates. If Euhemerus was planning to advocate the practice, then his chosen method was at least contradictory to such aspirations, as I have argued in this chapter.

Athenaeus's testimony could offer some proof pertaining to Euhemerus's possible ironic and satirizing disposition toward gods, kings, and—most importantly—kings claiming to be gods. The main problem with both Hitzel's and Holzberg's approach to the testimony in question is that they concentrated their interpretations solely on the latter. A more persuasive interpretation would be to take Euhemerus's possible ironic and satirizing stance toward all of the above and not merely toward kings who claimed to be divine. This can be deduced through both the centrality of (primarily) the theory of the origins of religion and (secondarily) the anti-ruler character of the *Sacred Inscription*, as I asserted in the previous section. The fact that Euhemerus was most likely inspired by the ruler cults solely indicates the starting point of his thought rather than his aim. The historization of the traditional gods in conjunction with the essentially inactive role of the unnamed king in Panara indicates Euhemerus's probable overall rejection of both traditional mythology and contemporary pretensions related to that mythology. Additionally, it cannot be overruled that Euhemerus used irony in his work only 'locally' rather than throughout the *Sacred Inscription*. After all, as Richard Rutherford has cogently shown, it is easier to recognize such restricted use of this trope than assigning it to a whole text.[52] Thus, if the Athenaeus's testimony could be seen as conveying irony, this does not necessarily imply or mean that the *Sacred Inscription* per se was a satire or filled with irony throughout. It all comes down, naturally, to how one decides to read or use the text based on particular circumstances and fueled by specific motivations.

Ancient Greek irony (*eironeia*), contrary to later adoptions of the trope, more clearly encountered in the Socratic method, was used not to ridicule or satirize but, rather, as a means to a specific end, which allowed Socrates to pretend (rather than actually being ignorant) in order to delve deeper into the discussion at hand—in itself a clear indication of "what is being said is *not meant*."[53] If Euhemerus was indeed utilizing irony in Athenaeus's testimony, this does not necessarily imply that he also intended or meant his irony as a means toward a specific end, that is, the rejection of Cadmus's traditional story. Just as in the case of Euhemerus's 'atheism' (see Chapter 4), the Messenean author could have well simply meant, paraphrasing Claire Colebrook, to present or 'mention' and not to intend a world-view.[54] The unsurpassable barrier, of course, remains the lack of context given the fragmentary and mostly indirect access we have to the *Sacred Inscription*. This certainly applies to the Athenaeus text as well, given that all we are left with is a mere four-line citation within another work that served its own specific agenda. This is where scholars like Winiarczyk justifiably raise their objections when theoretical interpretations go beyond the available sources. However, all historical and textual sources "do not 'speak' or present us with their intrinsic meaning and significance; rather we give them meaning and significance by interpreting them"[55] as Neville Morley has correctly put it. Thus, the question of whether we, later readers of fragmentary and objectively 'difficult' texts, are justified in reading them as ironic, satiric, or the like can only be answered within the context of theorizing and hypothesizing rather than by arguing of a text's irrefutable meaning. Hence, in the case of the Athenaeus testimony—as well as the rest of the summaries and testimonies of all the authors who decided to disseminate Euhemerus's ideas—solely based on the available sources, it is almost impossible to judge whether the Messenean author really meant what he seems to be saying.

In her excellent study *Irony's Edge: The Theory and Politics of Irony* (1994), Linda Hutcheon discusses how irony, as a literary trope, can irritate, mock, attack, ridicule, exclude, embarrass, or humiliate.[56] It is obviously one of the above reactions that the audience in Athenaeus has, when Ulpian's initial phrase ("You seem to me, O guests, to be ignorant that Cadmus, the grandfather of Bacchus, was a cook") is accompanied by dead silence ("no one made any reply") that urges Ulpian to provide further explanation.[57] This implies, of course, that the rest of the banqueters had no prior knowledge of such an interpretation—which could well also mean that Athenaeus here is implying a general lack of knowledge of Euhemerus's story among his intended readership and, thus, proceeds by offering further information. The silence Ulpian receives is most likely the puzzlement the *Deipnosophists* reader would have also felt when encountering this phrase. This demonstrates the truly radical nature of Euhemerus's work as well as its restricted circulation among the general public some six centuries after its compilation. The radicality of the *Sacred Inscription*, to return to my previous point, is closely related to how irony functions within the very system it criticizes. Ross Chambers has persuasively shown that irony tries to "use that system, with all the play the system allows, to produce different ends, that is, to change the products of the system,"[58] with the system here being both the Homeric and Hesiodic mythology of the gods and the Hellenistic rulers and their aspirations. It is only by combining these two elements that one can argue that Euhemerus was using irony and, eventually, satire in different parts of his work.

Marek Winiarczyk has rejected the satirical (and I include here ironic) nature of the *Sacred Inscription* based on the premise that it was not seen as one in antiquity.[59] Although Winiarczyk is correct, I can hardly agree with such a generalization given the nature of both irony and satire and how they function within texts. First, irony is very often conflated with humor—and, thus, often with satire.[60] If Euhemerus was using irony in certain parts of his work it does not mean that he must be seen as a satirist and his work as a satire throughout. Based on the Athenaeus testimony, the likelihood of 'localized' irony cannot be rejected at once. Second, irony is in the eye of the beholder rather than an explicit trait of a text, pronounced in the beginning of a work or evident in every possible instance. It is often the case that the reader (in the singular) might miss or not attribute irony in a given text or phrase and, mistakenly, take it in its literal form.[61] Third, the utopian nature of the *Sacred Inscription*, which Winiarczyk himself acknowledges as do most—if not all—scholars, allows for a satiric and/or ironic mood in the text. After all, as Quintero argues, "[s]atirists were our first utopians," which is based on the principal aim of the satirist who "either explicitly or implicitly, tries to sway us toward an ideal alternative, toward a condition of what the satirist believes should be."[62] Criticizing the existing condition practically requires some kind of irony and/or satire. Fourth, it is not merely the Athenaeus testimony that could be seen through an ironic and/or satirizing lens toward the royal cults. It could be traced in the wording of Lactantius as well, who presumably quotes from Ennius, when discussing the origins of kingship and, subsequently, gods. In the *Divine Institutes* we read:

> *Initio, inquit, primus in terris imperium summum Caelus habuit. is id regnum una cum fratribus suis sibi instituit atque paravit.*

'In the beginning,' he says, 'first Caelus held supreme sway on earth. He established and organized that kingship for himself together with his brothers.'[63]

If kingship is the result of one man and his siblings who concocted the ways to exercise and maintain power, their deification was subsequently originated from such crafty manipulations. It is possible (and, sometimes, necessary) to read such a text and interpret it as being ironic toward both kingship and traditional gods (and their stories). Thus, contemporary claims of divine ancestry or presence, as for example in the early Ptolemaic period in Egypt, must be seen as practically a 'joke' that should be dismissed. Potentates are mere humans, just as Caelus/Uranus and Jupiter/Zeus were. And if they managed, for whatever reason, to cross the threshold between human and divine, the same is not applicable with the unnamed king of Panara—and thus should not be with the Hellenistic rulers either.

The fifth and final point, also linked to the utopian nature of the *Sacred Inscription*, is the very practice of pseudo-documentarism in antiquity and its relation to 'ironic textual games' as Karen Ni-Mheallaigh characterizes them. The occurrence of such examples in Dictys, Antonius Diogenes, and Lucian, as she argues, "reveals implied readers who were complicit in ironic textual games, including the invention of pseudo-archaeological sources and traditions as authenticating strategies for fiction which played with authority with varying degrees of irony."[64] The golden stele in the temple of Zeus in Panchaea is another example of such pseudo-archaeological sources and traditions upon which Euhemerus based his own take on traditional religion and contemporary royal pretensions. If, as Emilio Gabba argued some years ago, the Hellenistic utopias were seen by their readers as if they were history, which also justifies Diodorus's insistence (5.41.4; 5.42.4) on calling them 'history,'[65] then the euhemeristic work had many reasons to employ those 'varying degrees of irony' when addressing the issue of the origin of the traditional gods.

It goes without saying that, given irony's delicate and usually veiled nature, the Athenaeus's testimony (and Lactantius's alike) can be seen as a non-ironic text; after all, this is how it has been dealt with by the vast majority of scholars. Notwithstanding these often justifiable objections, the plausibility of our interpretations can hardly be determined. After all, "[w]e cannot study directly the actual processes of ancient thought, only their products."[66] By the same token, the traditional view of the *Sacred Inscription* as a justification tool of the deification of the Hellenistic monarchs, as I have discussed in this chapter, is equally problematic—if not more easily dismissible—as I hope I have demonstrated in the preceding pages. If previous interpretative attempts focused on satirization against the practices encountered in the Hellenistic world, I maintain another view; one that takes irony and satire in a sense together, as complementary to each other when addressing and criticizing established systems and conditions within texts that have a utopian outlook as the *Sacred Inscription* did. If Euhemerus was indeed influenced by and wrote his novel as a reply to the royal divine pretensions of his time, as I strongly believe he did, then his theory of religion is stemming from a reaction to rather a confirmation of such practices. Such a view, naturally, entails even the subtlest hint of irony on behalf of the Messenean author. Given the way he chose to promote his theory, that is, via a narrative that shares a lot with other utopian works,[67] adding pseudo-documentarism in order to entwine it with a historical aura, localized irony can be acknowledged in some parts of the work (or, better, of its survived fragments and testimonies), such as in Athenaeus's testimony.

## Notes

1 Marcus 1992, 261; 301, emphasis added in both excerpts.
2 See the discussion in Winiarczyk 2013, 7 and n. 43.
3 It would be pointless to list all works that accept this view, since they tradition-ally constitute the vast majority. Some examples are Dörrie 1964, 218–224; Frazer 1972, I 294; Aalders 1975, 66; Gamble 1979, 13–14; Manuel and Manuel 1979, 89–90; Bietenholz 1994, 39; Littlewood 1998, 6–7; Stephens 2003, 37; Rüpke 2007, 123; Pachis 2014, who nevertheless approaches 'euhemerism' as implied in Diodorus's first book.
4 See Ferguson 1975, 108; Müller 1993, 279; Baumgarten 1996, 102; Honigman 2009, 29.
5 See Winiarczyk 2013, 59–64; 102; Schiebe 2014, 346–347. The literature on divine kingship during this period is extensive. For example, see Price 1984, 23–52; Shipley 2000, 156–163; Chaniotis 2005; Versnel 2011, 439–492. For a discussion of the top-down and bottom-up deification and the issue of whether those potentates were seen as gods, see Roubekas 2015.
6 Eusebius, *Preparation for the Gospel* 2.2.55 (W. T 3): Εὐήμερος μὲν οὖν φίλος γεγονὼς Κασσάνδρου τοῦ βασιλέως.
7 Winiarczyk 2013, 2; the discussion of dating Euhemerus is found in 1–5. Also see the classic Jacoby 1907, 953, who takes this information to be spurious. In a similar vein, Whitmarsh 2015, 154 argues that "it is likely enough that the whole story about Cassander is a fiction, like the rest of the story."
8 For example, see the criticism in Garstad 2003, 309, with which I agree.
9 Fraser 1972, I 292.
10 Peter Frazer (1972, I 289–290) has given strong evidence that indicates the Egyptian influence one encounters in Diodorus's description (5.44.1; W. T 38) of the temple of Zeus Triphyllian, which includes: a marble construction; priests dwelling in the sanctuary and wearing linen and occasionally wool; the existence of a long *dromos*, primarily a pharaonic feature; the existence of a spring and river quays, common around Egyptian temples; the singing within the temples of the gods' deeds. If we add to this the hieroglyphs used on the stele (cf. 5.46.7; W. T 37), we must assume that Euhemerus wrote his work having a very detailed knowledge of Egyptian religious culture and architecture. Cf. Whitmarsh 2013, 54.
11 Adams 1974, 101–103; Adams 2010; 214–218. Cf. the discussion in Gattinoni 2010, 113–116.
12 Errington 1990, 133.
13 Cassander's detestation toward Alexander's policies is eloquently presented in Diodorus's *Historical Library* 17.118.2 and 19.52.1–6. The latter, as nicely

discussed by Gattinoni 2010, 120, gives an explicit description of Cassander's anti-orientalizing practices that Alexander adopted; among them, of course, was the self-deification of the Kind of Macedonia.

14  Errington 1990, 133; Adams 2010, 217 n. 9; Winiarczyk 2013, 2.

15  Lund 1992, 162. Also see the general discussion in Hadley 1974.

16  On Demetrios of Phaleron and Demetrios Poliorketes, see Mikalson 1998, 46–104. Cf. O'Sullivan 2009; Harding 2015, 60–63.

17  The translation is drawn from Versnel, 2011, 446. This is not the place to expand on the content, motive, and goal of this hymn that holds a central role in the study of divine kingship during the Hellenistic era. See the excellent discussion in Chaniotis 2011.

18  Plutarch, *Demetrius* 10.3. Cf. the discussion in Versnel 2011, 451–452.

19  See Mikalson 1998, 83. I agree with Winiarczyk 2013, 102–103 in his criticism of Van Gils' assertion that Euhemerus wrote in order to prepare Cassander's deification. Given that by the time Euhemerus wrote his *Sacred Inscription* Cassander was most likely deceased—if, of course, we accept the hypothesis that he wrote in Egypt—it is highly unlikely to accept such an unfounded idea.

20  See Athenaeus, *Deipnosophists* 3.98d–f; cf. Strabo, *Geography* 7.1.162. Also, see Ferguson 1975, 108–110; Dubois 2006, 3–4; Winiarczyk 2011, 205–218.

21  For a discussion on the coins of the City of Uranids, see Mørkholm 1991, 60. On the possible relationship between Euhemerus and Alexarchus, see Baumgarten 1996, 93.

22  Diodorus's report (19.53.2) that Cassander endeavored to rebuild Thebes, assuming that in this way he would attain immortal fame (τυχεῖν ἀθανάτου δόξης) can hardly be seen as an indication of his wish to be deemed a god. Cf. Sulimani 2011, 72.

23  Diodorus Siculus, *Historical Library* 5.42.4; 5.46.3 (W. T 33; T35).

24  See Dowden 2006, 33.

25  Diodorus Siculus, *Historical Library* 5.70.

26  See Sakellarakis 1988, 212–213; Winiarczyk 2013, 36–37. On the importance of Crete in Zeus's biography also see Prent 2005; Whitley 2009, 277–282. Willetts 1962, 233–251 cites twenty-four epithets of Zeus associated with Crete.

27  Marinatos 2013, 252.

28  Garstad 2003, 310.

29  Lactantius, *Divine Institutes* 1.11.44–48 (W. T 69A).

30  Callimachus, *Hymn* 1.8–9. Cf. Acosta-Hughes 2002, 122.

31  See the discussion in Winiarczyk 2013, 34–35.

32  See Stephens 2003, 91.

33  Callimachus, *Iambus* 1.9–11 (W. T 1A; cf. 1C). Cf. Acosta-Hughes 2002, 23. The discussion regarding which temple the excerpt refers to is quite extensive, with no firm agreement. For example, see Winiarczyk 2013, 31–32, whereas an interesting alternative has been offered by De Angelis and Garstad 2006, 223 n. 82.

It is interesting here to point out a similar description that was used against Prodicus, the author most scholars see as Euhemerus's major influence (see the discussion in Chapter 2). In Aristophanes's lost work *Tagenistae* (Ταγηνισταί), the philosopher from the island of Ceos is characterized as a chatterer, who has corrupted a certain individual (Aristophanes fr. 490; cf. Drozdek 2006, 61): τοῦτον τὸν ἄνδρ᾽ ἢ βιβλίον διέφθορεν ἢ Πρόδικος ἢ τῶν ἀδολεσχῶν εἷς γέ τις [A book has corrupted this man, or Prodicus, or one of the chatterers]. Although the original wording is not the same (λαλάζων in Callimachus; ἀδολεσχῶν in the Aristophanes fragment), the underlying meaning, however, is virtually the same.

34 On Callimachus's life, see Gutzwiller 2007, 61; Weber 2011, 231; Depew 2013, 325–326.
35 On Arsinoe, see Fantuzzi and Hunter 2004, 42; Prioux 2011. On the *Hymn to Delos*, see Koenen 1993, 81–82; Barbantani 2011, 193–200.
36 Koenen 1993, 84.
37 A similar argument was recently supported by Depew 2013, 327: "[t]o direct criticism to the Olympians, as Euhemeros did, is to direct it to the beneficent monarchs, and in this particular case, to deny their divinity." I think that Callimachus's overall work denotes a belief in both the Olympians and the deified Ptolemies. Callimachus's praise of the Ptolemies was not mere adulation, but a strong belief that the Olympians themselves were true. Of course, these are not mutually exclusive, but I see Callimachus's work as strongly influenced by his beliefs and not merely as a struggle to support the divine nature of the Ptolemaic rulers.
38 Winiarczyk 2011, 117–180; Winiarczyk 2013, 19–21. I have extensively argued in favor of this position in Roubekas 2011. Also see Clay and Purvis 1999, 41–45; Campbell 2006, 124–127; Futre Pinheiro 2006. Whitmarsh 2013, 50 correctly draws attention to the lack of such terminology (i.e., utopia, utopianism) of literary works in antiquity.
39 Zumschlinge 1976; Bichler 1984; Müller 1993, 300.
40 Diodorus Siculus, *Historical Library* 5.42.5 (W. T 33).
41 See the discussions in Honigman 2009, 20 and Winiarczyk 2013, 79–89.
42 Schiebe 2014, 342 n. 6. Schiebe, however, ignores or overlooks my discussion in the article on which this chapter is based (see Acknowledgements).
43 Diodorus Siculus, *Historical Library* 5.42.1; 5.45.3–5 (W. T 30; T 35). Cf. Winiarczyk 2013, 81.
44 Honigman 2009, 21. Honigman here sees, as many before and after her, the deification of kings as only a post mortem phenomenon.
45 Diodorus Siculus, *Historical Library* 5.42.5 (W. T 33): ἄρχοντας δὲ καθιστᾶσι κατ' ἐνιαυτὸν τρεῖς. οὗτοι δὲ θανάτου μὲν οὔκ εἰσι κύριοι, τὰ δὲ λοιπὰ πάντα διακρίνουσι. καί αὐτοὶ δὲ οὗτοι τὰ μέγιστα ἐπὶ τοὺς ἱερεῖς ἀναφέρουσιν.
46 Winiarczyk 2013, 78 correctly rejects the idea of an ideal society and focuses on the origins of religion. For a discussion on ancient utopianism as a program meant to be put in action, see Dawson 1992, 5–10.
47 I find the conclusion of Winiarczyk 2013, 108 rather open-ended:

> I do believe that Euhemerus wanted to explain the origins of religion and thus engage in the discussion regarding the ruler cult at the start of the Hellenistic period. However, we cannot determine whether he merely intended to explain the origins of this cult or whether he also wanted to justify and promote it among Greeks.

Although I agree with his emphasis on the theory of religion, he seems to be very reluctant to proceed with a more persuasive and (admittedly) speculative proposal pertaining to the relationship between ancient euhemerism and deification. Euhemerus's engagement in the discussion related to the ruler cult seems like the key element. In the following pages I will try to reestablish the interpretation of the work as a satire on the ruler cult, but not solely based on previously promoted arguments that Winiarczyk himself rightly—to a certain degree—rejects (100–101 and n. 10–15).
48 Hitzel 1895, 394–396.
49 See Holzberg 2003, 625. The question of irony in the *Sacred Inscription* is not dismissed by Bolle 1970, 23 n. 15.
50 Athenaeus, *Deipnosophists* 14.658e–f (W. T 77). Cf. Hitzel 1895, 394.

51  Quintero 2007, 2.
52  See Rutherford 2011, 84.
53  See the excellent discussion in Colebrook 2005, 2; 7–8.
54  Ibid., 5.
55  Morley 2004, 1.
56  See Hutcheon 1994, 14.
57  Athenaeus, *Deipnosophists* 14.658e–f (W. T 77): ἀγνοεῖν μοι δοκεῖτε, ὦ ἄνδρες
    δαιταλῆς, ὅτι καὶ Κάδμος ὁ τοῦ Διονύσου πάππος μάγειρος ἦν. σιωπησάντων δὲ καὶ ἐπὶ
    τούτῳ πάντων.
58  Chambers 1990, 21. Cf. Hutcheon 1994, 16.
59  Winiarczyk 2013, 100–101.
60  See Hutcheon 1994, 2–3.
61  This is nicely discussed in Hutcheon 1994, 15–16 and Pavlovskis-Petit 2007,
    511–512.
62  Quintero 2007, 3.
63  Lactantius, *Divine Institutes* 1.13.14 (W. T 51A; cf. Lactantius, *Epitome of
    Divine Institutes* 14.2–4 [W. T 51B]).
64  Ni-Mheallaigh 2008, 422.
65  See Gabba 1981, 59.
66  Morley 2004, 100.
67  See Roubekas 2011.

# References

Aalders, Gerhard J. D. 1975. *Political Thought in Hellenistic Times*. Amsterdam:
    A. W. Hakkert.
Acosta-Hughes, Benjamin. 2002. *Polyeideia: The Iambi of Callimachus and the
    Archaic Iambic Tradition*. Berkeley, CA and Los Angeles, CA: University of
    California Press.
Adams, Winthrop L. 1974. "Cassander, Macedonia, and the Policy of Coalition,
    323–301 B.C." PhD diss., University of Virginia, VA.
Adams, Winthrop L. 2010. "Alexander's Successors to 221 BC." In *A Companion
    to Ancient Macedonia*, edited by Joseph Roisman and Ian Worthington, 208–224.
    Malden, MA and Oxford: Wiley–Blackwell.
Barbantani, Silvia. 2011. "Callimachus on Kings and Kingship." In *Brill's Com-
    panion to Callimachus*, edited by Benjamin Acosta-Hughes, Luigi Lehnus, and
    Susan Stephens, 178–200. Leiden and Boston, MA: Brill.
Baumgarten, Albert I. 1996. "Euhemerus' Eternal Gods: Or, How Not To Be
    Embarrassed by Greek Mythology." In *Classical Studies in Honor of David
    Sohlberg*, edited by Ranon Katzoff, Yaakov Petroff, and David Schaps, 91–103.
    Ramat Gan: Bar-Ilan University Press.
Bichler, Reinhold. 1984. "Zur historischen Beurteilung der griechischen Staat-
    sutopie." *Grazer Beiträge. Zeitschrift für die klassische Altertumswissenschaft* 11:
    179–206.
Bietenholz, Peter G. 1994. *Historia and Fabula: Myths and Legends in Historical
    Thought from Antiquity to the Modern Age*. Leiden and New York: E. J. Brill.
Bolle, Kees W. 1970. "In Defense of Euhemerus." In *Myth and Law Among the
    Indo-Europeans*, edited by Jaan Puhvel, 19–38. Berkeley, CA and Los Angeles,
    CA: University of California Press.
Campbell, Gordon L. 2006. *Strange Creatures: Anthropology in Antiquity*. London:
    Duckworth.

Chambers, Ross. 1990. "Irony and the Canon." *Profession* 90: 18–24.

Chaniotis, Angelos. 2005. "The Divinity of Hellenistic Rulers." In *A Companion to the Hellenistic World*, edited by Andrew Erskine, 431–445. Malden, MA and Oxford: Blackwell.

Chaniotis, Angelos. 2011. "The Ithyphallic Hymn for Demetrios Poliorketes and Hellenistic Religious Mentality." In *More than Men, Less than Gods: Studies on Royal Cult and Imperial Worship*, edited by Panagiotis P. Iossif, Andrzej S. Chankowski, and Catharine C. Lorber, 157–195. Leuven and Paris: Peeters.

Clay, Diskin and Andrea Purvis. 1999. *Four Island Utopias*. Newburyport, MA: Focus.

Colebrook, Claire. 2005. *Irony*. London and New York: Routledge.

Dawson, Doyne. 1992. *Cities of the Gods: Communist Utopians in Greek Thought*. New York and Oxford: Oxford University Press.

De Angelis, Franco and Benjamin Garstad. 2006. "Euhemerus in Context." *Classical Antiquity* 25 (2): 211–242.

Depew, Mary. 2013. "Connections, Origins, and the Construction of Belonging in the Poetry of Kallimachos." In *Belonging and Isolation in the Hellenistic World*, edited by Sheila L. Ager and Riemer A. Faber, 325–340. Toronto and London: University of Toronto Press.

Dörrie, Heinrich. 1964. *Der Königskult des Antiochos von Kommagene im Lichte neuer Inschriften-Funde*. Göttingen and Zürich: Vandenhoeck & Ruprecht.

Dowden, Ken. 2006. *Zeus*. London and New York: Routledge.

Drozdek, Adam. 2006. "Prodicus: Deifying Usefulness." *Myrtia* 21: 57–63.

Dubois, Page. 2006. "The History of the Impossible: Ancient Utopia." *Classical Philology* 101: 1–14.

Errington, R. Malcolm. 1990. *A History of Macedonia*. Translated by Catherine Errington. Berkeley, CA and Los Angeles, CA: University of California Press.

Fantuzzi, Marco and Richard Hunter. 2004. *Tradition and Innovation in Hellenistic Poetry*. Cambridge: Cambridge University Press.

Ferguson, John. 1975. *Utopias of the Classical World*. London: Thames and Hudson.

Frazer, Peter M. 1972. *Ptolemaic Alexandria*. Vol. I–II. Oxford: Clarendon Press.

Futre Pinheiro, Marilia P. 2006. "Utopia and Utopias: A Study on a Literary Genre in Antiquity." In *Authors, Authority, and Interpreters in the Ancient Novel: Essays in Honor of Gareth L. Schmeling*, edited by Shannon N. Byrne, Edmund P. Cueva, and Jean Alvares, 147–171. Groningen: Barkhuis.

Gabba, Emilio. 1981. "True History and False History in Classical Antiquity." *Journal of Roman Studies* 71: 50–62.

Gamble, Harry Y. 1979. "Euhemerism and Christology in Origen: 'Contra Celsum' III 22–43." *Vigiliae Christianae* 33 (1): 12–29.

Garstad, Benjamin. 2003. "Review of M. Winiarczyk: *Euhemeros von Messene. Leben, Werk und Nachwirkung*." *Classical Review* 53 (2): 309–311.

Gattinoni, Franca L. 2010. "Cassander and the Legacy of Philip II and Alexander III in Diodorus' *Library*." In *Philip II and Alexander the Great: Father and Son, Lives and Afterlives*, edited by Elizabeth Carney and Daniel Ogden, 113–121. Oxford: Oxford University Press.

Gutzwiller, Kathryn. 2007. *A Guide to Hellenistic Literature*. Malden, MA and Oxford: Blackwell.

Hadley, Robert A. 1974. "Royal Propaganda of Seleucus I and Lysimachus." *Journal of Hellenic Studies* 94: 50–65.

Harding, Phillip. 2015. *Athens Transformed, 404–262 BC: From Popular Sovereignty to the Dominion of the Elite*. New York and London: Routledge.

Hitzel, Rudolf. 1895. *Der Dialog: Ein Literarhistorischer Versuch*. Leipsig: Verlag vos S. Hirzel.

Holzberg, Niklas. 2003. "Novel-Like Works of Extended Prose Fiction II." In *The Novel in the Ancient World*, edited by Gareth L. Schmeling, 619–653. Leiden: Brill.

Honigman, Sylvie. 2009. "Euhemerus of Messene and Plato's Atlantis." *Historia* 58 (1): 1–35.

Hutcheon, Linda. 1994. *Irony's Edge: The Theory and Politics of Irony*. London and New York: Routledge.

Jacoby, Felix. 1907. "Euemeros." *Realencyclopädie der classischen Altertumswissenschaft* 6: 952–972.

Koenen, Ludwig. 1993. "The Ptolemaic King as a Religious Figure." In *Images and Ideologies: Self Definition in the Hellenistic World*, edited by Anthony Bulloch, Erich Gruen, Anthony A. Long, and Andrew Stewart, 25–115. Berkeley, CA and Los Angeles, CA: University of California Press.

Littlewood, Ronald. 1998. "In (Partial) Defence of Euhemerus." *Anthropology Today* 14 (2): 6–14.

Lund, Helen S. 1992. *Lysimachus: A Study in Early Hellenistic Kingship*. London and New York: Routledge.

Manuel, Frank E. and Fritzie P. Manuel. 1979. *Utopian Thought in the Western World*. Cambridge, MA: The Belknap Press of Harvard University Press.

Marcus, Joyce. 1992. *Mesoamerican Writing Systems: Propaganda, Myth, and History in Four Ancient Civilizations*. Princeton, NJ: Princeton University Press.

Marinatos, Nanno. 2013. "Minoan Religion." In *The Cambridge History of Religions in the Ancient World. Vol. 1: From the Bronze Age to the Hellenistic Age*, edited by Michelle R. Saizman and Marvin A. Sweeney, 237–255. Cambridge: Cambridge University Press.

Mikalson, Jon D. 1998. *Religion in Hellenistic Athens*. Berkeley, CA and Los Angeles, CA: University of California Press.

Mørkholm, Otto. 1991. *Early Hellenistic Coinage: From the Accession of Alexander to the Peace of Apamea (336–188 B.C.)*. Edited by Philip Grierson and Ulla Westermark. Cambridge: Cambridge University Press.

Morley, Neville. 2004. *Theories, Models and Concepts in Ancient History*. London and New York: Routledge.

Müller, Roland. 1993. "Überlegungen zur ΙΕΡΑ ΑΝΑΓΡΑΦΗ des Euhemeros von Messene." *Hermes* 121 (3): 276–300.

Ni-Mheallaigh, Karen. 2008. "Pseudo-Documentarism and the Limits of Ancient Fiction." *American Journal of Philology* 123 (3): 403–431.

O'Sullivan, Lara. 2009. *The Regime of Demetrius of Phalerum in Athens, 317–307 BCE: A Philosopher in Politics*. Leiden and Boston, MA: Brill.

Pachis, Panayotis. 2014. "The Discourse of a Myth: Diodorus Siculus and the Egyptian *Theologoumena* During the Hellenistic Age." In *Chasing Down Religion. In the Sights of History and the Cognitive Sciences: Essays in Honor of Luther H. Martin*, edited by Panayotis Pachis and Donald Wiebe, 303–336. Sheffield, UK: Equinox.

Pavlovskis-Petit, Zoja. 2007. "Irony and Satire." In *A Companion to Satire*, edited by Ruben Quintero, 510–524. Malden, MA and Oxford: Blackwell.

Prent, Mieke. 2005. *Cretan Sanctuaries and Cults: Continuity and Change from Late Minoan IIIC to the Archaic Period*. Leiden: Brill.

Price, Simon R. F. 1984. *Rituals and Power: The Roman Imperial Cult in Asia Minor*. Cambridge: Cambridge University Press.

Prioux, Évelyne. 2011. "Callimachus' Queens." In *Brill's Companion to Callimachus*, edited by Benjamin Acosta-Hughes, Luigi Lehnus, and Susan Stephens, 201–224. Leiden and Boston, MA: Brill.

Quintero, Ruben. 2007. "Introduction: Understanding Satire." In *A Companion to Satire*, edited by Ruben Quintero, 1–11. Malden, MA and Oxford: Blackwell.

Roubekas, Nickolas P. 2011. *Αναζητώντας τους Θεούς: Θρησκεία, Μύθος, και Ουτοπία στον Ευήμερο τον Μεσσήνιο*. Thessaloniki: Vanias.

Roubekas, Nickolas P. 2015. "Belief in Belief and Divine Kingship in Early Ptolemaic Egypt: The Case of Ptolemy II Philadelphus and Arsinoe II." *Religio: Revue pro religionistiku* 23 (1): 3–23.

Rüpke, Jörg. 2007. *Religions of the Romans*. Translated by Richard Gordon. Cambridge and Malden, MA: Polity.

Rutherford, Richard. 2011. "The Use and Abuse of Irony." In *Culture in Pieces: Essays in Ancient Texts in Honour of Peter Parsons*, edited by Dirk Obbink and Richard Rutherford, 84–103. New York and Oxford: Oxford University Press.

Sakellarakis, John A. 1988. "The Idaean Cave: Minoan and Greek Worship." *Kernos* 1: 207–214.

Schiebe, Marianne W. 2014. "Why It Should Be Obvious that Euhemerus Did Not Write His *Sacred History* to Bolster Ruler Cult." In *ΛΑΒΡΥΣ: Studies Presented to Pontus Hellström*, edited by Lars Karlsson, Susanne Carlsson, and Jesper Blid Kullberg, 341–350. Uppsala: Uppsala Universitet Press.

Shipley, Graham. 2000. *The Greek World After Alexander 323–30 BC*. London and New York: Routledge.

Stephens, Susan A. 2003. *Seeing Double: Intercultural Poetics in Ptolemaic Alexandria*. Berkeley, CA and Los Angeles, CA: University of California Press.

Sulimani, Iris. 2011. *Diodorus' Mythistory and the Pagan Mission: Historiography and Culture-Heroes in the First Pentad of the Bibliotheke*. Leiden and Boston, MA: Brill.

Versnel, Henk S. 2011. *Coping with the Gods: Wayward Readings in Greek Theology*. Leiden and Boston, MA: Brill.

Weber, Gregor. 2011. "Poet and Court." In *Brill's Companion to Callimachus*, edited by Benjamin Acosta-Hughes, Luigi Lehnus, and Susan Stephens, 225–244. Leiden and Boston, MA: Brill.

Whitley, James. 2009. "Crete." In *A Companion to Archaic Greece*, edited by Kurt A. Raaflaub and Hans van Wees, 273–293. Malden, MA and Oxford: Wiley-Blackwell.

Whitmarsh, Tim. 2013. *Beyond the Second Sophistic: Adventures in Greek Postclassicism*. Berkeley, CA and Los Angeles, CA: University of California Press.

Whitmarsh, Tim. 2015. *Battling the Gods: Atheism in the Ancient World*. New York: Alfred A. Knopf.

Willetts, Ronald F. 1962. *Cretan Cults and Festivals*. Westport, CT: Greenwood.

Winiarczyk, Marek. 2011. *Die Hellenistischen Utopien*. Berlin and Boston, MA: De Gruyter.

Winiarczyk, Marek. 2013. *The Sacred History of Euhemerus of Messene*. Translated by Witold Zbirohowski-Kościa. Berlin and Boston, MA: De Gruyter.

Zumschlinge, Marianne. 1976. "Euhemeros: Staatstheoretische und Staatsutopische Motive." PhD diss., University of Bonn.

# 6 Citing the Citations

## Anti-'Pagan' Euhemerism and Identity Formation

If history is written by the victors, truism notwithstanding, then texts and their embedded ideas and theories are likewise 'rewritten' by the victors. The emergence, spread, and eventual success and establishment of Christianity played the most decisive role in what euhemerism as a theory of religion came to mean, not only in the first centuries of our era but commonly thereafter. It is not a hyperbole to say that most—if not all—allusions to Euhemerus and euhemerism from this period were destined to permanently alter and essentially transform the theory, allowing us, for the first time, to refer to its plural form 'euhemerisms' with more confidence. This 'rewriting' was the result of specific motivations, as I will argue in what follows, mainly related to instituting an identity that could allow the early followers of the Christian teachings to establish themselves as a distinct group amidst existing ones.

In the third chapter I dealt with the variations of Euhemerus's theory as they manifest in the four main sources we have at our disposal, namely Diodorus, Ennius, Eusebius, and Lactantius. The latter two, as I argued, composed their works with a particular agenda linked to the three-centuries-old struggle of legitimating the Christian beliefs and way of life within the predominantly 'pagan' milieu of the Mediterranean world. However, these were not the only two authors who did so. The genre of Christian apologetics, developed after the first century CE, aimed at fending off the various attacks those early Christians received, both ideological as well as legal, which threatened not only the status quo of the movement but its followers very lives. Thus, various authors like Justin, Athenagoras, Aristedes, Tatian, Tertullian, Minucius Felix, and others engaged in the fierce battle of legitimation and survival. Traditionally, scholars have identified the theory of euhemerism in writings of virtually all apologetic authors solely due to a common phrase indeed encountered in many works: the pagan gods used to be mere human beings and their tombs are now their temples.[1] It is exactly the association of this idea with euhemerism, which was the result of a dual process, as I will discuss in this chapter, that eventually established itself as euhemerism proper.

The scholarly output on Christian apologetics is immense and I am not planning to attend to it here. Rather, I am more interested in two issues, quite interconnected eventually: first, what was the audience of the apologists and, second, what was accomplished by their writings. For many years, scholars have taken for granted that the apologetic works were directed to outsiders in order to both explicate Christianity's superiority and justify the place of Christians in the Mediterranean world. Although in many cases the addressees in the texts were indeed people outside the faith—at least according to what the writings maintain—those works were probably not much read outside the Christian communities, especially those written before the time of Constantine.[2] This, of course, does not mean that these authors did not deal with 'pagan' argumentations; on the contrary, their treatises were constructed around those argumentations, but hardly in order to persuade their enemies, as Wayne Kannaday has shown:

> His [Justin's] arguments, like those of most apologists of any ilk, seldom sound as if they would have proved compelling beyond the confines of his like-minded camp. Justin and his successors were, most of all, strengthening the belief of believers, not convincing antagonists. They were offering those of like mind but fragile faith some matrix of rationality on which to pin their piety. They sought to give those whose thoughts were being swayed some reasons to stay. They were providing those who doubted some semblance of an answer to their questions.[3]

If the main audiences of those works were primarily—if not, in cases, exclusively—existing, newly, or future converts, then what was their purpose? It is one thing to approach these texts as attempts to persuade outsiders and yet a completely different one if their contents were mainly addressing and influencing people who were already persuaded. The main topics of those works have been neatly summarized by Anders-Christian Jacobsen, and they include: accusations of atheism; designation of Christianity as a new religion that lacked tradition;[4] charges of political disloyalty and sectarianism; allegations of incestuous actions and sexual amoralities, accompanied by cannibalism.[5] Defenders of Christianity had a lot to deal with; but, primarily, had to cope with a group of people who not only rejected those accusations but mainly sought ways to feel at home and comfortable within their relatively newly formed communities. In this way, as Anders Klostergaard Petersen has argued, the very study of apologetics "gives us an extraordinary glimpse into different strategies of cultural intervention, social maintenance, and identity-formation in the ancient world."[6] The constantly growing field of the study of identity formation in antiquity, especially concerning Jewish-Christian-Pagan relationships, has demonstrated that this is a thorny yet rich area that has attracted a lot of attention lately.[7] Within this ambit, where Christians struggled to establish themselves not only as a distinctive group, but also as the one that holds the truth about the (both divine and natural) world, euhemerism seemed to have played an important role, albeit an indirect one in most cases; and it is through this usage and allusions to the theory of the Messenean author that euhemerism slowly managed to diffuse into the scholarly writings and discussions as merely a theory of post mortem deified kings.

## Whose Euhemerism? Citing the Citations

Marek Winiarczyk has put it bluntly:

> Only four Greek Christians (Theophilus, Clement, Eusebius and Theodoret) and four Latin Christians (Minucius Felix, Arnobius, Lactantius and Augustine) refer to Euhemerus and yet none of them had read the Ἱερὰ Ἀναγραφή or Ennius' translation, the *Euhemerus sive Sacra historia*.[8]

The argument that none of these authors had actually read either the original or the Latin translation is not new,[9] yet it is one that is constantly ignored by scholars when referring to Euhemerus and his theory of religion. Pertaining to this issue, the cases of Eusebius and Lactantius were dealt with in the third chapter, and it remains to be examined why this has been a common view regarding the other authors mentioned here by Winiarczyk and moreover how this affects the discourse on euhemerism.

Theophilus of Antioch (second century CE) mentions Euhemerus in his *To Autolycus*,[10] a three-volume work addressed to a 'pagan' friend, classifying him as an atheist (τοῦ ἀθεωτάτου), based obviously on one of the atheistic catalogues of antiquity.[11] What is more striking, though, is Theophilus's assertion that, according to Euhemerus, the universe was self-sustained and self-governed:

> For having made many daring assertions concerning the gods, he [Euhemerus] at last would absolutely deny their existence, and have all things to be governed by self-regulated action [τὰ πάντα αὐτοματισμῷ διοικεῖσθαι].[12]

This information could potentially be reconciled with Diodorus's report regarding the eternal and indestructible (ἀιδίους καὶ ἀφθάρτους) nature of the celestial gods; to claim, however, that Theophilus had access to the lost sixth book of the *Historical Library* means that he could not possibly miss Diodorus's distinction between earthly and celestial gods, which would in turn indicate that the charge of extreme atheism would be absolutely unfounded. Theophilus's lack of any direct contact with Euhemerus's work, however, is better exemplified in another excerpt, related to the famous Christian argument that all the ancient gods worshipped by the 'pagans' are dead men. In *To Autolycus* 1.9, he goes over a series of figures like Cronus,

Zeus, Dionysus, Apollo, Aphrodite, Ares, Osiris, Adonis, Serapis, and others. All these figures, he argues, were mere humans and, related to our discussion, when referring to Cronus and Zeus (excluding Uranus however) he adopts the traditional stories already known since the time of Homer and Hesiod. Hence, Cronus is accused of cannibalism, whereas Jupiter is accused of being an incestuous fornicator, a lust-driven man. If Theophilus had access to the *Sacred Inscription* why did he not utilize Euhemerus's theory here, which turns myth into history, thereby making his claim more solid and persuasive? After all, if euhemerism is merely the theory that all gods are dead kings, then this would have been the ideal place for Theophilus to allude to the Messenean and his work. Additionally, Theophilus could have resorted to the Ennian translation of the *Sacred Inscription* if he had had access to it. However, the Lactantian alleged verbatim narration regarding Cronus and Zeus has various differences with the conventional stories of the Olympians, making this hypothesis equally problematic.[13] On the contrary, Theophilus chooses to mention Euhemerus as an extreme atheist, which manifests his lack of direct knowledge of the original text or its translation.

Clement of Alexandria (late second century CE), on the contrary, adopts a rather different approach to Euhemerus and his theory. In his *Protrepticus*[14] he mentions Euhemerus among other known figures of antiquity designated as atheists.[15] Nevertheless, he does not stop there but, with a clever twist, he praises both Euhemerus and the other authors because, as he sees it, they managed to realize the fallacy of their ancestral traditions but failed to acknowledge the real God:

> Wherefore (for I must by no means conceal it) I cannot help wondering how Euhemerus of Agragas, and Nicanor of Cyprus, and Diagoras, and Hippo of Melos, and besides these, that Cyrenian of the name of Theodorus, and numbers of others, who lived a sober life, and had a clearer insight than the rest of the world into the prevailing error respecting those gods, were called Atheists; for if they did not arrive at the knowledge of the truth, they certainly suspected the error of the common opinion; which suspicion is no insignificant seed, and becomes the germ of true wisdom.[16]

Again, however, this is not sufficient evidence that Clement had read either the Greek or the Latin text. Similar to Theophilus, Clement does not employ Euhemerus's theory when discussing the common locus of all apologists: the gods are dead men. In 4.55.2, he uses the popular accusation (οἱ προσκυνούμενοι παρ' ὑμῖν, ἄνθρωποι γενόμενοι ποτε), which he practically implies in 3.44.4 and 4.49.3, where he claims that those figures' tombs have become temples for the 'pagans.' Yet again, Euhemerus's name is not invoked to give further credibility to his charge against the heathens. In Clement's case we can argue with confidence that he never read either the

Greek original or the Latin translation. In Lactantius's Ennian euhemerism, the issue of Zeus's entombment holds great importance,[17] which Clement could not have ignored if he had read the Latin version. Resorting to the famous scheme Euhemerus/atheism, as Winiarczyk has argued, only highlights Clement's knowledge of the doxographic tradition, as was the case with both Theophilus and Theodoret of Cyrus. This is even more apparent in the latter,[18] when in his *Cure of the Greek Maladities* he not only teams up with the other two Christian authors in designating Euhemerus (along with other figures, such as Diagoras of Melos and Theodorus of Cyrene) as an atheist, but gives us his source, namely Plutarch (ὡς ὁ Πλούταρχος ἔφη), the known enemy of Euhemerus's theory.[19]

In the Latin apologetics things are not very much different. Minucius Felix (early third century CE) refers explicitly to Euhemerus in his *Octavius*, a work that has been seen as introducing a new age in Christian apologetics and which was most likely addressed to outsiders, as it does not use any scriptural references nor discuss doctrinal matters.[20] Minucius gives a succinct description of Euhemerus's theory, according to which the Messenean author

> gives a list of gods accepted for their merits or their services; enumerates their birthdays, fatherlands, and places of sepulture, and province by province localizes Dictaean Jupiter, Delphic Apollo, Pharian Isis, and Eleusinian Ceres.[21]

At first sight Minucius gives the impression that he at least had the Latin translation at hand, given the mentioning of the gods' entombment, which reminds us of Lactantius's Ennian excerpt. Nevertheless, a few lines later (21.8), when referring to Jupiter in more detail, he places him in Crete where he presumably reigned, had offspring, and eventually died and was interred. Nowhere does he mention Panchaea or Jupiter's journeys around the world; on the contrary, he repeats the adverb "there" twice (*illic obit*; *illic filios habuit*), implying that Jupiter never left Crete. In both Eusebius's and Lactantius's versions, Zeus's journeys are the vehicle of his deification, and failing to employ this information essentially denudes Euhemerus's story of its most integral element. Moreover, right after mentioning Euhemerus, Minucius cites similar-minded (according to him) authors and works, like Prodicus, Persaeus, Alexander's letter to his mother Olympias, Cassius, and Diodorus (21.2–8). This led Don Cameron Allen, in an unfortunate reading of the passage, to argue that "Euhemerus's *Sacred History* was clearly provided with footnotes,"[22] which taking into account the nature of Euhemerus's work and its conveying theory seems not only unlikely but practically impossible. If Euhemerus had incorporated footnotes—meant here either literally, which, as we saw in the third chapter, does not constitute an element of writing in antiquity, or metaphorically by allusions to previous authors—it is almost unreasonable that it was not mentioned by Diodorus, Eusebius, Ennius, or Lactantius. Additionally, ancient critics of Euhemerus like, for example, Plutarch, would have instantly seized the opportunity to show Euhemerus's lack of novelty. What Minucius is doing here, on the contrary, is referring to the known list of authors found in the doxographic tradition (with some minor variations), which in turn indicates his indirect knowledge of the *Sacred Inscription*.

Arnobius of Sicca (late third century CE), along with Augustine as we will see, are the only two Christian authors who make a direct connection between 'pagan gods as dead men' and Euhemerus. Arnobius mentions the Messenean in his *Against the Pagans*, adding however in the same lot other authors like Nicanor, Leon of Pella, Theodorus of Cyrene, and Diagoras of Melos:

> And here, indeed, we can show that all those men whom you represent to us and call gods, were but men [*homines fuisse*], by quoting either Euhemerus of Acragas, whose books were translated by Ennius into Latin that all might be thoroughly acquainted with them.[23]

Although Arnobius provides us with the information of the translation by Ennius, this does not necessarily indicate that he had read the text itself—or any of the works of the other quoted names for that matter. Once again, the placement of Euhemerus among known 'atheists' of antiquity just further indicates that he as well only had access to the doxographic writings on ancient atheists (or to the *index atheorum* tradition).

Similarly, Augustine (354–430 CE) makes the explicit connection between Euhemerus and the known charge of 'pagan gods being dead men' in three different places, adding a fourth instance where he refers to Cicero, and thereby to Euhemerus in view of the context. The two first references are found in his monumental *City of God*, where we read:

> Did they not give evidence in support of Euhemerus who wrote, not as a garrulous story-teller, but as a careful historian who had diligently investigated the matter, that all such gods had once been men, and subject to death [*homines fuisse mortalesque*]?

> We see, then, that these select gods became better known than the rest, not, however, in order to glorify any merits of theirs, but rather in order not to conceal their shameful deeds. Hence it is all the more credible that they were once men [*homines fuisse*]. This tradition is preserved not only in poetry but also in history. For Virgil writes:

> *Saturn was first to descend from the heavenly heights of Olympus,*

> *Fleeing the bolts of Jove, an exile robbed of his kingdom.*

> Virgil goes on with the story, a story related in full by Euhemerus and translated into Latin by Ennius. But since a great deal has been set down

on this subject by those who have written before us, either in Greek or in Latin, against errors of this sort, I have decided not to dwell on the topic.[24]

I chose to provide the full citations from the *City of God* for the main reason that Augustine's influence was so great that whatever he conveyed about Euhemerus was, more or less, accepted (at least later on) as the correct version of the theory by Western Christianity and, thus, begs for a more careful examination. Augustine strips the *Sacred Inscription* of its utopian context in order to emphasize the historicity of Euhemerus's theory: instead of presenting him as a literary author (or a utopian writer), he calls him a historian in order to highlight the alleged credibility Euhemerus's theory had within the context of the *City of God*. Hence, the hitherto theorist of the origins of gods and religion was now explicitly transformed into a historian, regardless of the objections raised by other well-established thinkers of antiquity.[25] Moreover, we here clearly encounter the modification of euhemerism into 'pagan gods are dead men because of their immorality' (*merita, sed ne occultarentur opprobia*), a known version of the theory that Kees Bolle termed *euhemerismus inversus* almost half a century ago.[26] This improper euhemerism, first appearing in Athenagoras's *Embassy for the Christians*,[27] has its own merit in the long reception of euhemerism, which thenceforth also received a negative aspect related to wicked men often associated with demons.[28] However, Athenagoras can hardly be related to ancient euhemerism in view of his inability to relate Euhemerus with Callimachus in 30.3, where he attacks the Alexandrian poet without actually knowing to whom Callimachus's famous anathema was directed.[29]

Augustine, however, does not maintain a consistent approach in regards to his view of Euhemerus. In another context, he classifies him as a poet (*ille Euhemerus poeta fuit*), although he does not quote from nor refer to either the original Greek or the Latin translation. On the contrary, he is resorting to Cicero's assessment of Euhemerus's theory.[30] Yet again, in his *Epistle to Maximus of Madaura* he resorts to the same author to repeat the same charge (that is, the pagan gods were men), but he returns to the classification of Euhemerus as a historian.[31] Augustine's inconsistency does not cease here. If by the aforementioned standardized apologetic charge Augustine means Euhemerus's euhemerism, then his addition of "pagan gods were men who, due to their benefactions, were claimed posthumously to be stars" further complicates Augustine's understanding and exposition of the Messenean's theory.[32] This rather complicated picture of euhemerism therefore makes Gerard O'Daly's statement rather difficult to accept uncritically:

The notion that gods had been great humans, and that honour them had become cult was a convenient argument which had the advantages of deriving from a pagan source of being systematic [. . .]. Whether Euhemerus is cited or not, he lies behind similar arguments found, not just in Lactantius, but in Minucius Felix, Tertullian, Arnobius, and Prudentius, as well as Augustine himself.[33]

First, "whether cited or not" is quite an unreflective generalization, as I have already shown. Even when the authors cite Euhemerus, they do so only because they are using other sources who cite him. As such, we do not have here their own interpretation of Euhemerus's euhemerism but their utilization of someone else's "euhemerism without Euhemerus," as already argued by Jacobus Schippers many years ago, who deemed such practice a more or less corrupted euhemerism.[34] Consequently, this indicates how the theory, already from the very early Christian period, was altered to fit into a specific agenda and fulfill particular needs. Before attempting to relate Christian euhemerism to the issue of identity formation, which I think constitutes that underlying agenda, I need to slightly deviate in order to suggest that the known charge 'the pagan gods were mere humans' has another referent with which early Christian authors were most likely more familiar and which does not necessarily include or refer to Euhemerus.

## Interlude: Eternal and Immortal Gods in the Graeco-Roman World

In *Institutes of Oratory* (3.7.9), in his praise of Domitian, the Roman Quintilian (35–100 CE) highlights a familiar distinction encountered throughout the Mediterranean world: "Some [gods] [. . .] may be praised because they were born immortal, others because they won immortality by their valor." Quintilian was not introducing here something novel or bizarre. Rather, he alludes to a known ancient practice which became the vehicle for the deification of the most known figures of the Hellenistic era, like Alexander the Great, the Ptolemies in Egypt, Julius Caesar, and Augustus among others.[35] However, the concept of the immortals, that is, gods that did not exist eternally, is a classification already apparent in Herodotus (*Histories* 2.43), who discusses Herakles's and Dionysus's previous mortal state and subsequent immortalization. Both these influential and central figures of Greek mythology attained immortality and, eventually, became gods like the main great gods of the Greek pantheon. A similar known case is of course Asclepius. As Charles Talbert argued some forty years ago, the distinction between eternal gods and immortal figures was a characteristic trait of Mediterranean antiquity. The latter were originally mortals who, after their death, were transformed or ascended to heaven, thereby obtaining the honors only the eternal gods hitherto received.[36] The case of Herakles is, obviously, the most known example of a human becoming a hero and, finally, an immortal. The son of a divine father and a mortal mother (another common feature of the immortals), Herakles belonged to a long list of figures, such as Achilles, Theseus, Perseus, Dionysus, Asclepius, and others. However, not all of them received a post mortem immortalization. In the case of Herakles, there was a process of apotheosis, as Emma Stafford puts it, which gradually led to his final divine status, already existent around the year 600 BCE but further elaborated in literary works, such as Sophocles's *Philoktetes* (1418–1420).[37]

Diodorus Siculus, our foremost source of euhemerism, dealt with the concept of the immortals already in the beginning of his *Historical Library*, where he refers to Osiris (1.13), later turning to Greece and including in this group Dionysus, Herakles, Aristaeus, and Asclepius (4.1.5). Similarly, pivotal figures of Roman mythology, such as Aeneas and Romulus, were also included in this group of figures who were the offspring of a human and a god (or goddess). What all these figures had in common was their benefactions to mankind; they were good and benevolent kings, healers, powerful men, introducers of arts or skills that enhanced the civilization process.[38] This was not news to the early Christian authors. One of the earliest apologists, Justin Martyr (early second century CE), in a famous excerpt adopts these very examples in order to show the non-novelty of the Christian beliefs:

> When we claim also that the Word, which is the first offspring of God, was born without intercourse, Jesus Christ our teacher—and that he was crucified and died and rose again and ascended into heaven—we report nothing at all novel [οὐ ... καινόν τι] beyond those said by you to be sons of Zeus. For you know how many sons of Zeus your honored poets claim there are: Hermes, the interpreting Word and teacher of all; Asclepius, who—though he was a healer—was struck by a thunderbolt and ascended into heaven; Dionysus who was torn in pieces; Heracles, who in flight from his toils committed himself to the fire; the Dioscuri, the sons of Leda; Perseus, son of Danae; and Bellerophon, who, though from human beings, [rose to heaven] on the horse Pegasus. What do we say of Ariadne, and those who, like her, are said to have become stars? What of your deceased emperors, whom you deem fit to immortalize?[39]

In his book *Iesus Deus: The Early Christian Depiction of Jesus as a Mediterranean God* (2014), David Litwa has shown how early Christians, resorting to the concept of deification by exaltation, "constructed a divine Jesus with traits specific to deities in Greco-Roman culture" by using and adapting "widespread Hellenistic conceptions about divinity in order to understand and depict the divine status of Jesus."[40] Nevertheless, as all apologetic works demonstrate, this adaptation was only the initial step; the next one was the sophisticated presentation of Jesus "as unique and thus superior to any competitor";[41] this was accomplished by Justin, for example, by "identifying Jesus as the *logos*, demonstrating the superior antiquity of Christianity, emphasizing the monotheistic nature of the faith [...] and invoking the authority of prophecy."[42]

The early Christian authors' acquaintance with this widely spread concept cannot be simply overlooked, including in the cases where authors made references to Euhemerus. Given their lack of direct knowledge of the *Sacred Inscription*, as it was demonstrated in the previous section, it is likely that the commonly used phrase '*homines fuisse*' mainly referred to the concept of the immortals rather than to Euhemerus's theory. Taking into account the long-established notion of the concept, and its vibrant application during the same period in the Roman Empire with the discussions pertaining to the deification of the emperors, the early Christian authors had many reasons to make reference to the concept, relate it to Jesus, and then reflect further on it in order to demonstrate the uniqueness of their teachings. Finally, and with some reservations, it is plausible that when they encountered Euhemerus's name in their secondary sources it was mistakenly assumed that he belonged to the long tradition of authors who called attention to the concept of the immortals, thus confusing his theory with a well-established and known idea of antiquity.

## Why Resort to Euhemerism?

I began this chapter by arguing that the phrase 'the gods are dead men' eventually became the standardized version of what euhemerism is following a dual process. The first one, as I discussed, was related to the problem of indirect access to Euhemerus's work and consequently theory. I also supported this thesis by briefly discussing the popular distinction in antiquity between eternals (gods) and immortals (humans who became gods) that probably fueled the association between the aforementioned phrase and Euhemerus's ideas. The second one, to which I turn now, is linked to the reason the early Christian authors needed, in the first place, a 'pagan' view in order to talk about their own beliefs and worldview. Naturally, the answer is anchored to the many years of struggles between this new group of religious people and the traditional ones, that is, the Jews and Greeks primarily, with the Romans added due to their domination over the Mediterranean world within which this new movement arose. However, this is simply too vague to account for the eager adoption of Euhemerus's ideas and their eventual distortion by the early Christian authors. What I wish to argue, on the other hand, is that anti-'pagan' euhemerism became a valuable asset in a broader and more important debate, which exceeds the mere scope of demonstrating (or, to put it correctly, simply repeating) what the centuries-old established religious traditions already knew—and, among them, all existing, newly, or future converts. Rather, the utilization of a second-hand, distorted euhemerism needs to be seen as a precious tool in the ongoing process of (Christian) identity formation during the first centuries after Jesus's death.

In the writings of the early Christian authors we encounter—among others—two terms that are either straightforwardly or implicitly related to the issue of identity: *genos* (γένος) and *ethnos* (ἔθνος). These terms, as Denise Buell has shown, have various connotations and accompanying meanings; for example, *genos* can be translated as race, ethnicity, people, lineage, kind, class, or sex. Yet, whatever the translation might be, the term in antiquity "frequently demarcates groups whose members apparently share certain characteristics (which can include ancestors, rights of inheritance, knowledge, ritual practices, and ways of life, among other things)."[43] Both *genos* and *ethnos* were widely used by those early Christian authors in their attempt to legitimize their very existence. Eusebius employed the term *ethnos* already in the beginning of his monumental *Church History* in an excerpt that has great interest and which portrays two basic principles espoused not only by Eusebius but by all early Christian authors, as well as containing one known charge against the Christians:

> Even if we are obviously new, and this really new name of Christian is recently known among the *ethnoi* [ἔθνοι], nevertheless our life and method of conduct, in accordance with the percepts of our creeds [δόγμασιν], was not invented by us, but from the first creation of humans, as it were, has been upheld by the natural concepts of the ancient people who were friends of God.[44]

The two cherished principles are the understanding of the Christians as an *ethnos* different from the other *ethnoi*, and its superiority due to an unprecedented inheritance, which is not related to a prehistoric (or mythical) figure but is located in the very beginnings of the human race. On the contrary, the need for such a self-identification sprung from the 'pagan' precisely opposite argument: the Christians are not a distinct group exactly because they lack historicity, which is found among the Jews, Greeks, and Romans. As I discussed in Chapter 3, this was a famous accusation made by none other than Porphyry. The *Preparation* was a sophisticated and well-crafted response to Porphyry and his allegations, whereas Lactantius's *Divine Institutes* also refer to Porphyry (5.2). Lactantius was present in Nicomedia in 303, where Diocletian and Galerius authorized a public presentation by two men, Porphyry and Sossianus Hierocles, in light of the upcoming great persecution.[45] Lactantius's abhorrence for Porphyry cannot be better demonstrated. The main accusation launched against the Christians by Porphyry, as Eusebius informs us, was that the Christians "turned away from their fathers' gods, through whom each *ethnos* and *polis* has come together," thus abandoning the centuries-old religious norms set up and held by "all Hellenes and foreigners [. . .] all kings, law-givers, and philosophers alike."[46] As Porphyry continues, the Christians are not Hellenes nor foreigners (*barbaroi*) nor Jews, since they also rejected that group's (*ethnos*)[47] customs. On the contrary, this 'problematic' group of people seems to lie between the Greeks and the Jews without however having a clear-cut identity, hence being an illegitimate *ethnos*.[48] Such accusations demonstrate an important element in this ancient debate between 'pagans' and Christians: ethnicity—here taken as an identity of an *ethnos*, that is, a group of people seemingly sharing certain traits (to which I will return shortly)—is related to the worshipping of gods, making the discourse part and parcel of religious beliefs.[49]

Such argumentation also appeared in other contexts, although with different ends. During the Hellenistic period several 'ethnic histories,' as Jeremy Schott calls them, appeared by authors such as Diodorus Siculus, Hecataeus of Abdera, Manetho, Philo of Byblos, Berossos of Chaldea, Artapanus, Eupolemus, and Josephus, who extoled their own group vis-à-vis others, and in doing so "disparaged the histories, myths, and traditions of their neighbors."[50] In all these three aspects mentioned by Schott, what we today would call 'religion' is an inextricable element. For example, the Homeric poems for the Greeks were a vehicle of shaping their collective memory, by creating a clear image of prehistoric Greece (history), enriched with the stories of the gods (myths), and rituals (traditions).[51] However, identity (or collective memory, or ethnicity) in antiquity is not easy to pin down. The discussion on ancient ethnicity is complicated and far from any consensus due to the various ways the ancients identified and described themselves, contrary one would say to how moderns understand and define themselves—although modern self-identification is primarily seemingly straightforward. This self-identification and understanding, however, denotes the fluidity as well as the social aspect of ethnicity as a construction rather than an innate quality.[52] Scholars have identified several traits that transform a group of individuals into an *ethnos* in antiquity: kinship or descent and territorial homeland, linked to narratives (myths) and perform-ances (rituals, religious acts, observances).[53] Yet, as Kostas Vlassopoulos has cogently shown recently, the very term 'group' that could be called *ethnos* is itself an arbitrary one when it comes to the study of antiquity. He identifies four different kinds of groups in an ascending order that, as he argues, could each be described as an *ethnos*: the *polis* (e.g., Athens, Corinth, Thebes, etc.); regional communities (e.g., the Arcadians and the Phocians); trans-regional groups (e.g., the Dorians, Ionians, and Aeolians); and 'Hellenes,' the name under which all the aforementioned groups subsumed themselves.[54] If one adds here the more personal identity that was based on familial narratives linked to one's 'home' (*oikos*), in turn related to one's *oikos'* descend from a (mythological) ancestor thus being part of a *genos*, and adding the *phylai*, it becomes clear that in ancient discourse the myth of authenticity and membership into a group was vibrant and rather complicated.[55]

To return to the 'Pagan-Christian' opposition, it is exactly that myth of authenticity that is at stake. Denise Buell has effectively demonstrated how the early Christians managed to capitalize on that very myth by adopting and manipulating an existing yet precious understanding of belonging to an *ethnos*: one's identity, although ostensibly fixed, was simultaneously fluid and thereby mutable. As she puts it,

> [t]his juxtaposition of fluidity and fixity enabled early Christians to use ethnic reasoning to make *universalizing* claims, arguing that everyone

can, and thus ought to, become a Christian. By conceptualizing race as both mutable and "real," early Christians could define Christianness both as a distinct category in contrast to other peoples (including Jews, Greeks, Romans, Egyptians, etc.) and also as inclusive, since it is a category formed out of individuals from a range of different races.[56]

This was accomplished via conversion and the discourses accompanying the very practice of change (that is, baptism), that were seen

> [a]s both the transformation of one's ethnicity and the restoration of one's *true* identity [. . .]. Instead of positioning Christianness as not-race, or aracial, many early Christian texts defined their version of Christianity as a race or ethnicity, sometimes in opposition to other rival articulations of Christianness, and sometimes in contrast to non-Christian groups and cultures (including, but not limited, to those defined as "Jews").[57]

Those *universalizing* claims, promising the convert the opportunity to discover one's *true* identity, were the vehicles that led toward the legitimization of the Christians as an 'authentic' and thus 'unique' group that holds the 'right' beliefs and follows the 'true' God. In other words, early Christians sought to establish the notion of their *sui generis* identity that stems not from human norms, traditions, narratives, and historical (or mythical) figures, but from a preexisting and transcendent God. In this manner identity is in a way unhooked from its various determining elements and is now linked to a discourse on religion as the quintessential signifier of identity.

This is evident in our apologists who so eagerly seized both the notion of the immortals and what others said about Euhemerus, (intentionally or unintentionally) transformed the latter into an expression of the former, and thus composed an argumentation that, once accepted, it was not solely about religious beliefs but about religion-as-ethnic-identity. As such, in the Greek version of Aristedes's *Apology* (2.2) we read: "[f]or it is clear that there exist three *genoi* of humans: worshippers of so-called gods, Jews, and Christians." In Theophilus's *To Autolycus*, who is among the eight Christian authors to name Euhemerus, the issue of authentic vs. false is raised, by arguing that the Christian message "is not recent in origin, nor are our writings, as some think, mythical and false, but the most ancient and true" (3.29). The same argument, even more explicitly, is conveyed by Clement of Alexandria in his *Protrepticus* (1.6.4), where the Christians are portrayed as the one and only authentic *genos*: "Not one of these peoples existed before our world. But we were before the creation of the world, we [. . .] were begotten beforehand by God."[58]

Two from these three authors named Euhemerus within those very texts from which the above excerpts are taken. This cannot be simply overlooked as mere coincidence. The nature of those works indicates that their authors utilized whatever could intensify and bolster their arguments in their struggle to demonstrate the legitimacy of the Christian *ethnos*. As was the case with the earliest Christian writings, this identity formation process primarily was addressed to the members of the group rather than to outsiders. For example, Esther Kober has shown how communal meals played a crucial role in the life of the Johannine community, whereas the papers collected by Kathy Ehrensperger and J. Brian Tucker show how Paul worked toward the establishment and maintenance of this new identity.[59]

This 'rhetoric of authenticity,' to use Russell McCutcheon's phrase,[60] was thus an ongoing process, already apparent in the earliest Christian communities that functioned as a technique employed by their members in order to express and consequently affirm the Christian *ethnic(-religious)* supremacy in comparison to the other (deemed superior until then) *ethnoi*. Seen from this perspective, the corruption of Euhemerus's theory was not merely an accidental event, although lacking direct knowledge of the Messenean's work practically makes it indirectly non-accidental. On the contrary, it constitutes part of a broader and far more important discussion that sought to authenticate, reinforce, and legitimize the identity of their members both within their communities and in their exchanges with outsiders. Therefore, Eusebius's mission in the *Preparatio* or Lactantius's aim in the *Institutes* essentially dictated the incorporation of the *Sacred Inscription*'s content, albeit in a partial form since this is how those authors encountered it. We cannot, therefore, isolate what they convey the theory to be from the very content of their works, their agendas, and their overall argumentation. Likewise, as I discussed in the previous chapters, Euhemerus's theory cannot be crudely detached from its utopian narrative. If Euhemerus was only interested in delivering a theory, then why not choose a more straightforward and 'academic' way? Critias and Prodicus, as we saw in Chapter 2, did not employ a frame story to promote their theories, whereas Euhemerus's travelogue places the theory in a specific context. The sources in which the early Christian authors read about Euhemerus deliberately cherry-picked from the *Sacred Inscription* and, in turn, so did the apologists from those secondary sources. But as theories travel, they are transformed and—in some cases radically—changed to fit the needs of the victors, to return to the beginning of this chapter. It was Christianity's eventual success that transported this version of euhemerism all the way to the modern world, erroneously taking Euhemerus's theory to be all about the 'the gods being dead men' principle, although, as Diodorus informs us, Euhemerus was also interested in or talked about other gods: the heavenly or celestial ones. Adding to this the importance of Zeus as the protagonist of the work and his ante mortem deification, it becomes clear that, by referencing the references, the early Christian authors managed to mutilate an ancient theory of religion.

## Appendix: Euhemerism in Jewish Anti-'Pagan' Literature?

Scholars have long identified the use of Euhemerus's theory in Jewish anti-'pagan' literature, such as in the works of Pseudo-Eupolemus, Artapanus, Theodotus, and Mnaseas,[61] as well as in the *Wisdom of Solomon*, the *Letter of Aristeas*, and the third book of the *Sibylline Oracles*. Especially the latter three have been seen by most scholars as the primary examples of euhemerism in ancient Jewish writings. Marek Winiarczyk takes the three first aforementioned authors as "definite supporters of Euhemerism,"[62] adopting however a very broad understanding of what the theory is all about. As such, regarding Pseudo-Eupolemus, he sees euhemerism in the author's combination of biblical prehistory and Babylonian and Greek mythology, according to which Noah is identified with Belus and Cronus—also mortals—as well as Abraham as creator of culture and giver of astrology and divination, first to the Phoenicians and then to the Egyptians. Similarly, in Artapanus's work Winiarczyk sees euhemerism in the author's identification of Moses with Hermes-Thoth and Musaeus, while being the inventor of many crafts in addition to introducing the Egyptian religion. Finally, Winiarczyk sees euhemerism in Theodotus's work in which he identified god Hermes with Hamor, the king of Shechem.[63] It all comes down, once again, to what euhemerism is or, to put it more accurately, how far we want to go in our interpretation of the testimonies. In both Pseudo-Eupolemus and Artapanus, we encounter what is better known as syncretism, similar to the Hellenistic identification of Amun with Zeus in Egypt. Additionally, the protagonists of those works are deemed introducers and givers of skills and crafts, adding to the advancement of civilization. It is one thing to link euhemerism with benefactions and another with the known ancient concept of the first discoverer (πρῶτος εὑρετής) or culture hero (ἥρως εὑρετής).[64] Winiarczyk is obviously relating euhemerism with these narratives based on the Ennian version of the *Sacred Inscription*. However, the main feature of Euhemerus's theory (and that also includes the Ennian version) is the connection between deification and kingship as well as the process of deification being both ante and post mortem. As such, if scholars want to assign the euhemeristic theory to the aforementioned authors, then they must be willing to inform their readers of which version of the theory they are using and how loosely they do so.

A similar argument can be made regarding the third book of the *Sibylline Oracles*. In 108–158a the author describes the history of the first human generations, with Gaia and Uranus as the first human beings (πρώτιστοι μερόπων ἀνθρώπων), more or less in a Hesiodic fashion. The most important element of this passage is the etymology and origin of the names of the traditional gods: in 111b–113 we learn that Gaia (Earth) and Uranus (Heaven) were named as such by later generations (which in turn means that their original names remain unknown), whereas in 141 Zeus's name is etymologically explained as the result of being sent away (διεπέμφθη). In his monograph on the third book of the *Sibylline Oracles* Rieuwerd Buitenwerf associates these elements with the euhemeristic account, primarily as it is encountered in Ennius. It is interesting to see his conclusion:

> The incorporation of the tradition [Euhemerus's work] was merely needed for the author's purpose of explaining how people started to fight each other in spite of the fact that God created the world as a place of righteousness. He incorporated Euhemerus' story into his work because the story suited his purpose. From the Ennius quotation in Lactantius, it appears that the story had a sequel, but once the Sibylline author had attained his goal, he seems to have lost interest in the story. He breaks off the story rather abruptly and proceeds to another topic.[65]

In my view, this is precisely the problem. The author stops exactly where euhemerism would make sense: nowhere does he discuss these first humans as kings, benefactions are not mentioned, great royal power is not clearly indicated, whereas deification is absent or merely implied. The sheer fact that they are treated as historical figures does not necessarily mean that Euhemerus's theory is being used here. A simple reading of the Hesiodic works would have allowed the author of the *Sibylline Oracles* to reach the same conclusions.

Scholars have extensively argued about euhemerism in the *Letter of Aristeas*, especially according to the following excerpt:

> They make images of stone and wood, describing them as the images of those whose discoveries were of advantage to human life. They reveal all too clearly their lack of perception by worshipping these images. For that a person should become divine on account of some discovery that he has made is utterly senseless. Such people indeed took certain parts of creation and put them together and went on to demonstrate their usefulness, but they did not actually create them. It is thus idle and foolish for men to deify their fellows.
>
> (135–137)[66]

The most ardent supporter of euhemerism in this excerpt was Victor Tcherikover. He claimed that "the time of naïve polytheism had passed long since" and that educated Greeks of the Hellenistic period "knew that the gods were merely symbols."[67] I find such a generalization quite unwarranted. This contradicts both Plutarch and Callimachus, who openly attacked Euhemerus and his theory, as well as the various scholars who claim that Euhemerus functioned as justification for the deification of the Hellenistic monarchs. If the educated Greeks knew that their gods were nothing but symbols, then they would have also known that their kings were mere humans and would not allow for or would have fiercely attacked the long tradition of deified kings,[68] especially in Egypt where the *Letter of Aristeas* was most likely composed.[69]

A more realistic approach was promoted by John Collins. In discussing another text that is very often associated with euhemerism, the *Wisdom of Solomon*, he pointed out that both the *Wisdom* and the *Letter* are works primarily focusing on the denunciation of idolatry.[70] In the *Wisdom of Solomon* euhemerism has been indeed related to the discussion of the origins of idolatry (14.12–31). The two examples given are that of a father who makes an image of his deceased child, and of a ruler who requires the erection of his statue that must be worshipped while he is absent. As David Winston has rightly pointed out, these two cases "do not derive directly from" Euhemerus's work, but "probably from a later 'Euhemeristic' source [. . .] for the author [. . .] is more narrowly interested in explaining the origins of idolatry, whereas Euhemerus was concerned with the larger question regarding the origins of the gods of Greek mythology."[71] Winston's distinction is very important in our discussion of euhemerism in Jewish writings against the 'pagans.' He demonstrates nicely that the difference between Euhemerus's euhemerism and later adoptions of the theory is not to be taken lightly nor should we readily identify as ancient euhemerism whatever is related to the idea of 'the pagan gods were humans.'

Last but not least, euhemerism in anti-'pagan' Jewish works faces the same formidable problem encountered in some of the apologetic works: none of those writings cite Euhemerus's work or his theory as their source. In both cases, I believe, it is our later, arbitrary decision to see euhemerism in those works solely because they refer to the concept of dead men and women deemed divine. Both the ante mortem deification of Zeus as well as the existence of the celestial or heavenly gods are, by definition, exempted from what Euhemerus maintained according to those scholars: euhemerism is now only about post mortem deification wherever and whenever is encountered.

## Notes

1 Marek Winiarczyk (2013, 151 and n. 206–207) has offered excellent service to the student of euhemerism of the first centuries CE by collecting all the relevant passages: Justin, *1 Apology* 24.2; Theophilus, *To Autolycus* 1.9; Clement of Alexandria, *Protrepticus* 3.44.4; 4.55.2; 4.49.3; Eusebius, *Preparation for the Gospel* 2.4.1; Arnobius, *Against the Pagans* 6.6; Athenagoras, *Embassy for the Christians* 28.4; Lactantius, *Divine Institutes* 1.18.2; 2.1.5; 2.2.4; 2.2.9; Minucius Felix, *Octavius* 8.4; Augustine, *City of God* 8.26.
2 See the discussions in Edwards et al. 1999; Jacobsen 2009, 106–107; Graf 2011, 321.
3 Kannaday 2004, 40.
4 This was also discussed in Chapter 3 in relation to Porphyry's accusations and Eusebius's and Lactantius's responses.
5 See Jacobsen 2009, 86–101.
6 Klostergaard Petersen 2009, 16.
7 The bibliography on the issue is extensive. I indicatively mention here Lieu 2004; Buell 2005; Sandwell 2007; Rebillard 2012.
8 Winiarczyk 2013, 152.
9 This was initially argued by Zucker 1905.

10 On Theophilus and his work, see Palmer 1983, 246–251; Kannaday 2004, 48–49; Edwards 2008, 553–554 for a summary.
11 Winiarczyk 2013, 149 traces that list to Clitomachus of Carthage.
12 Theophilus, *To Autolycus* 3.7.6 (W. T 19). Allen 1970, 53–54 accepts uncritically Theophilus's information, although it is not supported by our sources.
13 Cf. Lactantius, *Divine Institutes* 1.14.1–8 (W. T 54).
14 For more on Clement, see Kannaday 2004, 51–52.
15 See the discussion in Chapter 4.
16 Clement of Alexandria, *Protrepticus* 2.24.2 (W. T 20). Cf. Allen 1970, 54; Winiarczyk 2013, 149.
17 Cf. Lactantius, *Divine Institutes* 1.11.44–48 (W. T 69A).
18 On Theodoret, see Pásztori-Kupán 2006.
19 See Theodoret of Cyrus, *Cure of the Greek Maladies* 3.4 (W. T 17B). Cf. Winiarczyk 2013, 149. On Plutarch's approach to Euhemerus and his theory, cf. Chapter 4.
20 See Kannaday 2004, 54. Cf. Von Albrecht 1987.
21 Minucius Felix, *Octavius* 21.1 (W. T 9).
22 Allen 1970, 54.
23 Arnobius, *Against the Pagans* 4.29 (W. T 21); cf. 6.6.
24 Augustine, *City of God* 6.7 (W. T 11); 7.27 (W. T 12).
25 Cf. Strabo, *Geography* 1.3.1 (W. T 4); 2.3.5 (W. T 7); 7.3.6 (W. T 6); Polybius, *History* 34.5 (W. T 5). The only exception is Diodorus himself, but only in Eusebius's testimony (*Preparation for the Gospel* 2.2.54 [W. T 8]), which also allows for some doubts. Honigman 2009 agrees with this later classification of Euhemerus and his *Sacred Inscription*, but correctly refuted by Winiarczyk 2013, 20–21. Of course, as we saw, the categorization of Euhemerus as a historian was also apparent in Minucius Felix (see above) and Lactantius (in *Divine Institutes* 1.11.33 [W. T 65]).
26 See Bolle 1970, 23; an argument he repeated in 2005, 2883.
27 29.1–2. Cf. Winiarczyk 2013, 150–151.
28 See Bolle 2005, 2883.
29 On Callimachus and Euhemerus, cf. Chapter 5. On Athenagoras against Callimachus, see Palmer 1983, 243–246, especially 246.
30 Augustine, *Harmony of the Gospels* 1.23.32 (W. T 13).
31 Augustine, *Epistle to Maximus of Madaura* 3 (W. T 94).
32 This appears in a psalm sermon as noted by Kahlos 2007, 155.
33 O'Daley 1999, 43–44.
34 See Schippers 1952. Unfortunately, his view is rarely employed. The dictum 'whether cited or not' seems to prevail after all. See the recent Alonso Venero 2013.
35 About these figures, see Klauck 2000, 250–330.
36 See Talbert 2011, 62–64.
37 See Stafford 2010, 239–244.
38 Cf. Talbert 2011, 64–68.
39 Justin, *1 Apology* 21.2–3. The translation is drawn from Litwa 2014, 2. Cf. Talbert 2011, 77. For a succinct presentation of Justin's apologetic work, see Kannaday 2004, 37–43.
40 Litwa 2014, 6; 18–19.
41 Ibid., 20.
42 Kannaday 2004, 39.
43 Buell 2005, 2. Cf. Hall 1997, 35–57.
44 Eusebius, *Church History* 1.4.4. The translation, with some minor changes, is drawn from Buell 2005, 77.

45 See DePalma Digeser 2006, 36–41.
46 Eusebius, *Preparation for the Gospel* 1.2.2. The translation, with some changes, is drawn from DePalma Digeser 2006, 43.
47 The categorization of the Jews as an ἔθνος was probably introduced by the Seleucids. See Lieu 2004, 244. For a more theoretical perspective, see the extremely influential Mason 2007.
48 See DePalma Digeser 2006, 44; 56.
49 Cf. the discussion in Nongbri 2013, 54–58, although he does approach the topic from a slightly different perspective.
50 See Schott 2008, 17–18.
51 See Finkelberg 2003, 84. Contrary to what one may think, there are inconsistencies in Homer that, most likely, did not affect what people thought about their gods and the stories told about them. The clearest example is how was Hephaestus injured. In *Iliad* 1.493–610, where Homer gives a very detailed (and anthropomorphic) picture of life on Olympus, Hephaestus attempts to calm his mother Hera by reminding her of Zeus's powers. After all, as he informs us, it was Zeus who snatched him by the foot and hurled him from Olympus, ending to his landing and injury on the island of Lemnos, only to be saved by the island's inhabitants. On the contrary, in 8.394–397, Hephaestus informs us that it was due to his mother's will that he was fallen from Olympus, only to be saved by Thetis. Such differences, however, probably had no impact on how the Greeks related to the Homeric poems as their 'scripture' that shaped their collective memory and identity.
52 Cf. Buell 2005, 6; Hall 1997, 24.
53 See Stratton 2013, 221; Antonaccio 2009, 33.
54 See Vlassopoulos 2015, 4–5.
55 See Antonaccio 2010, 8–9. Cf. the now-classic Sourvinou-Inwood 2000a and 2000b.
56 Buell 2005, 3, emphasis added.
57 Ibid., 9, emphasis added.
58 All translations are drawn, with minor changes from Buell 2005, 36, 70, and 74 respectively.
59 See Ehrensperger and Tucker 2010; Kober 2011.
60 For his highly critical take on the issue of authenticity, see McCutcheon 2003, 167–188 and 2005.
61 On Mnaseas, see the very interesting discussion in Bar-Kochva 2010, 210–215. He correctly, however, points out that Mnaseas's work contains "variations—indeed, reversals—of the Euhemerist interpretation of the world of gods" (215).
62 Winiarczyk 2013, 158.
63 Ibid., 154–156.
64 Cf. Pachis 2003. The same argument was made by Paul Hanson in his reading of *1 Enoch* 6–11. As he claimed,

> [t]he link between the ancient Mesopotamian tradition and the tradition of the *protoi heuretai* of the Greek-speaking world is to be found in the writings of the priest Sanchuniathon [. . .] [he] turns to a history of culture, where, in good euhemeristic fashion, he traces the various inventions and devices of culture to ancient heroes who had been awarded attributes by their grateful clients.
>
> (Hanson 1977, 228)

For a criticism, see Baumgarten 2014, 427 n. 94.
65 Buitenwerf 2003, 331 (and 172–178 for his analysis which I adopt here). The same stance, more or less, is employed by Barlett 1985, 39; Winiarczyk 2013, 156–158; Baumgarten 2014, 427.

66  The translation is drawn from Barlett 1985, 30.
67  Tcherikover 1958, 69.
68  Cf. my discussion in Roubekas 2015.
69  On the *Letter of Aristeas*, its context, audience, and time of composition, see Honigman 2003.
70  See Collins 1997, 209. However, he does see the *Letter of Aristeas* (135–137) as utilizing the euhemeristic approach. Yet, he relates euhemerism with deification of people "because they invented things" (211), which, again, should primarily be associated with the cultural heroes rather than with the euhemeristic deified kings.
71  Winston 1979, 270, although he too sees the *Letter of Aristeas* and the *Sibylline Oracles* (108–113) as directly influenced by Euhemerus. Collins 1997, 210–211 adopts Winston's perspective as well, when arguing that "[t]he worship of images to honor absent rulers was characteristic of the Roman era" (211) followed by two examples he then utilizes: Caligula's attempt to install his statue in Jerusalem and Josephus's report (*Antiquities of the Jews* 15.330) that Herod erected temples and statutes in the cities he built, although not in Jewish territory.

## References

Allen, Don C. 1970. *Mysteriously Meant: The Rediscovery of Pagan Symbolism and Allegorical Interpretation in the Renaissance*. Baltimore, MD and London: Johns Hopkins University Press.

Alonso Venero, Ana. 2013. "El Evemerismo como Motivo Retórico en la Literatura Apologética Cristiana." *'Ilu: Revista de Ciencias de las Religiones* 24: 91–116.

Antonaccio, Carla M. 2009. "(Re)defining Ethnicity: Culture, Material Culture, and Identity." In *Visual Culture and Social Identity in the Ancient Mediterranean*, edited by Tamar Hodos and Shelley Hales, 32–53. Cambridge: Cambridge University Press.

Antonaccio, Carla M. 2010. "Origins, Culture, and Identity in Classical Antiquity." In *When Worlds Elide: Classics, Politics, Culture*, edited by Karen Bassi and J. Peter Euben, 4–17. Latham, MD: Lexington Books.

Bar-Kochva, Bezalel. 2010. *The Image of the Jews in Greek Literature: The Hellenistic Period*. Berkeley, CA and London: University of California Press.

Barlett, John R. 1985. *Jews in the Hellenistic World: Josephus, Aristeas, The Sibylline Oracles, Eupolemus*. Cambridge: Cambridge University Press.

Baumgarten, Albert I. 2014. "The Rule of the Martian in the Ancient Diaspora: Celsus and His Jew." In *Jews and Christians in the First and Second Centuries: How to Write Their History*, edited by Peter J. Tomson and Joshua Schwartz, 398–430. Leiden and Boston, MA: Brill.

Bolle, Kees W. 1970. "In Defense of Euhemerus." In *Myth and Law Among the Indo-Europeans*, edited by Jaan Puhvel, 19–38. Berkeley, CA and London: University of California Press.

Bolle, Kees W. 2005. "Euhemerus and Euhemerism." In *Encyclopedia of Religion*, edited by Lindsay Jones, vol. 5, 2882–2884. New York: Macmillan.

Buell, Denise K. 2005. *Why This New Race: Ethnic Reasoning in Early Christianity*. New York: Columbia University Press.

Buitenwerf, Rieuwerd. 2003. *Book III of the Sibylline Oracles and its Social Setting*. Leiden and Boston, MA: Brill.

Collins, John J. 1997. *Jewish Wisdom in the Hellenistic Age*. Louisville, KY: Westminster John Knox Press.

DePalma Digeser, Elizabeth. 2006. "Christian or Hellene? The Great Persecution and the Problem of Identity." In *Religious Identity in Late Antiquity*, edited by Robert M. Frakes and Elizabeth DePalma Digeser, 36–57. Toronto: Edgar Kent.

Edwards, Mark. 2008. "Apologetics." In *The Oxford Handbook of Early Christian Studies*, edited by Susan Ashbrook Harvey and David G. Hunter, 549–564. Oxford: Oxford University Press.

Edwards, Mark, Martin Goodman, Simon Price, and Christopher Rowland. 1999. "Introduction: Apologetics in the Roman World." In *Apologetics in the Roman Empire: Pagans, Jews, and Christians*, edited by Mark Edwards, Martin Goodman, Simon Price, and Christopher Rowland, 1–13. Oxford: Oxford University Press.

Ehrensperger, Kathy and J. Brian Tucker. (Eds.). 2010. *Reading Paul in Context: Explorations in Identity Formation. Essays in Honour of William S. Campbell*. London and New York: T & T Clark.

Finkelberg, Margalit. 2003. "Homer as a Foundation Text." In *Homer, the Bible, and Beyond: Literary and Religious Canons in the Ancient World*, edited by Margalit Filkenberg and Guy G. Stroumsa, 75–96. Leiden and Boston, MA: Brill.

Graf, Fritz. 2011. "Myth in Christian Authors." In *A Companion to Greek Mythology*, edited by Ken Dowden and Niall Livingstone, 319–337. Malden, MA and Oxford: Wiley-Blackwell.

Hall, Jonathan. 1997. *Ethnic Identity in Greek Antiquity*. Cambridge: Cambridge University Press.

Hanson, Paul D. 1977. "Rebellion in Heaven, Azazel, and Euhemeristic Heroes in 1 Enoch 6–11." *Journal of Biblical Literature* 96 (2): 195–233.

Honigman, Sylvie. 2003. *The Septuagint and Homeric Scholarship in Alexandria: A Study in the Narrative of the Letter of Aristeas*. London and New York: Routledge.

Honigman, Sylvie. 2009. "Euhemerus of Messene and Plato's Atlantis." *Historia* 58 (1): 1–35.

Jacobsen, Anders-Christian. 2009. "Main Topics in Early Christian Apologetics." In *Critique and Apologetics: Jews, Christians and Pagans in Antiquity*, edited by David Brakke, Anders-Christian Jacobsen, and Jörg Ulrich, 85–110. Frankfurt and New York: Peter Lang.

Kahlos, Maijastina. 2007. *Debate and Dialogue: Christian and Pagan Cultures c. 360–430*. Aldershot, UK and Burlington, VT: Ashgate.

Kannaday, Wayne C. 2004. *Apologetic Discourse and the Scribal Tradition: Evidence of the Influence of Apologetic Interests on the Text of the Canonical Gospels*. Leiden and Boston, MA: Brill.

Klauck, Hans-Josef. 2000. *The Religious Context of Early Christianity: A Guide to Graeco-Roman Religions*. Translated by Brian McNeil. Edinburgh, UK: T & T Clark.

Klostergaard Petersen, Anders. 2009. "The Diversity of Apologetics: From Genre to a Mode of Thinking." In *Critique and Apologetics: Jews, Christians and Pagans in Antiquity*, edited by David Brakke, Anders-Christian Jacobsen, and Jörg Ulrich, 15–41. Frankfurt and New York: Peter Lang.

Kober, Esther. 2011. *Dining With John: Communal Meals and Identity Formation in the Fourth Gospel and Its Historical and Cultural Context*. Leiden and Boston, MA: Brill.

Lieu, Judith M. 2004. *Christian Identity in the Jewish and Graeco-Roman World*. Oxford: Oxford University Press.

Litwa, M. David. 2014. *Iesus Deus: The Early Christian Depiction of Jesus as a Mediterranean God*. Minneapolis, MN: Fortress Press.

McCutcheon, Russell T. 2003. *The Discipline of Religion: Structure, Meaning, Rhetoric*. London and New York: Routledge.

McCutcheon, Russell T. 2006. *Religion and the Domestication of Dissent: Or, How to Live in a Less than Perfect Nation*. London and Oakville, CT: Equinox.

Mason, Steve. 2007. "Jews, Judaeans, Judaizing, Judaism: Problems of Categorization in Ancient History." *Journal for the Study of Judaism* 38: 457–512.

Nongbri, Brent. 2013. *Before Religion: A History of a Modern Concept*. New Haven, CT and London: Yale University Press.

O'Daly, Gerard. 1999. *Augustine's City of God: A Reader's Guide*. Oxford: Clarendon Press.

Pachis, Panayotis. 2003. Ἥρως Εὑρετής: Γεωργία και Πολιτισμός στον Αρχαιοελληνικό Κόσμο. Thessaloniki: Vanias.

Palmer, D. W. 1983. "Atheism, Apologetic, and Negative Theology in the Greek Apologists of the Second Century." *Vigiliae Christianae* 37 (3): 234–259.

Pásztori-Kupán, István. 2006. *Theodoret of Cyrus*. London and New York: Routledge.

Rebillard, Éric. 2012. *Christians and Their Many Identities in Late Antiquity, North Africa, 200–450 CE*. Ithaca, NY and London: Cornell University Press.

Roubekas, Nickolas P. 2015. "Belief in Belief and Divine Kingship in Early Ptolemaic Egypt: The Case of Ptolemy II Philadelphus and Arsinoe II." *Religio: Revue pro religionistiku* 23 (1): 3–23.

Sandwell, Isabella. 2007. *Religious Identity in Late Antiquity: Greeks, Jews and Christians in Antioch*. Cambridge: Cambridge University Press.

Schippers, Jacobus W. 1952. *De Ontwikkeling der Euhemeristische Godencritiek in de Christelijke Latijnse Literatuur*. Groningen: J. B. Wolters.

Schott, Jeremy M. 2008. *Christianity, Empire, and the Making of Religion in Late Antiquity*. Philadelphia, PA: University of Pennsylvania Press.

Sourvinou-Inwood, Christiane. 2000a. "What is Polis Religion?" In *Oxford Readings in Greek Religion*, edited by Richard Buxton, 13–37. Oxford: Oxford University Press.

Sourvinou-Inwood, Christiane. 2000b. "Further Aspects of Polis Religion." In *Oxford Readings in Greek Religion*, edited by Richard Buxton, 38–55. Oxford: Oxford University Press.

Stafford, Emma. 2010. "Herakles Between Gods and Heroes." In *The Gods of Ancient Greece: Identities and Transformations*, edited by Jan N. Bremmer and Andrew Erskine, 228–244. Edinburgh, UK: Edinburgh University Press.

Stratton, Kimberley B. 2013. "Identity." In *The Cambridge Companion to Ancient Mediterranean Religions*, edited by Barbette Stanley Spaeth, 220–251. New York and Cambridge: Cambridge University Press.

Talbert, Charles H. 2011. "The Concept of Immortals in Mediterranean Antiquity." In *The Development of Christology During the First Hundred Years and Other Essays on Early Christology*, 61–82. Leiden and Boston, MA: Brill.

Tcherikover, Victor. 1958. "The Ideology of the Letter of Aristeas." *Harvard Theological Review* 51 (2): 59–85.

Vlassopoulos, Kostas. 2015. "Ethnicity and Greek History: Re-Examining Our Assumptions." *British Institute of Classical Studies* 58 (2): 1–13.

Von Albrecht, Michael. 1987. "M. Minucius Felix as a Christian Humanist." *Illinois Classical Studies* 12 (1): 157–168.

Winiarczyk, Marek. 2013. *The Sacred History of Euhemerus of Messene*. Translated by Witold Zbirohowski-Kościa. Berlin and Boston, MA: De Gruyter.

Winston, David. 1979. *The Wisdom of Solomon*. New York: Doubleday.

Zucker, Friedrich. 1905. "Euhemerus und Seine ἱερά ἀναγραφή bei den Christlichen Schriftstellern." *Philologus: Zeitschrift für Klassische Philologie* 64: 465–471.

# 7 Turning the Tables

## Anti-Christian Euhemerism in Celsus

Although euhemerism has been mostly recognized within anti-'pagan' and apologetic Christian writings, it is no surprise that scholars have also traced Euhemerus's theory within anti-Christian writings during the 'Pagan-Christian' debates in the first centuries after the emergence of the new religious movement. For obvious reasons, the vast majority of the anti-Christian treatises have not survived, whereas the apologetic literature is more than sufficient in order to provide us with a clear view of the early Christian thinking and reaction against the accusations as were articulated by the numerous 'non-persuaded' ones. The most known anti-Christian writings coming from the early centuries are Celsus's *True Doctrine* or *True Word*, Porphyry's *Against the Christians*, and Emperor Julian's[1] *Against the Galileans*. Just like the *Sacred Inscription*, these works do not survive. We only have excerpts found in Christian authors, who by responding to the criticisms incorporated parts of those works in their own treatises. Celsus's work can be largely reconstructed via Origen's *Against Celsus*, whereas Julian's attack on Christianity can be partly restored from Cyril of Alexandria's *Against Julian*. Porphyry's work, however, is the most problematic case, since its reconstruction can only be accomplished with considerable reservations via numerous Christian authors of the fourth and fifth century CE. It is widely accepted that Porphyry was the most threatening voice against Christianity, which is reflected on the very fact that many early Christian authors wrote against him but his work did not survive.[2]

Julian and Porphyry dealt with the Christian and Jewish theological concepts and teachings, but they also dedicated extended space and argued against the divine nature of Jesus. Nevertheless, their works do not contain a line of argumentation that can be somehow explicitly related to Euhemerus's theory or its influence on their own thought. It is widely accepted that Porphyry was a more competent and educated author, who had a good knowledge of the Christian writings, and launched a cogent and coherent attack on what the Christians held to be true, whereas Julian was more interested in diminishing the Christian movement into a localized (Judea) and *ethnos*-bound religious tradition (thus, against the 'Galileans,' as the title of his work demonstrates); his approach places the Christian movement amidst the two traditional religions that Julian himself acknowledges as valid based on their antiquity, that is, Judaism and Greek religion. Deserting the long-established traditions, as the Christians did, was a clear indication of the fallacies the Christians maintained,[3] a view that was presumably held by Porphyry as well according to the known and still disputable testimony offered by Eusebius.[4]

Julian seems to echo an aspect of the euhemeristic theory in his discussion of how heaven is related to the origins of religion, although such an assertion should be deemed implausible considering that Julian was influenced by Neoplatonism rather than Euhemerus, whom he does not even mention by name nor gives any hint that he actually knew his work or theory. In a rather detailed and long excerpt, Julian discusses the centrality of the heavens in the conceptualization of the existence of divinity and thereby the emergence of religious belief:

> There exists no man who does not stretch out his hands toward the heavens when he prays; and whether he swears by one god or several, if he has any notion at all of the divine, he turns heavenward. And it was very natural that men should feel thus. For since they observed that in what concerns the heavenly bodies there is no increase or diminution or mutability, and that they do not suffer any unregulated influence, but their movement is harmonious and their arrangement in concert; and that the illuminations of the moon are regulated, and that the risings and settings of the sun are regularly defined, and always at regularly defined seasons, they naturally conceived that the heaven is *a* god and the throne of *a* god.[5]

Plato, as I have discussed, could probably have influenced Euhemerus's theory of heavenly gods (cf. Chapter 2), but the Neoplatonic notion of one God, the All, as it was elaborated by Plotinus, most likely lies behind Julian's words here. Euhemerus's relevant theory, on the other hand, even though it maintained the same observational process, most likely took each celestial object to be divine—or, at least, this is the prevalent understanding of Uranus's role in how religion originates.[6]

Porphyry's systematic treatment of Christianity is in many regards different from that of Celsus and Julian, especially in relation to Jesus. Although Porphyry maintains that the Christian teachings are to be condemned, there is an apparent distinction between Christianity and Jesus in his criticism. Porphyry's remarkable knowledge of the Jewish and Christian scriptures is portrayed throughout his *Against the Christians*, which must be seen as exactly as its title indicates: a refutation of what others told, thought, and believed about Jesus rather than a severe attack on Jesus himself. It goes without saying of course that by refuting the Christian writings he also denied Jesus's divinity. But contrary to Celsus's and Julian's attacks on Jesus, Porphyry in his *Philosophy of the Oracles* adopted a different—and seemingly euhemeristic-like—view, according to which Jesus was seen as "extremely devout," a wise man, a mortal who attained the status of a hero, a sage, but a mere human nevertheless. Yet it was his decision to pronounce an immortal status upon Jesus that came as a surprise. Porphyry's attempt to reconcile the figure of Jesus with examples from antiquity of other mortals who attained immortal honor and status demonstrates, as Jeffrey Hargis has eloquently put it, that "if Jesus was going to be included in the realm of the blessed, it would be on pagan terms."[7] As such, Porphyry attempted to incorporate Jesus into the long tradition of wise men (like Pythagoras or Herakles) who received immortality of the soul (not of the body) but who, nevertheless, were not gods. In this way, just as in *Against the Christians*, Porphyry launched an astute attack against Christianity and Christians, since it was the disciples of Jesus who led them away from the truth, which was none other than Jesus being a mere human that ought to be praised for his piety and wisdom but not honored or worshipped as a god.[8]

Celsus's work and Origen's response to it, as was articulated in his work *Against Celsus*, is probably the most famous theological contention of antiquity. It is due to Origen that we have several excerpts of Celsus's work still available, even though one should not uncritically accept that Origen did indeed use verbatim citations from the now lost *True Doctrine*. Related to this is the issue of Origen's reliability in regards to which parts of Celsus's work he chose to incorporate in his response and, more importantly, which ones he decided not to address and thus omitted. From what we do have available via Origen, Celsus attacks Christianity and Christian doctrines covering every possible angle. From accusations about sorcery and seeing Jesus as a magician—in itself enough proof for his readers that Jesus held no noble divine essence whatsoever—to dealing with the new religious movement as the epitome of what constituted superstition for the ancients, it is clear that Celsus had no aspirations to reconcile Jesus with the traditional religious ideas as Porphyry did in his *Philosophy of the Oracles*.[9] In an article published almost forty years ago, however, Harry Gamble argued that Celsus employed the euhemeristic theory in order to prove the falsity of the Christian beliefs regarding Jesus's divine nature. As he put it, "we find [Celsus] lodging against the Christian estimate of Jesus the very euhemeristic considerations which Christian apologists brought to bear on paganism."[10] As such, Celsus attacks the Christian creeds by utilizing the very argument the early Church fathers used against the traditional religious beliefs: "However, [the Christians] themselves are clearly refuted for the reason that they worship not a god, nor even a daemon, but a corpse."[11] Although Gamble successfully differentiates between Euhemerus's theory and versions of euhemerism based on the various interpretations his theory received by the doxographic tradition, the Skeptic-Academic circles, the Stoics, and the Christian apologists, he nevertheless acknowledges these different readings, exploitations, and presentations of Euhemerus' theory as 'euhemerism.'

Having already discussed in the previous chapter how and why the Christian arguments can hardly qualify as ancient euhemerism, in this chapter I wish to argue that Gamble, as many before and after him, makes a loose use of both Euhemerus's theory and Celsus's (alleged) euhemerism, as is often the case whenever and wherever the theory is used. This, in turn, raises certain problems when one wishes to include Celsus among the euhemerists.

## Celsus, Origen, and Euhemerism

Although Origen's responses to Celsus's arguments are of great importance for understanding the apologetic rhetoric employed by the early Christian writers, I will largely concentrate in this chapter on Celsus's arguments and examine whether his positions represent a euhemeristic approach when he is defying the divine nature of Jesus.[12] As Gamble has noted, in *Against Celsus* 3.22–43 the main question is "whether anyone who was once a human being might properly be regarded as divine."[13] It could well be argued that this is a question that could have also been the crux of Euhemerus's own motivation for composing the *Sacred Inscription*. There are eleven statements by Celsus that Gamble takes to be euhemeristic:

1. *He* [Celsus] *says that we* [Christians] *do not tolerate the opinion that they* [the Dioscuri, Heracles, Asclepius, and Dionysus] *are gods because they were human in the first place, even though they performed many noble acts on behalf of mankind; yet we say that after Jesus died he appeared to his own confraternity.* [. . .] *he* [Jesus] *appeared even then only as a phantom.* (3.22)
2. *[A] great multitude of men, both Greeks and barbarians, confess that they have often seen and still do see not just a phantom, but Asclepius himself healing men and doing good and predicting the future.* (3.24)
3. *Then as for Aristeas the Preconnesian who both vanished so miraculously from men and again clearly appeared, and a long time afterwards visited many parts of the world and related amazing tales, so that Apollo even commanded the Metapontines to regard Aristeas as a god, nobody still thinks him a god.* (3.26)
4. *No one thinks Abaris the Hyperborean to be a god, though he had such power that he was carried along by an arrow.* (3.31)
5. *Do they not say that his* [the Clazomenian] *soul often left his body and wandered about in a bodiless state? Yet men do not think that even he was a god.* (3.32)
6. *[H]e* [Cleomedes the Astypalean] *got into a chest and after shutting himself inside was not to be found in it; but by some miraculous providence he had vanished from it when people broke the chest in pieces to arrest him.* (3.33)
7. *[B]ecause we* [Christians] *worship the man who was arrested and died, we behave like the Getae who reverence Zalmoxis, and the Cilicians*

who worship Mopsus, the Acarnanians Amphilochus, the Thebans
Amphiaraus, and the Lebadians Thophonius. (3.34)

8. *[T]he honour which we give to Jesus is no different from that paid to
   Hadrian's favourite* [i.e. the boy Antinous]. (3.36)
9. *And if you compare him with Apollo or Zeus, they will not tolerate it.*
   (3.37)
10. *But when he* [Jesus] *had put off his flesh perhaps he became a god? Then
    why not rather Asclepius, Dionysus, and Heracles?* (3.42)
11. *[W]e* [Christians] *ridicule those who worship Zeus because his tomb is
    shown in Crete, without knowing how and why Cretans do this; none
    the less we* [Christians] *worship one who rose from the tomb.* (3.43)

With the exception of 9 and 11, the discussion does not include the Olympians but, rather, a number of infamous heroes and demigods of traditional religion. It must be thus noted from the outset that the dispute revolves around figures that are absent from our sources that discuss the *Sacred Inscription*. It is evident from the available testimonies that Euhemerus did not include heroic figures but prominent kings in his work, with Zeus being the main figure. Such an account could be seen as not representative of our available testimonies, since it does not take into consideration certain secondary sources that maintained that Euhemerus treated many other figures apart from mere kings. Plutarch's attack on Euhemerus in *Isis and Osiris* 360a–b is the most illustrative case. But as I argued in Chapter 4, Plutarch's additions could be interpreted as a form of trivializing Euhemerus's ideas and not necessarily as an indication of a better—let alone direct—knowledge of the *Sacred Inscription*. A counter-argument here can be linked to Diodorus's testimony, as transmitted by Eusebius, which *prima facie* is indeed pointing toward a euhemeristic adoption by Celsus in his argumentation. The names of "Heracles, Dionysus, Aristeas, and others like them"[14] that are included among the group of Diodorus's earthly gods are repeated here by Celsus (via Origen). However, major reservations pertaining to these names and whether they were included in Euhemerus's work have been raised by several scholars. Marek Winiarczyk has successfully shown that it is justifiable to doubt Euhemerus's usage of those names in his *Sacred Inscription*, and the possibility that they were added by Diodorus should be taken quite seriously.[15]

The Dioscuri, Herakles, Asclepius, and Dionysus constitute peculiar figures in Greek religion. The Dioscuri were known mythological figures, sons of Zeus and Leda, who belonged to the intermediate sphere, that is, neither mere humans nor gods. Herakles constitutes the most prominent heroic figure of Greek mythology. Like Achilles, he was among the very few mortals that received panhellenic honors, initially as a hero and eventually as a god.[16] Asclepius was a mortal who went through the stages of human, hero, and finally god. He became the healing god par excellence of the Greeks by displacing the traditional major healing deity (and his father), Apollo.

Celsus uses the example of Asclepius in other instances as well.[17] The posthumous appearance of Asclepius throughout the world, as argued in point 2, is most likely here based on the widely spread tradition of incubation, with healing taking place through dreams in the god's sanctuaries. The god would appear in a dream and either touch the ill part of the sufferer's body or give instructions regarding the healing process. The Graeco-Roman world was full of sanctuaries dedicated to Asclepius and great personages were devotees of his cult, such as Alexander the Great, Pausanias, and Aelius Aristides.[18] Asclepius's remedial powers were so popular that many believed that he could raise the dead. As Xenophon informs us, "Asclepius won yet greater preferment—to raise the dead, to heal the sick; and for these things he has everlasting fame as a god among men."[19] It is surprising that Celsus does not use this ability of Asclepius in his argumentation against Jesus's relevant supernatural power. Nevertheless, the transition from hero to god, which is advocated by Celsus in response to the Christian understanding of Jesus, could hardly be taken as a euhemeristic argument. The assertion that Euhemerus himself could have dealt with these figures is highly doubtful, whereas Celsus was drawing from the vast pool of ancient heroes rather than benevolent or powerful kings. As we have seen, the deified heroes constituted the most common examples utilized by the early Christian authors when attacking Greek religion, and it is likely that Celsus was simply responding to Christian arguments on specific examples rather than introducing new ones. It is known, for instance, that Justin in his *First Apology* (21.1–3) referred explicitly to Asclepius and Herakles. The comparison between heroes who were transformed into gods and Jesus constituted the crux of the debates between Christians and their opponents during these first centuries of the common era,[20] and one needs to keep in mind that seeing such conversations as based on euhemeristic argumentations misses the basic principle that conditions Euhemerus's theory: the origins of belief in gods (and, thus, religion) lies in the deification of prominent and powerful kings—either by self-deification or external proclamation.

The figures Celsus mentions in points 3 to 6 are related to mythological stories and legends that are even less relevant to Euhemerus's theory. Aristeas the Preconnesian and Abaris the Hyperborean constitute semi-legendary figures. The former was known to be raised from the dead and appear in different places in different time periods, and it was Apollo that requested Aristeas's worship. The latter is related to the mythical land of the Hyperboreans, a mythological place located at the far north from where the cold winds come.[21] The association of both figures with Apollo is of minor importance regarding the question of whether they could fit into a euhemeristic interpretation. Celsus himself acknowledges the non-divine nature of these two semi-mythological figures, by pointing out that nobody thinks of them as gods. It is clear that Celsus is more interested in showing that resurrection or return from the realm of the dead did not simultaneously mean deification; an argument that is completely detached from any possible euhemeristic connotation. Finally, Hermotimus of Clazomenae (point 5), a philosopher of the sixth century BCE, is related to a story wherein his soul could leave his body,[22] whereas Cleomedes of Astypalea (point 6) is a strange case of hero. A man that was a "deranged mass-murdering athlete," as Robert Parker put it, certainly surprises us when he was believed "to have become a hero."[23] In both examples there is very little that can be said from a euhemeristic point of view. Hermotimus's case is similar to that of Aristeas and Abaris, who were not revered nor deemed gods, whereas Cleomedes is by default against any euhemeristic interpretation. Nowhere in the *Sacred Inscription*, or even in tertiary or later sources, is Euhemerus portrayed as discussing figures that could be seen as gods due to their detrimental actions.

Mopsus, Amphilochus, Amphiaraus, and Trophonius that Celsus mentions in point 7 were all (mythological) figures, the historicity of whom was at times called into question. Mopsus, according to the relevant myth, was the older half-brother of Amphilochus and they were both connected to Apollo, just like Aristeas and Abaris were. It is once again apparent that Celsus was interested in replying to the claims already made by earlier authors pertaining to the relationship between Apollo, Zeus, and humans/heroes related to them, versus the Christian God and Jesus. Such an argument was employed by Justin, as is demonstrated in his famous statement that "we introduce nothing stranger than those you call the sons of Zeus."[24] However, the debate obviously revolved around the resurrection incident, with both camps arguing in favor of their own traditions and against those of their opponents.[25] All four figures mentioned here by Celsus were never deemed gods by the Greeks, and certainly do not fall into the pool of the divine agents that Euhemerus discusses in his *Sacred Inscription*. One encounters numerous stories in Greek mythology that were apparently not enduring enough to receive wide propagation and popularity in order to be taken as conveying truths or, more importantly, to allow their protagonists to be elevated into the divine realm. Bruce Lincoln has convincingly argued that "we would do better to classify narratives not by their content but by the claims that are made by their narrators and the way in which those claims are received by their audience(s)."[26] Stories such as those accompanying the figures already discussed did not generate the same response from their audiences as the stories of Homer and Hesiod did regarding the Olympian gods, a position that is more or less implied by Celsus's own depreciation of those legends mentioned in points 3 to 7. Zalmoxis, the god of the Getae, also constitutes such a mythical figure, who went from being a slave to becoming a local god. Celsus's choice here to mention Zalmoxis was probably not coincidental. Already since the early second century CE, the Christian authors used this god as an example for exposing the inferiority of the traditional deities when compared to Jesus.[27] But Zalmoxis was never deemed god by the Greeks, whereas his original social status of a slave can hardly be seen through a euhemeristic lens.

The reference to Hadrian's favorite, found in point 8, refers to the young boy Antinous, who "was drowned in the Nile [. . .] [and] Hadrian founded Antinoopolis in memory of him, and he was formally deified."[28] The deification of Antinous, first in Egypt, where he enjoyed wide acceptance as a god, and later in other parts of the Roman Empire, never actually received the popularity of other eastern cults. Could it be argued that Celsus uses here the ancient euhemeristic argumentation? First, we need to be reminded that Celsus, like Plutarch, was a (Middle) Platonist,[29] and such a deification practice would be, to his eyes at least, detestable. Considering that Plutarch explicitly condemned the euhemeristic approach, it is somehow paradoxical to accept that Celsus was in favor of it. The deification that Euhemerus described in the *Sacred Inscription* was the result of deeds or power that exceeded the narrow limits of a personal relationship, or the borders of a single city or country; the Olympians were kings deified due to their actions that had beneficial consequences for the whole world—or, due to their kingly power, when recalling Eusebius's rendition of the theory. Antinous, on the other hand, was not a king, let alone a prominent one. His elevation to the heroic and, subsequently, the divine sphere was the result of Hadrian's ululation for the loss of the young boy. Additionally, the fact that Antinous had "no divine ancestry, no noble blood, and [. . .] no heroic deeds" soon raised suspicions regarding his relationship with the Roman emperor, with people whispering "that the apotheosis was no more that the whim of the boy's distraught and unbalanced imperial love."[30] The caprices of an almighty ruler, such as Hadrian, do not coincide with the ancient euhemeristic interpretation regarding the origins of the gods as probably Euhemerus formulated it. One could, of course, reply that in Lactantius's version Zeus is deified due to his cunning plan. Yet, as I have discussed in Chapter 3, it is debatable whether this version, which contradicts both Diodorus and Eusebius, was indeed part of the Ennian translation or of the original.

Point 9 is among the most problematic ones when we deal with an underlying euhemerism in Celsus's arguments. For Origen, the pronoun 'him' in 3.37 refers to Antinous, while Henry Chadwick maintains that it must refer to Jesus and not to the young boy.[31] If the pronoun means Antinous, then there is little to be said; no form of comparison between Zeus and Antinous can be made as I mentioned above. For Euhemerus, the former was a prominent king deified for his deeds and/or his overwhelming power, whereas the latter was a mortal young boy deified by his patron and, most likely, lover. We must also take into consideration that Euhemerus promoted a vertical top-down deification, where a descendant deifies his predecessor, that is, Zeus deifying Uranus. In Zeus's case, this process is discontinued and, instead, we encounter a bottom-up sequence, with his own deification being the result of consensus among his contemporaries—at least according to Diodorus and Eusebius. In Antinous's case, none of the two processes apply. If, on the other hand, what Celsus does here is to compare Jesus with Zeus (or Apollo), then the discussion needs to be shifted once again toward the issue of resurrection. Its centrality in Celsus's treatise is undeniable but does not fit into Euhemerus's work. It could be argued that Celsus is euhemerizing Jesus, since, like Zeus, he was also a mortal that was deified and entombed. However, this implies that Celsus knew of the *Sacred Inscription* and, additionally, shared the work's view regarding the traditional deities. The fact of Jesus's resurrection is effectively what distinguishes him from Euhemerus's Zeus. None of our sources even imply a resurrection in the *Sacred Inscription*; on the contrary, it is explicit that for Euhemerus (as Lactantius transmits) the very death and burial of Zeus in Crete signifies his mere human nature. To argue that Celsus is here euhemerizing Jesus simultaneously means that he shared Euhemerus's idea of Zeus not being a god. Such a far-fetched claim not only is not justified in *Against Celsus* but, on the contrary, should be altogether dismissed based on the debate in connection to point 11.

The seemingly outright euhemeristic statement found in 3.43 (point 11), pertaining to Zeus's tomb in Crete, is probably the only case where one could with some certainty argue of Celsus employing Euhemerus's views. The story about the existence of Zeus's tomb in Cnossus was supposed to be found in the *Sacred Inscription*. The uncertainty implied here stems from the very fact that such information comes to us only from Lactantius, whereas Diodorus and Eusebius do not mention anything about the death and entombment of Zeus.[32] Considering, however, that Lactantius's testimony can be partly but not conclusively refuted, one could draw the conclusion that Celsus was indeed employing euhemerism, basing this assumption on the comparison and the similarities between Zeus and Jesus, who both lived, died, and were interred. As a matter of fact, Celsus does indeed return the ball to the Christian court when he argues that they worship a corpse (7.36; 7.68). But if Celsus was a euhemerist, then how could such a statement be reconciled with Euhemerus's seemingly identical claim toward those who worshipped Zeus? It is the reply to this question that demonstrates how Celsus deviates from Euhemerus's theory. Origen sheds light on this matter when he essentially de-euhemerizes Celsus's argument at this point, by concentrating on the phrase "without knowing how and why the Cretans do this." Celsus's assertion, which embraces an allegorical explanation to the Cretan tradition of Zeus's entombment, is not only foreign to Euhemerus's view but also against it. Euhemerism and allegory are two distinct interpretations, and it is known that Plutarch, one of the most notorious despisers of Euhemerus's theory, employed allegory and rejected euhemerism as well.[33] For Gamble, "Celsus' point, as the context shows, is not to justify the Cretan tradition but to illustrate the hypocritical selectivity of Christian logic."[34] Even if that was the ultimate goal, it is nevertheless evident that Celsus did not take the Cretan tradition at face value and obviously promoted allegorical interpretations of it. As Origen, in his reply, put it: "Notice that he [Celsus] here defends the Cretans' account of Zeus and their story about his tomb by hinting that there are hidden allegorical meanings which, it is said, the myth of Zeus was invented to convey."[35] Origen supports his argument by mentioning Callimachus, who called the Cretans liars precisely due to their story of Zeus's entombment. As we saw in Chapter 5, Callimachus was a known enemy of Euhemerus's ideas, describing him as "the old man who fashioned the ancient Panchaean Zeus" and who dwells "to the shrine before the wall, where [. . .] [he] chatters and scratches out his unrighteous books."[36] If Celsus was following Euhemerus, then he would have accepted Zeus's tomb in Crete as a historical fact rather than a statement that should be approached according to the allegorical methods. By employing the latter, Celsus is presented by Origen as accepting the story but not its historical veracity, which in turn rejects the euhemeristic explanation and maintains the reality of Zeus as a god.

Pertaining to allegorical interpretation, Celsus did not hold a consistent stance. He rejected any allegorical interpretation of biblical stories that created difficulties for the Jews and Christian interpreters. Those allegorical interpretations "are far more shameful and preposterous than the myths, since they connect with some amazing and utterly senseless folly ideas which cannot by any means be made to fit."[37] On the other hand, Celsus could have meant here that the existing allegorical interpretations fail to adequately respond to what was embarrassing to the sophisticated Jews and Christians. This does not, as it were, dismiss allegory as an interpretative device altogether but only specific allegorical renditions that are unsuccessful according to Celsus's reading of such interpretations. For example, Celsus rejects altogether the book of Genesis, in which God is portrayed in an anthropomorphic form. As a true (Middle) Platonist, Celsus maintains that God cannot adopt a human body, contrary to the *daimones*, who are the ones able to descend to the world; as such, Jesus cannot possibly be deemed god.[38]

## What Would Euhemerus Say?

The fact that Celsus explicitly states that no one believes that Aristeas, Abaris, Hermotimus, and the other infamous figures discussed in his treatise are gods, despite their miraculous actions and the stories accompanying them, is most likely a stance that Euhemerus himself would have taken as well albeit in a different manner. If the most revered agents of Greek religion, like Zeus, Apollo, Hermes, and Artemis were not real gods but mere humans, then apparently those minor and less important figures of Greek mythology do not belong to the divine sphere. Celsus's argumentation follows a comparative approach in order to prove Jesus's non-divine nature. It becomes clear that, by following his comparison between Jesus and Zeus (or Apollo and Asclepius), Celsus depreciates the former. If we accept that the pronoun 'him' in point 9 referred to Jesus, it is obvious that Celsus claims that the Christians introduce nothing new that the Greeks did not already maintain or were unaware of. However, an ancient euhemeristic discussion of Jesus would have followed a completely different path.

The issue of Jesus's resurrection, and contrary to its centrality in Celsus's thought, would have played a secondary—if at all—role if Euhemerus were to discuss the divinity of Jesus. For the Messenean author, the historicity of an individual demonstrates the lack of divine essence. First, the process of deification in the *Sacred Inscription* follows two paths that cannot be reconciled with the Jesus narrative. The elevation into the divine realm is closely related to blood lines—as in the case of Uranus being deified by his grandson—and benefactions or power as in the case of Zeus. Jesus had no political or military power whatsoever, whereas the argument of divine ancestry related to the house of David could have been disputed by the problematic genealogies offered in Matthew 1.1–16 and Luke 3.23–38. Even if Jesus's genealogical problem could be reconciled, in the gospels we encounter the reverse process from the one we find in the *Sacred Inscription*. Zeus is not claimed to be divine due to Uranus's divinity, which he himself established; on the contrary, he is deified by his contemporaries throughout the world, even though the process appears to be the result of his own crafty ideas in one of our sources.[39] Jesus, on the other hand, is claimed to be divine due to his relationship with the Jewish God. His divinity is not the result of some process employed by his peers and fellow men and women; on the contrary, he is deemed divine by birth (cf. Luke 1.35) or divine prior his birth (John 1.1). Euhemerus, of course, would dispute such claims, based on the very fact that divine and human conditions cannot be reconciled. One can either be human or divine according to his view.

Second, Euhemerus would have directly refuted Jesus's divinity due to his death and entombment. In that respect, Zeus and Jesus are identical according to the euhemeristic view. With resurrection holding no importance, Jesus's death and burial would have been sufficient proof for his non-divine nature. The story of Zeus and his tomb in Cnossus, which made both Callimachus and Plutarch react fiercely to Euhemerus's theory, lies at the crux of Euhemerus's euhemerism, at least according to the Lactantian version. It can be argued that Celsus touches upon euhemerism in point 9, without however expanding to encompass the whole of the theory. Euhemerus, on the other hand, would in this case argue that these figures are indeed, to a certain extent, comparable as human beings but not as gods. The same would apply to Celsus's question in point 10. But, again, Euhemerus would simply refute any divine nature of Asclepius, Dionysus, and Herakles, given their human nature. It becomes apparent that miracles and miraculous events held no special importance in Euhemerus's thought. He does not discuss any such incidents in the available testimonies, which implies that he would simply not take into consideration Jesus's miracles as portrayed in the gospels. The prevailing method in Euhemerus's work is to strip Zeus of all stories accompanying him and found in the traditional myths and concentrate solely on his human nature, which is also disseminated via the most ancient myths. It is apparent that earthly birth, in Euhemerus's thought, means earthly death and, thus, lack of divine essence.

A third and very important element in Euhemerus's theory is of course the relationship between kingship and divinity. Euhemerus refutes the possibility of earthly kings becoming gods and, for that reason, he would probably reject the idea that Jesus could be deemed divine. Jesus is seen as a king in the Christian writings with his kingdom however, as argued in John 18.36, not being of this world. The narrative offered by Mark 15.1–5, where Jesus remains silent even when asked by Pontius Pilate if he is a king, could have helped Euhemerus argue that Jesus had nothing in common with Zeus. The deconstruction of the traditional Greek religious ideas with regard to the Olympians was based on diminishing Zeus and other traditional gods to the level of historical kings. As we learn in the *Sacred Inscription*, Zeus traveled throughout the known world, with his deification occurring without any apparent justification (Eusebius), as the result of his own aspirations (Lactantius), or as a result of his benefactions to mankind (again Lactantius).[40] If Jesus is to be seen as a king, then in Euhemerus's view he could hardly qualify as one who deserved to be deified or treated as a god. Euhemerus's argument regarding Zeus's divinity is that it emerges out of his accomplishments and deeds that are easily acknowledged by every nation of the earth (according to Eusebius and partly Lactantius). In this way, as he argued, people erroneously took Zeus to be a god, a practice which he himself rejected. If Zeus, with all his accomplishments and his extraordinary power, should not be considered a god, Jesus's deeds in a more restricted geographical area, that of Judea, could hardly allow him to be seen as a god by the Messenean author. The premise upon which Zeus is mistakenly seen as a god is his actions or his royal power and the subsequent appreciation by the recipients of his actions. The execution of Jesus would have been seen by Euhemerus as a failure to receive broad acceptance and praise—as well as explicit proof of the absence of any substantial or extraordinary royal power. The theory of the non-divine nature of Zeus is, at least partly, founded upon the principle of a mistaken evaluation by the people of the potentate's nature due to his ability to bestow gifts and benefit mankind—or due to his kingly power and his crafty plan. Euhemerus would have probably simply ignored or rejected Jesus and all Christian teachings regarding his divine nature.

\* \* \*

One can hardly claim that Celsus was responding with euhemeristic arguments to the Christian allegations, because the latter, as I argued in the previous chapter, did not actually utilize such argumentation. What they did, however, was to employ and further twist a distorted euhemeristic theory, which is heavily biased and piecemeal. Most of these authors, as we saw, did not claim to be using Euhemerus's theory. Likewise, Celsus does not mention Euhemerus nor explicitly state that he is euhemerizing Jesus. Furthermore, we have no reason to believe, as was the case with the Christian authors, that Celsus had any direct knowledge of Euhemerus's work and theory. The frequent mingling of Euhemerus's theory with what was later on called 'euhemerism' by interpreters and scholars has led the study of Euhemerus and his theory to misapprehensions and false conceptions of what euhemerism is all about. Thus, the Christian version of Euhemerus's theory, which scholars have uncritically detected in the works of the early Christian authors and, as I argued in this chapter, in Celsus's treatise, has managed to find its way into the history of Christian and anti-Christian polemic literature as euhemerism per se.

Belonging to this tradition, Harry Gamble's paper acknowledges a euhemeristic approach on behalf of Celsus. This loose usage of Euhemerus's theory is highly problematic for two reasons. First, Gamble—just like other scholars—continues the long process of identifying the distorted euhemeristic theory that the early Christian writers utilized with what Euhemerus most likely claimed. This approach, erroneously defined as euhemerism, fails to take into consideration the two groups that Euhemerus mentions: earthly or human and heavenly or celestial gods. Second, just as with the various Platonic philosophical schools, it is one thing to identify that a writer is 'platonizing' and another to see Plato's exact theories in the work of such a writer. Thus, it is known that philosophical schools that derived from or are closely connected to the Academy belong to different Platonic traditions, such as Middle Platonism, Neoplatonism, Christian Platonism, etc. Such a distinction and classification is unfortunately not evident nor proposed when dealing with euhemerism. On the contrary, the Christian version of 'euhemerism proper,' as scholars have taken it, has managed to establish itself as a representation of Euhemerus's thought.

The need to distinguish between what was said or written and that which is said to have been said or written, to paraphrase Michel-Rolph Trouillot,[41] is a fundamental process when classifying texts or identifying authors as euhemeristic. The very distinction that Gamble himself makes in his article, which includes the different usages of Euhemerus's theory—although he fails to recognize that those were partial adoptions, but rather sees them as simple variations—forces us to make a similar distinction between Euhemerism with a capital 'E' and euhemerisms. In my view, these versions of the original theory constitute distortions rather than variations and should be treated as such.

## Notes

1 I deliberately avoid the adjective 'Apostate' with which Julian is widely known in the relevant literature, since it was a Christian designation rather than a title Julian himself espoused. On how he was presented by the (Christian) historians of late antiquity, see Rohrbacher 2002, 237–273.

2 See the excellent discussion in Wilken 1979, 117–118.

3 See Smith 1995, 197–198. On how Julian uses Jesus as a local rather than a universal religious figure, see ibid., 202–203. Smith's work is probably the best

discussion of Julian's religious beliefs. A classic work on Julian's life and significance remains Athanassiadi 1992. A reading of Porphyry's *Against the Christians* indicates his good knowledge of Christian scriptures, since he consistently invokes excerpts from the gospels to further strengthen his arguments. For a translation of the text, see Hoffmann 1994. For a discussion of the anti-Christian writings during this period, see Hargis 1999; Cook 2000; Hartog 2010.

4 Eusebius, *Preparation for the Gospel* 1.2.1–4:

> How can men not be in every way impious and atheistic who have apostasized from the customs of our fathers, through which every nation and city is sustained? [. . .] What types of pardon will they be worthy of who have turned away from those recognized as Gods from the earliest times among all Greeks and Barbarians, both in cities and in the country, with all types of sacrifices, and mysteries and initiations by all, kings and lawgivers and philosophers, and have rather chosen what is impious and atheistic among men [. . .]?

The translation is drawn from Wilken 1979, 119. The issue of whether this excerpt is indeed coming from Porphyry or not remains problematic. For a discussion, cf. Morlet 2011, 120–122.

5 Julian, *Against the Galileans* 69b–c (emphasis added). The translation is drawn from the third volume of W. C. Wright's LOEB edition.

6 See Eusebius, *Preparation for the Gospel* 2.2.58–59 (W. T 49). Also, see my discussion in Chapter 1.

7 Hargis 1999, 85.

8 See ibid., 83–89. Cf. the position held by Augustine in *Harmony of the Gospels* 1.15.23. Wilken 1979 persuasively argued that the *Philosophy of the Oracles* had a twofold function: to defend the traditional religions of the Graeco-Roman world while, simultaneously, acting as refutation of Christianity. Thus, it should be added to the quintessential anti-Christian treatise, *Against the Christians*.

9 On Jesus as a magician and the Christians as practitioners of sorcery, see Origen, *Against Celsus* 1.6; 1.38; 1.71; 6.40. Cf. Benko 1984, 103–139; 150–151. On superstition as the main accusation in Celsus's work, see Martin 2004, 140–159. On Porphyry's rejection of the idea that Jesus was a magician, see Wilken 1979, 122.

10 Gamble 1979, 15.

11 Origen, *Against Celsus* 7.68 (all translations throughout the chapter are drawn from Chadwick 1953).

12 On Origen, see Trigg 1998; Frede 1999; Heine 2010.

13 Gamble 1979, 16–17.

14 Eusebius, *Preparation of the Gospel* 2.2.53 (W. T 25).

15 Winiarczyk 2013, 27–28 and n. 7.

16 See the excellent discussion in Stafford 2010.

17 Origen, *Against Celsus* 3.3; 7.53.

18 See Martin 1994; Graf 2009, 77–81. Cf. Burkert 1985, 214–215.

19 Xenophon, *On Hunting* 1.6: Ἀσκληπιὸς δὲ καὶ μειζόνων ἔτυχεν, ἀνιστάναι μὲν τεθνεῶτας, νοσοῦντας δὲ ἰᾶσθαι. διὰ δὲ ταῦτα θεὸς ὡς παρ' ἀνθρώποις ἀείμνηστον κλέος ἔχει. On the phenomenon of resurrection in Greek religion and with a thorough discussion of Asclepius, see the detailed study by Endsjø 2009.

20 See the excellent study by Litwa 2014. Cf. Talbert 2011.

21 On the Hyperboreans, see Bridgman 2005, and on the relationship between the Hyperborean land and Apollo, see Graf 2009.

22 See Chadwick 1953, 149 n. 1.

23 Parker 2011, 104–105.
24 Justin, *1 Apology* 21.1. Cf. Litwa 2014, 147.
25 See Endsjø 2009, 100–104.
26 Lincoln 1989, 24.
27 On Zalmoxis and his place in the works of early Christian authors, see Dan 1999/2000. Cf. the now classic Eliade 1972.
28 Chadwick 1953, 152 n. 1. On the cult of Antinous, see Lambert 1984; Jones 2010, 75–83.
29 On Celsus's (Middle) Platonism and its importance in his refutation of Christian claims, see Hargis 1999, 41–61; Martin 2004, 152.
30 Lambert 1984, 2.
31 Chadwick 1953, 153 n. 2.
32 Lactantius, *Divine Institutes* 1.11.44–48 (W. T 69A).
33 See Chapter 4.
34 Gamble 1979, 22.
35 Origen, *Against Celsus* 3.43.
36 Callimachus, *Iambus* 1.9–11.
37 Origen, *Against Celsus* 4.51. Cf. the discussion in Martin 2004, 143.
38 On Celsus's attack to biblical anthropomorphism and the *daimones*' ability to acquire human form, see Origen, *Against Celsus* 5.2; 6.61; 6.63; 7.34. Cf. the discussions in Benko 1984, 149; Martin 2004, 142–148.
39 This is only found in Lactantius, *Divine Institutes* 1.22.21–27 (W. T 64A).
40 See Chapter 1.
41 Trouillot 1995, 3.

# References

Athanassiadi, Polymnia. 1992. *Julian: An Intellectual Biography*. London and New York: Routledge.

Benko, Stephen. 1984. *Pagan Rome and the Early Christians*. London: B. T. Batsford.

Bridgman, Timothy P. 2005. *Hyperboreans: Myth and History in Celtic-Hellenic Contacts*. London and New York: Routledge.

Burkert, Walter. 1985. *Greek Religion: Archaic and Classical*. Translated by John Raffan. Oxford: Blackwell.

Chadwick, Henry. 1953. *Origen: Contra Celsum*. Cambridge: Cambridge University Press.

Cook, John Granger. 2000. *The Interpretation of the New Testament in Greco-Roman Paganism*. Tübingen: Mohr Siebeck.

Dan, Dana. 1999/2000. "Zalmoxis in Christian Context." *Ephemeris Napocensis* 9/10: 275–305.

Eliade, Mircea. 1972. *Zalmoxis: The Vanishing God*. Translated by Willard Trask. Chicago, IL: University of Chicago Press.

Endsjø, Dag Øistein. 2009. *Greek Resurrection Beliefs and the Success of Christianity*. New York: Palgrave MacMillan.

Frede, Michael. 1999. "Origen's Treatise *Against Celsus*." In *Apologetics in the Roman Empire: Pagans, Jews, and Christians*, edited by Mark Edwards, Martin Goodman, and Simon Price, 131–155. Oxford: Oxford University Press.

Gamble, Harry Y. 1979. "Euhemerism and Christology in Origen: 'Contra Celsum' III 22–43." *Vigiliae Christianae* 33 (1): 12–29.

Graf, Fritz. 2009. *Apollo*. London and New York: Routledge.

Hargis, Jeffrey W. 1999. *Against the Christians: The Rise of Early Anti-Christian Polemic*. New York: Peter Lang.

Hartog, Paul. 2010. "Greco-Roman Understanding of Christianity." In *The Routledge Companion to Early Christian Thought*, edited by D. Jeffrey Bingham, 51–67. London and New York: Routledge.

Heine, Ronald E. 2010. "Origen." In *The Routledge Companion to Early Christian Thought*, edited by D. Jeffrey Bingham, 188–203. London and New York: Routledge.

Hoffmann, R. Joseph. 1994. *Porphyry's Against the Christians: The Literary Remains*. Amherst, MA: Prometheus.

Jones, Christopher P. 2010. *New Heroes in Antiquity: From Achilles to Antinoos*. Cambridge, MA and London: Harvard University Press.

Lambert, Royston. 1984. *Beloved and God: The Story of Hadrian and Antinous*. London: Weidenfeld and Nicolson.

Lincoln, Bruce. 1989. *Discourse and the Construction of Society: Comparative Studies of Myth, Ritual, and Classification*. New York and Oxford: Oxford University Press.

Litwa, M. David. 2014. *Iesus Deus: The Early Christian Depiction of Jesus as a Mediterranean God*. Minneapolis, MN: Fortress Press.

Martin, Dale B. 2004. *Inventing Superstition: From the Hippocratics to the Christians*. Cambridge, MA and London: Harvard University Press.

Martin, Luther H. 1994. "Religion and Dream Theory in Late Antiquity." In *The Notion of "Religion" in Comparative Research: Selected Proceedings of the XIth Congress of the IAHR, Rome 3rd–8th September 1990*, edited by Ugo Bianchi, 369–374. Rome: L'ERMA di Bretschneider.

Morlet, Sébastien. 2011. "Eusebius' Polemic Against Porphyry: A Reassessment." In *Reconsidering Eusebius: Collected Papers on Literary, Historical, and Theological Issues*, edited by Sabrina Inowlocki and Claudio Zamagni, 119–150. Leiden and Boston, MA: Brill.

Parker, Robert. 2011. *On Greek Religion*. New York: Cornell University Press.

Rohrbacher, David. 2002. *The Historians of Late Antiquity*. London and New York: Routledge.

Smith, Rowland. 1995. *Julian's Gods: Religion and Philosophy in the Thought and Action of Julian the Apostate*. London and New York: Routledge.

Stafford, Emma. 2010. "Herakles Between Gods and Heroes." In *The Gods of Ancient Greece: Identities and Transformations*, edited by Jan N. Bremmer and Andrew Erskine, 228–244. Edinburgh, UK: Edinburgh University Press.

Talbert, Charles H. 2011. "The Concept of Immortals in Mediterranean Antiquity." In *The Development of Christology During the First Hundred Years and Other Essays on Early Christology*, 61–82. Leiden and Boston, MA: Brill.

Trigg, Joseph W. 1998. *Origen*. London and New York: Routledge.

Trouillot, Michel-Rolph. 1995. *Silencing the Past: Power and the Production of History*. Boston, MA: Beacon.

Wilken, Robert L. 1979. "Pagan Criticism of Christianity: Greek Religion and Christian Faith." In *Early Christian Literature and the Classical Intellectual Tradition: In Honorem Robert M. Grant*, edited by William R. Schoedel and Robert L. Wilken, 117–134. Paris: Beauchesne.

# 8 Seeing 'Euhemerism' Everywhere

In his *Exploring Greek Myth* (2012), Matthew Clark notes:

> In the process of telling and retelling, the original author loses control of the story, as elements are added or changed or deleted. It is almost possible to say that a myth is a story that has escaped from its author.[1]

In a similar vein, in this chapter I wish to give additional examples of how euhemerism escaped from its original context and author, whereby in the case of the lost *Sacred Inscription* I refer to how that context and author is represented in our available testimonies, thereby further complicating our understanding and usage of the theory. I trace three such paths that have led to the considerable alteration of ancient euhemerism. The first one is related to the academic study of myth, with euhemerism being often seen as a theory of myth or—in an even more complicated fashion—as an instance of rationalization of myths. The second refers to the way euhemerism was used in a long process that started in the medieval period and continued through the Renaissance and the Enlightenment in an attempt to 'rescue' ancient mythology by simultaneously meddling with it. Lastly, the third path is related to how the theory of euhemerism qua theory of religion (or of myth in most cases) has been utilized by scholars dealing with different religious traditions—apart from the examples of early Christianity, Judaism, and 'pagan' religions addressed in the previous two chapters. The basic example I will be discussing is stemming from Nordic mythology and the famous *Edda* composed by Snorri Sturluson, whose prologue has been interpreted as a clear example of euhemerism outside the Graeco-Roman world.

These three divergent but somehow overlapping processes owe much of their interpretational predispositions to the way the theory of Euhemerus was corrupted already in the first centuries after the *Sacred Inscription* was composed. The treatment of the theory was almost immediately based on partial adoptions and outright ignorance, which not only continued in the centuries after the early Christian period, but also made its way into modern studies. Although this is a vast topic to be covered in just one chapter, I will attempt to sketch this misappropriation of Euhemerus's theory based on specific interpretational desires that scholars had and still have when it comes to utilizing what Euhemerus said about 2,500 years ago. It is hardly an exaggeration to say that a lack of acquaintance with the available testimonies, in addition to the tendency to isolate Euhemerus from both his utopian novel and his time, has led to a confusion that still remains and which has prompted me throughout this book to imply or explicitly make a distinction between Euhemerism (with a capital 'E') and euhemerism.

## Euhemerus on Myth

A common understanding of euhemerism is its mission to explain away myth by rationalizing and historicizing it.[2] Theories of myth are as difficult to deal with as theories of religion. Similar to the questions pertaining to religion, theorists of myth seek to answer the fundamental questions of the origin (why and how myth arises) and function of myth (why and how myth lasts), adding the issue of its subject matter (whether myth should be read literally or symbolically).[3] The question, however, is whether Euhemerus promoted a theory of myth as a generalization for all myths. This depends on the way we wish to read the available testimonies. Marek Winiarczyk does not include such an interpretation of Euhemerus's work in his possible motives for the writing of the *Sacred Inscription*, whereas Albert Baumgarten has taken the theory to be a reinterpretation of Greek mythology rather than a theory of myth.[4] If we wish to universalize what Euhemerus says about the Greek religious myths, then it could potentially allow us to deem his work as a theory of myth per se, although its application to non-religious myths would pose a certain challenge. On the other hand, if we see his theory as one dealing with the origins of the gods, and thus religion, then it simply encompasses myths as the means by which the stories of the traditional Greek gods were conveyed. In a sense, an ancient theory of religion is also a theory of myth given their interconnections.[5] What is more interesting to examine, however, is whether Euhemerus's theory leads to effectively explaining away myth or rationalizing it. The former implies that for Euhemerus (Greek) myth is erroneous, improbable, and thus pointless and unnecessary. We can hardly subsume Euhemerus under this rubric; his twisting of the traditional stories and his proposal of an alternative version of the known stories about the gods does not allow for explaining away those narratives. As such, he maintains numerous elements of the traditional credos, including Crete as Zeus's place of birth, the genealogical tree of the Olympians, and their names; if we also add here the extensive narrative given by Lactantius (cf. 1.14.1–8; W. T 54), then we hardly see how Euhemerus can reject myth by simultaneously employing it. Historicizing and humanizing the mythical figures but maintaining their frame stories indicates Euhemerus's opposite mission: to explain myths historically in order to respond to a contemporary practice, that is, the deification of Hellenistic potentates. In this sense, Euhemerus can hardly be taken as explaining myth away. This common misconception has often led scholars—already from antiquity as we have seen—to characterize Euhemerus as an atheist: explaining away Greek myth means explaining away Greek religion.

The rationalization of myth, on the other hand, needs further attention. It is a common mistake to include Euhemerus in the list of rationalists, mainly due to the problem of what one means by 'rationalization' in this context. Related to the issue of subject matter, rationalization is linked to the problem of literal or symbolic reading of myth. Rationalizing myth virtually means reading myth not literally but symbolically, thereby making it rational and comprehensible. However, Euhemerus does not read myth symbolically; rather, he transforms myth into history, making adjustments, incorporating these stories in a utopian work, and creating a new story altogether with new elements. Symbolical reading of myths, on the contrary, is an attempt to peel off all supernatural or implausible elements of a story in order to encounter its truth underneath its various distorting layers. The most famous rationalist of myths in antiquity was no other than the author of *On Incredible Tales*, Palaephatus. The work, which is survived in fragmentary form, contains fifty-two brief sections on various Greek myths. Palaephatus functions as a corrector rather than rejecter of the myths he deals with in his work, denuding them of all fantastical elements in order not to explain them away but to make them more credible and acceptable.[6] This, in turn, implies that for Palaephatus myths contain historical truth which has been obscured by material added by the various readers, narrators, and compilers of such stories. Up to this point one can hardly see how or why Euhemerus does not fit into this classification of figures dealing with myths. Contrary to Euhemerus, however, Palaephatus deals with heroes, monsters, and heroines in his work but leaves out the gods of the traditional pantheon. He distances himself from all the stories that include the gods and does not apply his rationalistic method to those by arguing, as he does for the other stories, that they are silly, false, impossible, or laughable.[7] Euhemerus only deals with a specific group of agents but does so not by trying to decipher their underlying meaning; on the contrary, he is basing the new form of the stories on allegedly hard evidence rather than mere speculation. For Palaephatus myth is full of past misunderstandings, whereas for Euhemerus it is about the wrong sources. "The Euhemeristic tradition must be carefully distinguished from the Palaephatean" argued Jacob Stern about fifteen years ago, a position shared by the best recent publication on rationalization of myth in antiquity by Greta Hawes, who rightly points out that euhemerism is primarily "a critique of Greek religion; myth criticism is of subsidiary concern."[8] Stern, however, takes euhemerism as atheistic aiming to create disbelief, whereas Hawes is more attentive and connects the theory with the royal cultic practices of Euhemerus's time. If, however, euhemerism is to be seen as a critique of Greek religion by "revisionist descriptions of the historical development of civilization"[9] then it must be also seen as a critique of the royal and dynastic cults of his time, which in turn agrees with my own assessment in Chapter 5. In a sense, rationalists resemble allegorists, as both seek the most possible original form of the story that makes sense; Euhemerus, on the other hand, relies upon new findings, that is, a new version of the story that essentially diminishes the prior versions as mistaken, maintaining, however, elements of those older accounts.

## Rescuing the Gods, Altering (Further) the Theory

The habitual overlapping of euhemerism with rationalism has not been the only common mistake in scholarship on euhemerism or on works that employ 'euhemerism.' Often scholars would classify euhemerism as another form of allegory, such as in the case of the Latin writer of the sixth century Fulgentius. Many authors of the middle ages and the Renaissance used Fulgentius's work which was seen as "full of the flowers of allegories" as Robert Edward has noted. Nevertheless, even in more contemporary works, Fulgentius is portrayed as using euhemerism although the examples employed to demonstrate his euhemerism are but instances of allegory.[10] Similar misconceptions of what euhemerism was all about persisted even more fiercely between the fourteenth and nineteenth centuries.

In a publication that basically complements Jean Seznec's now classical *The Surviving of the Pagan Gods* (1953), Luc Brisson examines how classical myths survived from the middle ages onwards due to the allegorizing method employed by philosophers. He points out that in the sixteenth century euhemeristic interpretation was used by authors (such as Giovanni Nannio of Viterbo and Walter Raleigh among others) as a tool in exposing Greek mythology as "a distortion of history stolen from Moses."[11] Even more interesting, nevertheless, is that those authors merged corrupted traditional euhemerism—that is, the known dictum that gods were dead men of antiquity—with etymological research and comparative biographies. Thus, Raleigh's *Historie of the World*, as Brisson demonstrates, identified Adam with Saturn, Cain with Jupiter, Eve with Rhea and so on. This practice of establishing "agreements between biblical figures and the pagan gods" became the standardized form of what euhemerism meant after, more or less, the fourteenth century.[12]

How exactly were those works euhemeristic? And, moreover, who decided to call these works euhemeristic and why? The answer is quite straightforward: not euhemeristic at all—at least not in the ancient sense and content of the ancient theory. In the Renaissance the trend of associating the 'pagan' gods with biblical figures in addition to etymological research flourished. This at least is the position employed by scholars like Arthur Ferguson who, however, misinterprets ancient euhemerism when he sees Palaephatus as Euhemerus's successor.[13] I agree however with his position that euhemerism, already in the middle ages, was "undergoing subtle changes in emphasis,"[14] although 'subtle' is a very modest adjective he employs due to his own misconception of ancient euhemerism. Biblical scholars of this period, throughout Europe, undertook a very ambitious mission: the aim now was not to demonstrate the superiority of the Christian God against the 'pagan' ones—this was accomplished (successfully or not depends on the stance one takes) by the early Christian authors—but to show that both the language and religion of the Jews antedates those of the Greeks. They identified the mythological figures with those of the biblical narratives, similarly to Raleigh's project, but promoted other associations as well. The examples are numerous: Saturn and Janus had originated in the biblical Noah; Moses had incarnations in the pagan world as Bacchus and Pan; Janus and Bacchus were types of Noah; the Garden of Adonis was a type of Eden.[15] This is in itself problematic; but it becomes even more so when such manipulations of traditional stories are defined by scholars as euhemeristic.

This is the case, for example in A. M. Cinquemani's treatment of Henry Reynold's *Mythomystes* (1636). The following phrase gives a straightforward description of what euhemerism here means:

> Unlike the Church Fathers, who wished to subject pagan myth to analysis with a view to rejecting it, Reynolds wishes to unify and synthesize mythic elements with a view to finding [. . .] the latent principles of Scripture in paganism. His Euhemerism is tied to a kind of typology.[16]

This is hardly euhemerism, to say the least. Another example comes from Bart Van Es's monograph on the English poet Edmund Spenser (1552/3–1599). In analyzing Elizabethan antiquarianism and the search of prehistory, Van Es identifies three basic principles. First, the superiority of Moses as the greatest of all historians; second, the frustratingly partial nature of the biblical account for making sense of prehistory; and third, the need of Christian chronographers to devise a way to incorporate the 'false' or 'corrupted' Graeco-Roman writings in the 'true' biblical account, given that the Bible contained the actual facts from the very beginning of the world. Euhemerism, in this scheme, provided such a device. Ancient gods and monstrous characters became genuine historical figures, whose accompanying stories were being changed by storytellers and, by using 'euhemerism,' it was possible to retrieve the actual names and events of that dimmed prehistory.[17] However, it is evident that here we find a loose usage and adoption of ancient euhemerism, which now included stories of mythical monsters, recovery of actual names and incidents, and a tool for accessing a distorted prehistory whereas Euhemerus solely offered the actual accounts of particular individuals, who were kings rather than heroes or mythical creatures. Van Es also makes an association between allegory and euhemerism when he identifies two levels of allegory. The first one is the known practice from antiquity, according to which "mythical figures could be read as direct moral allegory—their actions or characters being interpreted as

abstract qualities," whereas the second one—which for him is euhemerism
—sought to decode the traditional stories differently as "veiling the actions
of men who were once true enforcers of justice."[18] It is known already from
antiquity that euhemerism was the opposite method of interpretation when
compared to allegory. This was shown by Plutarch's attack on Euhemerus
and maintained by scholars of euhemerism as we have already seen (cf.
Chapter 5). David Harvey recently put such interpretations in their right
place. What we are dealing with is nothing but diffusionist theories, which
traced all religions and all peoples back to the book of Genesis by creating
"lines of transmission through the establishment of linguistic similarities on
the flimsiest of evidence."[19] It is difficult, if not impossible, to reconcile such
approaches with Euhemerus's theory.

The examples are not exhausted here. Different from the biblical scholars'
agenda, euhemerism has been identified by scholars in artistic and literary
works as well, probably nowhere more clearly than in John Milton's
*Paradise Lost* (1667). In an article published about forty years ago, Philip
Gallagher reached the following interesting conclusion: "Although Milton's
characteristic position with respect to the Semitic and Greek gods is that
they are not men but fallen angels in disguise, euhemerism remains for him
a useful (though very occasional) tool in the construction of *Paradise Lost*."[20]
The same argument was promoted some twenty years later by Bruce
Boehrer.[21] Yet, what we are dealing with here is the concept of demonology
and fallen angels which, in essence, is reverse euhemerism, that is, divine
benevolent beings becoming demons—although in order to qualify as proper
reverse ancient euhemerism it should make humans into gods, no matter
how bizarre that might seem. Nonetheless, both Gallagher and Boehrer
acknowledge the existence of euhemerism in *Paradise Lost*, which follows
an older tradition in studies on Milton which seems to have perished lately.[22]
The most apparent contradiction between ancient euhemerism and 'alleged
euhemerism' in *Paradise Lost* is that the fallen angels are seen as introducers
of malevolent deeds, which cannot be correlated to what our sources tell us
about the *Sacred Inscription*. Another example of finding euhemerism everywhere is evident in the artistic works of Diego Velázquez, the seventeenth
century painter and leading artist in the court of King Philip IV. In discussing
various paintings of Velázquez, John Moffitt relates the depiction of the
'pagan' gods in Velázquez's works as influenced by a work found in the
artist's library, entitled *Philosofía Secreta* and written by Perez de Moya in
1585.[23] The *Philosofía Secreta*, as it turns out, is a treatise on allegory which,
nevertheless, is here merged with euhemerism in Moffitt's reading. Citing
from de Moya's work, Moffitt demonstrates the content of the work, worthy
of reciting here: "An example: Hercules, the son of Jupiter (according to
poetic conventions), was placed in the Heaven once his victorious labors
were concluded. [. . .] But, according to Allegory or Morality, by Hercules
there is understood a victory against vices."[24] It is indeed surprising how
Moffitt then goes on to argue that this work "still remains our best guide

to Velázquez's naturalistic-moralising, or 'euhemeristic' mythologies."[25] Historicizing and humanizing the traditional major deities of the Olympian pantheon cannot be deemed equivalent to the allegorical interpretation of the stories that informed the readers and audiences of storytellers of the works and days of their gods.

During the Enlightenment, the tendency to connect and fuse the biblical narratives with 'pagan' mythology did not cease overnight. Authors such as Samuel Shuckford in his *The Sacred and Profane History of the World Connected* (1728) continued this tradition, although the scope of euhemerism was now further expanded.[26] In his now classical *The Eighteenth Century Confronts the Gods* (1959), Frank Manuel argued that:

> Euhemerists of the narrow persuasion are truly rare. [. . .] But if Euhemerism is broadened to include those who recognized in most pagan myths the elaboration of ancient political and other historic events of great moment, then the concept would encompass the majority of mythographers and chronologists who flourished in the first half of the eighteenth century.[27]

Yet, Manuel makes the same mistake Sextus Empiricus did centuries ago. He is relating ancient euhemerism with Critias's theory of religion which saw the gods as divine agents of law enforcement. As he claims, "[t]he eighteenth century had a natural affinity for Sophist theory and the view that a state religion was a necessary political institution."[28] Based on this misinterpretation of Euhemerus's theory, he adds Issac Newton (1643–1727) among the euhemerists, although Newton accepted the syncretistic practice of merging Greek and Egyptian gods and heroes "with the traditional kings of Greece and Egypt," which meant that "Sesostris was at once Osiris, Bacchus, Hercules, and Belus; Thoas, King of Lemnos, had forged arms for the monarchs of Egypt and was deified as Vulcan."[29] The concept of the genealogies being national political histories is a projection of the Enlightenment that saw, as Newton did as well, "organized religion as political institutions founded by princes,"[30] which is quite distanced from how Euhemerus conceptualized the origin of religion as belief in gods rather than as a political institution—at least according to Diodorus's and Eusebius's version and mainly in connection to Uranus's deification.

The nineteenth and twentieth centuries are equally full of euhemerisms that need our attention. The English classicist Herbert Rose (1883–1961), in an essay discussing the Frazerian idea of divine kings in ancient Greek mythology, concentrates on the nature of Zeus in Euhemerus's work by employing only the theory's branch pertaining to the Olympians and neglecting any discussion on the celestial or heavenly gods, or Uranus's deification by Zeus. However, Rose is probably among the very few scholars who do not add variations to the story about Zeus but remains faithful to the story as it is portrayed in our sources, although he does not expand too much on what is euhemerism for him.[31] Similarly, the American classicist Joseph Fontenrose (1903–1986) dealt with euhemerism in his criticism of the theory's usage by Lord Raglan (1885–1964). He accuses Raglan of only having consulted secondary sources and thereby concentrating on the post mortem deification of the Panchaean kings, whereas according to Fontenrose "Euhemerus did *not* say that the first gods were dead kings: he said that they were *living* kings."[32] However, Fontenrose here misses the actual information conveyed by our available testimonies: Euhemerus said that the first gods were both dead (Uranus) and living (Zeus) kings. Nevertheless, Fontenrose should be credited for making the distinction between euhemerism and palaephatism which Raglan obviously misinterpreted or overlooked.[33]

Perhaps the most interesting encounter with euhemerism is promoted by Jan Assmann in his study of Freud's analysis of Moses. By referring to *Moses and Monotheism* (1936), Assmann calls Freud's idea of 'the man Moses,' who is acknowledged by Freud as the creator of the Jewish nation, a "compelling (if not convincing) new version of Euhemerism."[34] Ironically, Freud nowhere in *Moses and Monotheism* mentions the name of Euhemerus or his theory. On the contrary, he relates Moses with the notion of 'the father as the great man,' who is admired, loved, and trusted by the Jews, but simultaneously causes fear to them—although, as he notes, the question of Moses's historicity is of great importance.[35] In my view, in order to reconcile Moses and euhemerism one needs to start with the idea that Moses was a mythical or prehistoric figure who became the king of the Jewish people and, later on, deified due to his benefactions or power (based on the Diodorian/ Eusebian, and partly Lactantian version), or his crafty character (based on the Lactantian/Ennian version). This can hardly be justified according to the biblical narrative. Moses for Freud is not considered divine, nor does Judaism consider him to be a god. A great man is not a god. Freud's approach to Moses is psychological: an instance of Freud's favorite trope of the Oedipus complex, but not of the notion of God as a substitute for the father which was promoted in detail in his *Totem and Taboo* (1913).

A final example is here drawn from a recent article by Thomas Barden on the famous American author John Steinbeck (1902–1968). Barden concentrates on a phrase encountered in a piece that Steinbeck wrote in 1967 dealing with an agriculture agent he met during a visit in Laos. As we learn, this man in Laos was working with the indigenous Meo people. It is worth quoting an abbreviated version of Barden's excerpt of choice:

> Pop Ewell personally founded the Sam Thong village. [. . .] Pop is an example of how the ancient gods were born and preserved in the minds and the carven images of people all over the world. Remember, Alicia, how the story invariably goes—in olden times the people did not live well as they do now and they practiced abominations. Then a stranger appeared and he taught us to use the plow and how to sow and how

to harvest. He brought us writing so we could keep records. And he gave us healing medicines to make us healthy, and he gave us pride so we would not be afraid and when we had learned these things he went away. *He was translated* [. . .]. Well, I don't think Pop is likely to be taken up in a sweet chariot, even if he had the time or the inclination, but that ancient story is Pop Ewell's story.[36]

Barden is quick to add that the phrase "he was translated" rang a bell; it was encountered in the King James Bible (Hebrews 11.5), in which Enoch "was translated" in order not to experience death and, thus, he was not to be found.[37] Although this is a very interesting case, it can hardly qualify as an instance of euhemerism. First, both Steinbeck's character and the biblical Enoch are not kings, nor are they proclaimed gods by their peers. Second, Barden seems to neglect the common pattern of heroization in antiquity. The myth of Herakles is a clear case of 'being translated.' Third, Steinbeck's description is closer to the notion of cultural heroes rather than benevolent (or crafty) kings. Euhemerus's Uranus and Zeus are not 'translated' but proclaimed gods and for completely different reasons compared to the cases of Enoch or Pop Ewell.

In most instances, as is manifested in these examples, it is later, modern scholars who find euhemerism in the works of those middle ages, Renaissance, and Enlightenment figures, which is further repeated in studies on twentieth century scholars and authors. In some occasions, on the other hand, Euhemerus or euhemerism is indeed invoked, albeit with a different and widely distorted content. This resembles what we encountered in the early Christian usage of the theory, where it is subsequent scholars who assign euhemerism to specific phrasings—with the Christian authors who cite Euhemerus, as we have seen, doing so via secondary sources. Hence, ever since the compilation of the (lost) original *Sacred Inscription*, we are witnessing the accumulation of misrepresentations and transformations of euhemerism—likewise, a term later scholars assigned to Euhemerus's theory—that began already in antiquity, further reinforced in the early Christian period, and even further distorted from the middle ages onwards.

## Finding Euhemerism in Other Religious Traditions

Perhaps the most common misrepresentation of Euhemerus's theory of the origin of belief in gods and religion is its association with the learned English scholar Herbert Spencer (1820–1903). In an essay published in 1870, Spencer outlined his own theory of religion which he further developed in his *Principles of Sociology* (1898): "The rudimentary form of all religion is the propitiation of dead ancestors, who are supposed to be still existing, and to be capable of working good or evil to their descendants."[38] Spencer's theory, linked to the evolutionary trend of his time, is considerably different from Euhemerus's approach. Yet, the two figures are often presented side by side, with Euhemerus seen as Spencer's predecessor. This linkage is often seen in connection with ancestor-worship that is widely encountered in African tribal traditions. In his treatment of the subject, Bolaji Idowu almost half a century ago argued that Spencer did not actually promote a new theory when he saw ancestor-worship as the root of all religion; he was simply restating Euhemerus's theory.[39] Similarly, in his article on "Myth" in the *Guide to the Study of Religion* (2000), Russell McCutcheon makes the same connection, taking Spencer as the re-introducer of Euhemerus's theory, a position also supported by Fiona Bowie in her textbook on the anthropology of religion, who sees euhemerism as an early version of Spencer's theory.[40] Much of the confusion is perhaps related to the severe criticism Spencer's theory received by Friedrich Max Müller in the Gifford Lectures he delivered at the University of Glasgow in 1891, published as a monograph the following year. In confronting Spencer's theory of ancestor-worship, Müller labeled this approach as euhemerism and accused Spencer of applying the idea to Zeus without however explaining how "a divine character could have been ascribed" to a powerful figure "by people who had as yet no knowledge of divine beings."[41]

The misconception of euhemerism in all these cases is based on the corrupted version of the theory as was promulgated by the early 'pagan' and Christian authors who criticized or employed the theory in their own writings. In this fashion, euhemerism is seen as the deification of dead men of antiquity, and ancestor-worship in Africa naturally fitted this corrupted version of euhemerism. Notwithstanding any other apparent problems, Spencer's theory entails not merely the worshipping of dead people but also their continuing presence among the living. Usually, after three to five generations, the ancestors' memory seems to dissolve and they are transformed into mere dead humans given that new members of the family and of the community cross the threshold of death, thereby replacing the older generations of ancestors. Additionally, throughout Africa ancestors are dealt with as supernatural agents but hardly as gods, despite the veneration and worship they receive. An important aspect of the ancestor cult, however, is the belief that these agents mediate between the living and God, who in African conception most of the time remains unnamed or is described by an ancient term or a unique word only assigned to that deity. Ancestors are inferior agents compared to God and lack the divine characteristics of God.[42] Ancient euhemerism cannot be applied to such traditions considering the theory's subject matter: benevolent, powerful, or cunning kings who are deified both ante and post mortem and are henceforth deemed fully fledged gods. Even in cases that seemingly resemble Euhemerus's view, such as in the apotheosis of certain ancestors in African traditions, the ancestor in question only absorbs the characteristics and powers of an existing deity—for example, as Idowu informs us, the deification of Sango of the Yoruba tradition, who assumes Jakuta's attributes, the deity of the Yoruba related to the sun and thunder.[43]

Again, divinity preexists in this scheme, whereas euhemerism offers an answer to the origins of (belief in) gods and religion.

A similar case of misusage of ancient euhemerism is observed in the study of Mesoamerican religious traditions. Yet, ancestor worship in this context, as Joyce Marcus has shown, is restricted to the genealogies of rulers, who in their attempt to legitimize their right to be and remain in power invoked a chain of descent that expanded from the near ancestors (who could be easily remembered and identified), to the distant ones (whose memory was maintained mainly through oral traditions or written records), all the way to mythical ancestors (supernatural beings).[44] In Marcus's view this lineage can be best understood through the euhemeristic method. She gives as an example the transformation of the Aztec rulers into gods after their death, which could not be also claimed by the nobles of Aztec society.[45] As I argued in the beginning of Chapter 5, Marcus is again employing the Christian version of euhemerism without taking into account the overall theory—let alone the case of Zeus, who is deified while alive. In the Mayan culture, on the other hand, although the power of kingship is well linked with and emanates from ancestors, the kings are seen as the center of the cosmos: they are responsible for the maintenance of balance between heaven and earth, as well as the regulators of every aspect of social life, from agriculture and warfare to life-style, developments of social status and stratification, and ceremonial cycles and rituals.[46] Even though the kings are deemed sacred, their role is "to align the social world of the humans with the supernatural world of the gods,"[47] making explicit that they cannot be counted themselves among the gods. This distinction indicates that godlike honors do not equate kings with gods.

What is more interesting, however, in the study of Mesoamerican religions and euhemerism, is how the colonists approached and interpreted the indigenous gods. Much of the connection between Mesoamerican kingship and gods with euhemerism comes from the interpretation of the Spaniards after conquering the New World. This is evident in the work of the missionary priest and Franciscan monk Bernardino de Sahagún (1499–1590). In his famous work *Historia General de las Cosas de la Nueva España*, written shortly after Mexico's conquest, Bernardino engaged in a syncretistic enterprise in which he identified the traditional Mexican deities with the Graeco-Roman ones. As such, Paynal was seen as another Mercury, Tezcatlipoca as Jupiter, etc., in a way similar to Julius Caesar's identification of the Celtic gods with the Roman ones (cf. *Gallic Wars* 6.11–20). However, contrary to Caesar's motive, Bernardino sought to demonstrate the wicked nature of those alleged divinities when compared to the Christian God. As such, identifying Huitzilopochtli with Herakles, Bernardino mentions not only his great physical strength but also characterizes Huitzilopochtli as destructor of villages and a massive murderer. After his death, his Mexicans, who respected and were afraid of him, honored him as a god and offered him slaves as gifts. Guilhem Olivier characterizes

Bernardino's method as euhemeristic,[48] although he neglects the fact that for Euhemerus the promotion to the divine sphere is the result of power and good deeds (or even crafty planning) rather than fear, destruction, and massacres. Moreover, Olivier cites Bernardino's decision to identify Tezcatlipoca with Jupiter, calling him a real god, who was omnipotent, invisible, and creator of both heaven and earth, which he nevertheless calls euhemeristic.[49] Considering the leading role of Zeus/Jupiter in Euhemerus's work, as both Diodorus/Eusebius and Ennius/Lactantius inform us, in which Jupiter is the primary figure stripped away of his divinity, it is indeed problematic to trace the ancient euhemeristic method in Bernardino's *Historia General*.

Some thousand miles away, in East Asia, scholars have also recognized the workings of euhemerism in the discussion of Japanese and Chinese mythology. In an ambitious and rich volume on how Japanese historians between 1600 and 1945 interpreted and approached the stories pertaining to the origins of the Japanese people and their imperial house, John Brownlee offers a learned study of the reception of the Japanese myths that first appear in the ancient works *Kojiki* (Account of Ancient Matters) and *Nihon Shoki* (The Chronicles of Japan). These works, composed in the eighth century, narrate

> the creation of Japan by deities, the activities of the deities during the Age of the Gods, the founding of the imperial line by the Sun Goddess, and the reign of the first emperor, Jinmu, a direct descendant of the Sun Goddess, beginning in 660 BC according to *Nihon Shoki*.[50]

By focusing mainly on the various interpretations offered during the Tokugawa period (1603–1868), in which the Neo-Confucian rationalistic philosophy was imported to Japan from China, Brownlee traces a euhemeristic interpretation of those origin myths in the works of Aral Hakuseki (1657–1725), a Confucian and anti-superstition historian of this period.[51] Hakuseki's euhemerism, as Brownlee calls his interpretation, was based on the idea that the figures called gods in those chronicles were human beings. Therefore, the appropriate way of approaching those narratives was by taking "the Age of the Gods as a record of the actions of humans," which for Brownlee corresponded to "a more general preoccupation among Confucian scholars with the reality or otherwise of gods and spirits of the dead" due to their rationalism that did not allow much space for gods and spirits.[52] Similar, in a way, to what we encountered in the brief overview of the Christian practice in Europe during the Renaissance, Hakuseki's method for proving the mortality of those agents was based on a linguistic explanation according to which, as he argued, humans came to misunderstand those ancient records. Although seeing the gods of prehistory as deified humans resembles Christian euhemerism, the same cannot be argued about ancient euhemerism. First, Hakuseki's linguistic and orthographic explanation does not coincide with Euhemerus's method, that is, not the mere rejection of the traditional stories but their correction as historical records and the creation of new versions based on new evidence. Second, Hakuseki's Neo-Confucian rationalism here does not act as a theory of religion but as a palaephatean interpretation that stems from his own reluctance toward the supernatural. Third, as Brownlee informs us, Hakuseki did not maintain a uniform approach to these stories. In another source, a letter to Sakura Dogan in 1721, he supported the idea that those myths were not actual records but manipulated texts that sought to provide legitimacy to the imperial house. As Brownlee rightly points out, "[t]o contend that the Age of the Gods was concocted to support the imperial house was quite different from arguing that it had come to be misunderstood through linguistic confusion."[53] Yet, he calls both of Hakuseki's views 'euhemerism.' The second view does not really lie afar from Isaac Newton and other scholars and thinkers of the Enlightenment that saw institutionalized religion as political institutions founded by princes. From a euhemeristic point of view, such a suggestion can only be established according to the Lactantian version of the origins of religion (*Divine Institutes* 1.22.21–27; W. T 64A)—and again, only partially—but cannot be justified by the Diodorian or Eusebian version of the theory.

"*Euhemerism* in the proper Greek sense is the belief that myth is nothing more than forgotten history, and what the Greeks enjoyed as their mythological heritage was [. . .] just remote Greek history imperfectly remembered."[54] This is how William Boltz defines euhemerism in his treatment of the Chinese Flood story that occurs in the *Shu ching* (Book of History), one of the Five Classics of Chinese literature.[55] The known Flood story describes how Emperor Yao seeks a competent individual to deal with the state affairs. One of his advisors proposes Kung Kung, whom Yao immediately rejects due to Kung Kung's arrogance. The ongoing deluge, now reaching its ninth year, leads Yao to the execution of Huan Tou and Kun—the persons in charge of controlling the Flood—but also of Kung Kung.[56] In his interpretation of this myth, Boltz employs euhemerism, yet defined in the aforementioned manner. First, for Euhemerus myth is not forgotten history, let alone imperfectly remembered. On the contrary, Euhemerus partly rejects the traditional stories of the Olympian gods in favor of his own version that is supported by the putative hard evidence he found in Panchaea. Second, Boltz's method essentially corresponds to rationalizing the Flood myth in order to demonstrate how things must have happened. As such, as he claims, although the original motive for the creation of the Flood myth was to represent the "tension between the desire for a stable and orderly society [. . .] and a sense of perpetual disorder beyond human control," later on the story was "euhemerized, that is, transformed into a human struggle between an allegedly historical ruler, Yao, and his irresponsible functionary, Kung Kung, and the entire incident was seen in human bureaucratic terms."[57] This is vintage Palaephatus. The transformation of the myth into a rationalized replacement is the typical method of Palaephatus as argued earlier in this chapter. Lastly, Boltz extends Euhemerus's method to stories that do not include gods. This is a common practice among scholars, as we have already seen. Euhemerism, in this sense, is now the interpretative tool of any kind of myth that is seen as a distorted version of a historical event that can include any form of activity but not necessarily gods alone.

In the Indian mythology, Indra is one of the most peculiar cases of a deity: initially a powerful warrior and hero, he was elevated to the status of solar god settling the heaven and the earth, became the highest god, only to be degraded in a god of trickery and a mere leader of demigods, eventually becoming "a mere clown with the honorary title of king of the gods."[58] This known transformation of Indra's status is surprisingly seen as euhemerism by Uma Chakravarty: "This phenomenon of change in the character of a god hints at his euhemeristic nature also."[59] Although Chakravarty acknowledges that Indra's status was changed due to the cultural evolution encountered among the nomadic Aryans, who were now transformed from warriors into agriculturalists and thereby Indra's depiction of a king warrior naturally started to fade, she nevertheless approaches Indra's career from a euhemeristic perspective. It is interesting, I think, to see how Indra could be related to euhemerism rather than to the Graeco-Roman tradition of eternal and immortal gods (cf. Chapter 6). As Chakravarty informs us, Indra was a benevolent leader, but only toward his Aryan followers. Armed with the powerful and indestructible weapon *vajra*, he is seen as "(i) the destroyer of cities and killer of *dasyus* [the earlier inhabitants], (ii) bestower of prosperity on humanity (i.e., his people) and (iii) the lord of heaven."[60] In the stories accompanying Indra we learn that he owed his strength to the drink *soma*, brought to him from heaven by a hawk, and with the help of which he managed to kill Vritra, an ancient monster and his most powerful enemy. Additionally, he also received Visnu's help. After killing Vritra, he released the enclosed waters, thus destroying his enemies' economy and making the Aryans the most powerful people in the region, which resulted in his treatment by his people initially as a culture hero and then as a god.[61] There is hardly anything euhemeristic in this depiction of Indra's deeds and subsequent deification. On the contrary, and from a comparative perspective, Indra is here similar to Herakles of Greek mythology, the quintessential immortal who became a god—or, one could argue, Thor of Nordic mythology. The changes of Indra's status we encounter in writings that come from different periods cannot be reconciled with ancient euhemerism or Greek mythology in toto. Nowhere in our testimonies is Zeus experiencing multiple changes of status, apart from his deification. Moreover, Euhemerus's main figures are not gifted with supernatural power, utilize mythical weapons, bring prosperity only to their own people, kill and destroy other peoples and their habitat, or identified with celestial beings. Furthermore, according to the accompanying mythologies, Indra had many reasons to be deemed a god, whereas the euhemeristic kings are mere humans. Finally, Indra receives the assistance of existing gods (for example, Visnu), which means that even if we would like to apply ancient euhemerism to this deity in order to explain the origins of religion, the barrier of the divinity's preexistence (in whatever form) is unsurpassable.

A different but very interesting approach to the issue of seeing euhemerism everywhere is unwittingly promoted by Gannath Obeysekere in his study on the apotheosis of captain James Cook (1728–1779). When reaching the coasts of Hawaii, Cook was welcomed with ceremonies and prostrations that were interpreted by the Europeans as expressions of worship, adoration, or devotion. However, as Obeysekere argues, none of these ceremonies the Hawaiians performed had the connotation of worship or adoration in the European Christian sense; on the contrary, "Cook was simply accorded the ceremonial obeisance known as *kapu moe* by which their own important chiefs were honored" rather than making any connections, as was later argued, between Cook and the god Lono.[62] Obeysekere offers as proof the absence of any such connections by the accompanying officers—with only one exception, an officer called Rickman—but they did recognize that he was honored in the same way a local chief was revered.[63] It is worth citing in full Obeysekere's explanation of how Cook came to be seen as a divine figure in Hawaii:

> Thus, the very beginnings of the voyages of discovery carried with them the tradition of the apotheosis of redoubtable European navigators who were also the harbingers of civilization. This cultural structure occurs against a larger background of ancient Indo-European values pertaining to euhemerism, to gods in human shape appearing among mortals, to men becoming gods and gods becoming men and so forth. [. . .] The popular shipboard narratives of Europeans who were divine figures to natives is thus an old tradition, and one that has continued to this very day [. . .].[64]

In other words, Obeysekere offers a stimulating example of how (corrupted) euhemerism and other Graeco-Roman ideas managed to work as tools serving particular viewpoints that stemmed from the notion of European superiority, which is attached to issues that emerged during the colonial era. As he puts it:

> It is unlikely that educated eighteenth-century Europeans thought that Cook was "deified" like a European saint or that at death he ascended to heaven. Contrast with this, however, the European perception of savage people: *They* were capable of direct and unabashed deification of the intrepid explorer in their midst.[65]

Such a view reminds us of Russell McCutcheon's treatment of myth, who insists on its study but not as an enterprise of finding, recognizing, or expounding any truth claims; on the contrary, myths must be seen as

> the products and the means of creating authority by removing a claim, behavior, artifact or institution from human history and hence from the realm of human doings. A rectified study of myths thus turns out to be study of mythmaking.[66]

The mythmaking process, which led to the establishment of the idea that Cook was seen as god Lono, can then be further elaborated to include issues of superiority/inferiority between Europeans and Polynesians and Hawaiians, with ideas such as the Christian corrupted version of euhemerism acting not as an interpretational or theoretical tool but, rather, as a means of justifying such claims.

### We Are Like You: Euhemerism in Snorri

Perhaps nowhere else can one encounter distorted euhemerism 'in all its glory' than Snorri Sturluson's *Edda*. A medieval text, the *Edda*—and particularly its Prologue—has been almost unanimously described as Snorri's euhemeristic explanation of the Nordic traditional gods. Indeed, the Prologue has many elements that resemble euhemerism; but, as I will show, euhemerism in this context is defined as the ante mortem deification of people who were sorcerers and powerful warriors.

In the Prologue we immediately encounter an admiration of Asia, which is seen as the richest part of the world. We learn that Thor (initially named Tror in connection to Troy), son of Priam's daughter Troan and King Munon (or Mennon), was raised in Thrase by a war-duke called Lorikus. Already from the age of ten, Thor was able to carry the weapons of his foster father, and at the age of twelve had reached his full strength. He killed Lorikus and his wife Lora (or Glora) and became the ruler of Thrace, which Snorri associates with Trudheim. Subsequently, Thor is portrayed as a hero who slaughters berserks and giants, a dragon, and many beasts. Thor married Sibyl and, after many generations, Voden, that is Oden as Snorri informs us, was born. Oden married Frigida (Frigg) and both had 'second sight,' which allowed them to foreknow the future. Oden, in the company of many people, called the Æsir, journeyed outside Turkland toward the north and wherever they went "many glorious things were spoken of them, so that they were held more like gods than men."[67] The Æsir reached Sweden and married local women and spread their language throughout Saxland.

The question, which also preoccupied Heinrich Bech, is whether Snorri was a euhemerist. Bech argued that by presenting the traditional gods as deified men, Snorri was indeed using one aspect of euhemerism. However, as he goes on to add, by not dismissing 'paganism' as a delusion, he is not employing euhemerism, which for Bech equals dismissal of traditional religion.[68] Such an evaluation of euhemerism is of course stemming from the negative way the theory was used by both its early critics (for example, Plutarch) and the later Christian apologists. If we wish to acknowledge euhemerism in the *Edda*'s Prologue, we first need to clarify that this was not a tradition that preceded Snorri; on the contrary, as Antony Faulkes demonstrated, Icelandic genealogies do not assign any divine status to the figures in them but are rather treated as human kings. It was due to the coming of Christianity that Christian euhemerism was introduced.[69] But the question still persists: was Snorri a euhemerist in the ancient sense?

The Prologue contains elements of euhemerism but deviates considerably from any consistent and honest ancient euhemeristic account. Thus, Snorri follows in a sense the tradition I discussed when referring to the Renaissance, in which biblical scholars engaged in a linguistic explanation of the traditional Graeco-Roman myths in their attempt to reconcile them with the biblical narrative. Snorri, however, is not interested in relating the Nordic gods to biblical figures. However, he does promote a linguistic approach— Troy-Tror-Thor; Thrace-Trudheim[70]—in order to promote a different claim: the Nordic gods and mythological figures were historical agents whose origins are to be found in the broader area of Asia, which includes in his description the Mediterranean basin. His motive is not so much religious but (primarily) political and (overall) cultural. Antony Falkes, who sees the placement of Odin at the head of the Nordic pantheon, suggested that this occurred after English influence, whereas the linking of Scandinavian dynasties "through Odin and fiórr, to Priam of Troy" anticipated the transformation of their ancestry, thus becoming "as noble as those of the Frankish and British kings."[71] Moreover, Snorri's work has been recently well studied in regards to his own political activities and aspirations in Norway and Iceland, thereby making the text not so much about antiquarianism or religious criticism but a strategic practice aiming at the preservation and protection of skaldic poetry, as well as the placement of the Nordic countries into a European historical continuity.[72] This is further portrayed in Gro Steinsland's words: "Now [that is, from the twelfth century onwards] writers did not merely construct the histories of dynasties anymore, but the histories of peoples."[73] This, as he further argues, led to the adoption of a euhemeristic interpretation—although I will discuss its validity shortly—which was "of more interest to historiographers than to theologians."[74]

But what kind of euhemerism—if we can call Snorri's method as such— is at work here? Thor, similar in a way to Herakles, is an extraordinary human with overwhelming physical power, which is evident already from his childhood and early teens. His life is full of battles with mythical monsters and giants, whereas he is not portrayed as a god but merely as a hero. Oden and Frigg, on the other hand, are capable of knowing the future due to their second sight, a trait usually assigned to magicians and sorcerers. The journeys and actions of the Æsir in the north results in being regarded "more like gods than men," but Snorri is not clear whether they are understood or proclaimed gods by those peoples or simply treated *like* gods. Euhemeristically, Thor does not fit the theory, but is a suitable candidate of the group of immortals encountered in the Graeco-Roman world. The acknowledgment of magical powers, as in the case of Oden and Frigg, does not simultaneously elevate mythical figures to a divine status. Magic and sorcery is often related to trickery, whereas in the ancient euhemeristic tradition the deified kings were worthy of such honor (that is, deification) due to their deeds or power. Moreover, Snorri does not address the issue of deities existing in the heavenly realm, like Euhemerus did as the information pertaining to Uranus's actions indicate.

The connection of magic powers and euhemerism was also promoted by John Lindow in an article on Saxo's euhemerism. Lindow draws on Saxo's *History of the Danes* 1.170, where we read that, in the past, "certain individuals, initiated into the magic arts, namely Thor, Odin and a number of others who were skilled as conjuring up marvellous illusions, clouded the minds of simple men and began to appropriate the exalted rank of godhead."[75] In Lindow's view, euhemerism is not any more about benefactions or power, but is related to sorcery that tricks people, which is evident not only in Saxo but in Snorri as well.[76] Once again, euhemerism is transmuted into merely an idea of ancient humans becoming divine through whatever medium, motivation, and intention.

The equation of euhemerism with rejection of 'pagan' religion, as Bech interprets it, which first appears in Plutarch and the lists of atheists of antiquity and later on in the early Christian apologists, is more evident, as Christopher Abram has shown, in the *Gylfaginning*. Snorri adds here the so-called 'advice to young poets':

> Now it is to be said to young skalds who are desirous of acquiring the diction of poetry, or of increasing their store of words with old names, or, on the other hand, are eager to understand what is obscurely sung, that they must master this book for their instruction and pastime. These sagas are not to be so forgotten or disproved as to take away from poetry old periphrases which great skalds have been pleased with. But christian men should not believe in heathen gods, nor in the truth of these sagas, otherwise than is explained in the beginning of this book, where the events are explained which led men away from the true faith, and where it, in the next place, is told of the Turks how the men from Asia, who are called asas, falsified the tales of the things that happened in Troy, in order that the people should believe them to be gods.[77]

Here Snorri, contrary to what he mentions in the Prologue, takes the myths of antiquity as manipulated by the Æsir in order to fool people into believing that they were indeed divine. In Abram's view, "one of the aims of *Gylfaginning* is to explain away the divinity of the pagan gods as a delusion: a delusion that has been promulgated by falsifying accounts of universal history,"[78] which makes even more difficult the connection of this narrative with ancient euhemerism. If deification for Euhemerus according to the available testimonies is either a unanimous decision by the people who have seen the power and benevolence of Zeus, as Diodorus and Eusebius claim (and, partly, Lactantius), then Snorri's 'advice to the young poets' does not qualify as a euhemeristic instance. On the other hand, the Lactantian (and possibly Ennian) version does deal with Zeus's deification as the result of a well-instrumented plan that was conceived by Zeus and executed each time he was about to depart from the different peoples that he visited. However, what Snorri introduces here is not the manipulation of the deification process per se but the falsification and misrepresentation by the people from Asia of the actual past events in Troy. If we would like to draw parallels, then this could only be applied to ancient euhemerism if Zeus was presenting false or manipulated stories about Uranus's deification that would allow him to be a descendant of gods and thus a god himself—which, as we have seen, does not occur in any of our available testimonies.

It is such diverse versions of the ancient theory of the origin of gods and religion that one documents in Snorri's *Edda*. The utilization of a distorted or corrupted euhemerism to promote the Nordic affiliation to the European historical continuity is also evident in other works. For example, a similar version of euhemerism used as a method of etymological roots of certain figures such as Odin and Apollo in connection to magical arts is apparent in Tero Antilla's recent dissertation on the myth of the Hyperboreans and its adoption for the purposes of creating, maintaining, and promoting a national antiquity in early modern Swedish research.[79] Hence, the ancient theory of the origins of religion has largely been altered into a method and interpretative tool of cultural and historical endeavors that serve different agendas, just as it did in the early Christian period, the middle ages, the Renaissance, and the Enlightenment. In this sense, euhemerism is indeed everywhere; the question is: whose euhemerism?

## Notes

1 Clark 2012, 3.
2 See Coupe 1997, 63. Explaining away myth here is rather problematic. Practically, explaining away means that myth does not exist. Otherwise, even the historicization of myth is still an explanation, that is, accounting for myth by giving its historical origins. If such an approach reduces myth into reality, silliness, error, etc., this is still explaining it rather than explaining it away. In this case, however, historicization or rationalization acts as an exposé, which is not a theory but simply a reinterpretation of myth.
3 See Segal 2015, 172; 2004, 2.
4 Cf. Winiarczyk 2013, 106–107; Baumgarten 1996.
5 This is not restricted to antiquity. As Segal 1999, 2 notes

> [f]or many theorists, myth is a subset of religion. For Tylor, Smith, Frazer, Harrison, and Hooke, religion is the primitive counterpart to modern science, and myth is part of the religious explanation of the world or part of the

religious means of controlling the world. For Bultmann, myth is part of the religious worldview, itself eternal rather than merely primitive.

Yet, for many theorists, like Eliade or Tylor, there are no non-religious myths. In this sense, based on how the theorist approaches the definition of myth, then the acceptance or not of non-religious myths will also determine whether the interconnection is indeed valid. Not all theorists of myth are interested in religion or vice versa.

6　See Stern 1999, 215.
7　Ibid., 216; 218–219.
8　Ibid., 219; Hawes 2014, 27.
9　Hawes 2014, 27.
10　See Edwards 1990, 141; for a misusage of euhemerism as allegory in Fulgentius's work, see Whitbread 1971, 18.
11　Brisson 2004, 152.
12　Ibid., 153.
13　See Ferguson 1993, 15.
14　Ibid., 22.
15　See ibid., 35; Cinquemani 1970, 1047; Killeen 2008, 103–105. Cf. Manuel 1959, 115.
16　Cinquemani 1970, 1046.
17　See Van Es 2002, 113–114.
18　Ibid., 124–125; cf. 138.
19　Harvey 2014, 38.
20　Gallagher 1978, 17.
21　See Boehrer 1996, 29.
22　This 'demonology as euhemerism' also appeared in Osgood 1901, whereas in the 2007 edition of *Paradise Lost* (cf. Milton 2007), edited by Barbara Lewalski, the term 'euhemerism' is not mentioned at all throughout the book. The concept of the fallen angels, demonology, and the connection with 'paganism' goes back to Justin Martyr, although he did not adopt a euhemeristic stance, as I maintain. As Reed 2004, 143 has shown, for Justin "the teachings of the fallen angels serve to explain the origins and continued practice of Greco-Roman religions," although she did take such a method as euhemeristic in Reed 2005, 186.
23　See Moffitt 1989, 161–162.
24　Ibid., 162.
25　Ibid., 166; cf. 173.
26　On Shuckford's work, see Manuel 1959, 118–119.
27　Ibid., 103–104.
28　Ibid., 104.
29　Ibid., 117.
30　Ibid.
31　See Rose 1998, 386.
32　Fontenrose 1998, 451, emphasis in the original.
33　Ibid., 435.
34　Assmann 1997, 164. On his criticism of the idea of Moses as the creator of the Jewish nation, which he deems a far more complex process, see 163–164.
35　See Freud 1939, 11, 174.
36　Barden 2014, 40, emphasis in the original.
37　Ibid.
38　Spencer 1870, 536.
39　See Idowu 1973, 178.
40　See McCutcheon 2000, 194; Bowie 2006, 12.

41 Müller 1892, 137; cf. 134–141 for the complete criticism. For an equally fierce attack on Müller's criticism of Spencer, see Grant 1897, 171–172 who accepts Spencer's 'euhemerism.'
42 For a general overview of African religions, see Beyers 2010; Olupona 2014 (who does not cite euhemerism in his study).
43 See Idowu 1973, 186.
44 See Marcus 1992, 262.
45 Ibid., 269.
46 See the discussion in Carrasco 1990, 103–104.
47 Ibid., 104.
48 See Olivier 2010, 396, from which I draw Bernardino's syncretistic examples and his narration on Huitzilopochtli and Herakles. Cf. the discussion in López Austin 2000/2001, 9–10 who also sees here euhemerism being at work, which he classifies as a rationalistic method.
49 See Olivier 2010, 397.
50 Brownlee 1999, 1.
51 On Neo-Confucianism's rationalism, which of course played a significant role in Hakuseki's interpretation of the stories encountered in *Kojiki* and *Nihon Shoki*, see ibid., 16–18.
52 Ibid., 45.
53 Ibid., 48.
54 Boltz 1981, 142, emphasis in the original.
55 For a concise presentation of the Five Classics, see Littlejohn 2011, 7–10.
56 See Boltz 1981, 142–143. For more on this incident, cf. Lewis 2006, 21–29.
57 Boltz 1981, 151–152.
58 See Williams 2003, 157. On Indra and his deterioration cf. Shattuck 1999, 22–23.
59 Chakravarty 1997, 152.
60 Ibid., 95.
61 Cf. ibid., 96–100; 115–118; Williams 2003, 156–157.
62 Obeysekere 1992, 120. Lono was one of the four major eastern Polynesian and Hawaiian deities along with Kū, Kāne, and Kanaloa. For a brief description of their traits, see Kirch 2010, 57 (with further bibliography).
63 See Obeysekere 1992, 122.
64 Ibid., 124.
65 Ibid., 130, emphasis in the original.
66 McCutcheon 2000, 207.
67 I am using Snorri's text from Rasmus B. Anderson's translation (1901), 46.
68 See Bech 2001. Bech's approach is, obviously, referring to Christian euhemerism.
69 See Faulkes 1978/1979, 3–5.
70 In a way, we can argue of an *interpretatio Nordica*, similar in a sense to Herodotus's *interpretatio Graeca* and Caesar's *interpretatio Romana*. Cf. Lincoln 2012, 17–29.
71 Ibid., 6, 12.
72 See the discussions in Lincoln 2012, 53–62; 2014, 32–40; cf. Wanner 2008.
73 Steinsland 2011, 19.
74 Ibid., 20.
75 Cited in Lindow 2013, 250.
76 Ibid., 244–255.
77 Sturluson 1901, 167.
78 Abram 2009, 7. However, this does not explain why people accept it; fooling people bypasses the explanation. For example: how do you get people to be fooled? And what happens once they have been fooled?
79 See Antilla 2014, 109; 113–114.

# References

Abram, Christopher. 2009. "*Gylfaginning* and Early Medieval Conversion Theory." *Saga-Book* 33: 5–24.

Antilla, Tero. 2014. "The Power of Antiquity: The Hyperborean Research Tradition in Early Modern Swedish Research on National Antiquity." Ph.D. Diss., University of Oulu.

Assmann, Jan. 1997. *Moses the Egyptian: The Memory of Egypt in Western Monotheism.* Cambridge, MA and London: Harvard University Press.

Barden, Thomas E. 2014. "'He was Translated': Euhemerism in Steinbeck's Work and Worldview." *Steinbeck Review* 11 (1): 39–45.

Baumgarten, Albert I. 1996. "Euhemerus' Eternal Gods: Or, How Not To Be Embarrassed by Greek Mythology." In *Classical Studies in Honor of David Sohlberg*, edited by Ranon Katzoff, Yaakov Petroff, and David Schaps, 91–103. Ramat Gan: Bar-Ilan University Press.

Bech, Heinrich. 2001. "War Snorri Sturluson ein Euhemerist?" In *Mythos und Geschichte: Essays zur Geschichtsmythologie Skandinaviens in Mittelalter und Neuzeit*, edited by Gerd Wolfgang Weber, 61–71. Trieste: Edizioni Parnaso.

Beyers, Jaco. 2010. "What is Religion? An African Understanding." *HTS Teologiese Studies* 66 (1): 1–8.

Boehrer, Bruce. 1996. "'Female for Race': Euhemerism and the Augustinian Doctrine of Marriage in *Paradise Lost* VII." *South Atlantic Review* 61 (4): 23–37.

Boltz, William G. 1981. "Kung Kung and the Flood: Reverse Euhemerism in the *Yao Tien*." *T'oung Pao* 67 (3–5): 141–153.

Bowie, Fiona. 2006. *The Anthropology of Religion: An Introduction.* Second edition. Malden, MA and Oxford: Blackwell.

Brisson, Luc. 2004. *How Philosophers Saved Myths: Allegorical Interpretation and Classical Mythology.* Translated by Catherine Tihanyi. Chicago, IL and London: University of Chicago Press.

Brownlee, John S. 1999. *Japanese Historians and the National Myths, 1600–1945: The Age of the Gods and Emperor Jinmu.* Vancouver, BC: UBC Press and University of Tokyo Press.

Carrasco, David. 1990. *Religions of Mesoamerica: Cosmovision and Ceremonial Centers.* San Francisco, CA: HarperCollins.

Chakravarty, Uma. 1997. *Indra and Other Vedic Deities: A Euhemeristic Study.* New Delhi: D. K. Printworld.

Cinquemani, A. M. 1970. "Henry Reynold's *Mythomystes* and the Continuity of Ancient Modes of Allegoresis in Seventeenth-Century England." *Publications of the Modern Language Association of America* 85 (5): 1041–1049.

Clark, Matthew. 2012. *Exploring Greek Myth.* Malden, MA and Oxford: Wiley-Blackwell.

Coupe, Lawrence. 1997. *Myth.* London and New York: Routledge.

Edwards, Robert. 1990. "The Heritage of Fulgentius." In *The Classics in the Middle Ages*, edited by Aldo S. Bernardo and Saul Levin, 141–151. Binghamton and New York: Centre of Medieval and Early Renaissance Studies.

Faulkes, Anthony. 1978/79. "Descent from the Gods." Online: www.vsnrweb-publications.org.uk/Descent-from-the-gods.pdf (access 11 May 2015) [Originally published in *Mediaeval Scandinavia* 11: 92–125].

Ferguson, Arthur B. 1993. *Utter Antiquity: Perceptions of Prehistory in Renaissance England.* Durham, NC and London: Duke University Press.

Fontenrose, Joseph. 1998. "The Ritual Theory of Myth." In *The Myth and Ritual Theory: An Anthology*, edited by Robert A. Segal, 428–459. Malden, MA and Oxford: Blackwell.

Freud, Sigmund. 1939. *Moses and Monotheism*. Translated by Katherine Jones. Letchworth: Hogarth Press.

Gallagher, Philip J. 1978. "Milton and Euhemerism: *Paradise Lost* X. 578–584." *Milton Quarterly* 12 (1): 16–23.

Grant, Allen. 1897. *The Evolution of the Idea of God: An Inquiry Into the Origins of Religions*. London: Grant Richards.

Harvey, David A. 2014. "The Rise of Modern Paganism? French Enlightenment Perspectives on Polytheism and the History of Religions." *Historical Reflections* 40 (2): 35–55.

Hawes, Greta. 2014. *Rationalizing Myth in Antiquity*. Oxford: Oxford University Press.

Idowu, E. Bolaji. 1973. *African Traditional Religion: A Definition*. London: SCM Press.

Killeen, Kevin. 2008. *Biblical Scholarship, Science and Politics in Early Modern England: Thomas Browne and the Thorny Place of Knowledge*. Farnham, UK and Burlington, VT: Ashgate.

Kirch, Patrick V. 2010. *How Chiefs Became Kings: Divine Kingship and the Rise of Archaic States in Ancient Hawai'i*. Berkeley, CA and London: University of California Press.

Lewis, Mark E. 2006. *The Flood Myths of Early China*. New York: SUNY Press.

Lincoln, Bruce. 2012. *Gods and Demons, Priests and Scholars: Critical Explorations in the History of Religions*. Chicago, IL and London: University of Chicago Press.

Lincoln, Bruce. 2014. *Between History and Myth: Stories of the Harald Fairhair and the Founding of the State*. Chicago, IL and London: University of Chicago Press.

Lindow, John 2013. "Some Thoughts on Saxo's Euhemerism." In *Writing Down the Myths*, edited by Joseph Falaky Nagy, 241–255. Turnhout: Brepols.

Littlejohn, Ronnie L. 2011. *Confucianism: An Introduction*. London and New York: I. B. Tauris.

López Austin, Alfredo. 2000/2001. "Fray Bernardino de Sahagún: Frente a los Mitos Indígenas." *Ciencia* 60/61: 6–14.

McCutcheon, Russell T. 2000. "Myth." In *Guide to the Study of Religion*, edited by Willi Braun and Russell T. McCutcheon, 190–208. London and New York: Cassell.

Manuel, Frank E. 1959. *The Eighteenth Century Confronts the Gods*. Cambridge, MA: Harvard University Press.

Marcus, Joyce. 1992. *Mesoamerican Writing Systems: Propaganda, Myth, and History in Four Ancient Civilizations*. Princeton, NJ: Princeton University Press.

Milton, John. 2007. *Paradise Lost*. Edited by Barbara K. Lewalski. Malden, MA and Oxford: Blackwell.

Moffitt, John F. 1989. "The 'Euhemeristic' Mythologies of Velázquez." *Artibus et Historiae* 10 (19): 157–175.

Müller, Friedrich Max. 1892. *Anthropological Religion*. London and New York: Longmans, Green, and Co.

Obeysekere, Gannath. 1992. *The Apotheosis of Captain Cook: European Mythmaking in the Pacific*. Princeton, NJ: Princeton University Press.

Olivier, Guilhem. 2010. "El Panteón Mexica a la Luz del Politeísmo Gregolatino: El Ejemplo de la Obra de fray Bernardino de Sahagún." *Studi e Materiali di Storia delle Religion* 76 (2): 389–410.

Olupona, Jacob K. 2014. *African Religions: A Very Short Introduction.* Oxford: Oxford University Press.

Osgood, Charles G. 1901. "Milton's Classical Mythology." *Modern Language Notes* 16: 282–285.

Reed, Annette Yoshiko. 2004. "The Trickery of the Fallen Angels and the Demonic Mimesis of the Divine: Aetiology, Demonology, and Polemics in the Writings of Justin Martyr." *Journal of Early Christian Studies* 12 (2): 141–171.

Reed, Annette Yoshiko. 2005. *Fallen Angels and the History of Judaism and Christianity: The Reception of Enochic Literature.* Cambridge: Cambridge University Press.

Rose, Herbert J. 1998. "The Evidence of Divine Kings in Greece." In *The Myth and Ritual Theory: An Anthology*, edited by Robert A. Segal, 381–387. Malden, MA and Oxford: Blackwell.

Segal, Robert A. 1999. *Theorizing About Myth.* Amherst MA: University of Massachusetts Press.

Segal, Robert A. 2004. *Myth: A Very Short Introduction.* Oxford: Oxford University Press.

Segal, Robert A. 2015. "Myth in Religion." In *International Encyclopedia of the Social and Behavioral Sciences*, edited by James D. Wright, second edition, vol. 16, 172–178. Oxford: Elsevier.

Shattuck, Cybelle. 1999. *Hinduism.* London and New York: Routledge.

Spencer, Herbert. 1870. "The Origin of Animal-Worship, etc." *The Fortnightly Review* 7 (n.s.): 535–550.

Steinsland, Gro. 2011. "Origin Myths and Rulership. From the Viking Age Ruler to the Ruler of Medieval Historiography: Continuity, Transformations and Innovations." In *Ideology and Power in the Viking and Middle Ages*, edited by Gro Steinsland, Jón Viðar Sigurðsson, Jan Erik Rekdal, and Ian Beuermann, 15–67. Leiden and Boston, MA: Brill.

Stern, Jacob. 1999. "Rationalizing Myth: Methods and Motives in Palaephatus." In *From Myth to Reason? Studies in the Development of Greek Thought*, edited by Richard Buxton, 215–222. Oxford: Oxford University Press.

Sturluson, Snorri. 1901. *The Younger Edda.* Translated by Rasmus B. Anderson. Chicago: Scott, Foresman and Company. Online: www.gutenberg.org/files/18947/18947-h/18947-h.htm (accessed 14 June 2015).

Van Es, Bart. 2002. *Spenser's Forms of History.* Oxford: Oxford University Press.

Wanner, Kevin J. 2008. *Snorri Sturluson and the "Edda": The Conversion of Cultural Capital in Medieval Scandinavia.* Toronto and London: University of Toronto Press.

Whitbread, Leslie G. 1971. *Fulgentius: The Mythographer.* Columbus, OH: Ohio State University Press.

Williams, George M. 2003. *Handbook of Hindu Mythology.* Santa Barbara, CA and London: ABC Clio.

Winiarczyk, Marek. 2013. *The Sacred History of Euhemerus of Messene.* Translated by Witold Zbirohowski-Kościa. Berlin and Boston, MA: De Gruyter.

# Afterword
## On the Use and Abuse of a Theory

In 1962, Edward Evans-Pritchard delivered the Sir D. Owen Evans Lectures at the University College of Wales (now Aberystwyth University), on the topic of theories of primitive religion, which four years later were published in a monograph that still remains one of the most important studies on psychological, anthropological, and sociological theories of religion. In the introduction of those lectures he fiercely criticized the eighteenth and nineteenth century theorists like Tylor, Durkheim, Freud, and others based on two important facts: First, none of those theorists actually had some kind of a personal contact with the very peoples they studied and theorized about. On the contrary, they merely relied on information transmitted by travelers, missionaries, traders, and other Europeans. Second, the material they used was based not on accurate descriptions but, rather, on reports that were selective according to what drew those travelers' attention, or what they deemed important and worthy of being recorded.[1] Although Evans-Pritchard's criticism here stems from the fact that he did spend a considerable period of time with indigenous tribes in Africa, thus contrasting his 'real' method to the armchair approach of those previous thinkers, I find his dissatisfaction intriguing when seen from the lens of this book's approach to euhemerism's exploitation from antiquity onwards.

In the preceding chapters I have argued that euhemerism, somehow, had the fate of those remote peoples' traditions, beliefs, and practices studied by the classical theorists. In euhemerism's case, however, the problem of its reception and usage is more complicated, because, although we are left, like the aforementioned theorists, with the reports of authors who were obviously writing down what they deemed important and worthy of recording in order to serve the needs of their own works, in the course of time there were additional layers put on top of those ambiguous testimonies. Many thinkers and authors from antiquity, like Plutarch, Callimachus, Cicero, Sextus and others, interpreted and disseminated a version of Euhemerus's theory that eventually found its way into the works of the early Christian authors. Once again, the theory was further pitched, this time in order to address a completely different issue, that of a new religious movement's ideas and very survival. By approximately the fifth century CE, thereby, there already were three levels of alterations, corruptions, and modifications of what presumably Euhemerus said back in the late fourth or early third century BCE. The process of changing, adapting, modifying, selectively choosing, and in some cases misconstruing the most ancient forms of the theory continued in subsequent periods, as we saw, which transformed the theory into the principle of 'gods being deified humans.' If texts contain explicit data, that is, the information found in a given text, and implicit data, that is, information that one must infer through the analysis of that text, as Gerhard van den Heever has argued,[2] then Euhemerus's text also contains a third set of data that could be called 'external data.' These are the ones that were probably inserted in the existing text (or, alternatively, the modification of the explicit data), by the author(s) who decided—for whatever reason—to propagate the text. In the previous chapters I tried to demonstrate this slow but critical transformation of the theory which I detected not only in how the theory was misrepresented but, largely, in how it managed to crawl into modern scholarship in an unreflective manner that took its already altered form as the most ancient and thus accurate one.

Furthermore, most scholars who utilize euhemerism seem to neglect or ignore altogether not only the source problem and, thus, the reception of the theory, but also the peculiar nature of the *Sacred Inscription*. Above all, Euhemerus told a story rather than straightforwardly offering a theory of the origin of (belief in) gods and thus religion, which has its own value and broaches another set of problems; still, the rationale behind the frame story remains concealed and thereby in a sense impossible to decipher. In his *On Stories* (2002), Richard Kearney argued that "no matter how distinct in style, voice or plot, every story shares the common function of *someone telling something to someone about something.*"[3] Unfortunately, in the case of the *Sacred Inscription*, we only know the name of the teller (Euhemerus), somewhat know the tale (the theory and the frame story partially told or even distorted by the earliest sources available), and do not know the recipient of the story. According to Eusebius's testimony, the recipient of the story (and the theory therein) could have been Cassander, that is, the Macedonian King who ordered Euhemerus to embark on his journey. However, from what we can gather from the available testimonies, it is more possible that Euhemerus wrote for a larger audience, and most likely did so in Alexandria rather than in Macedonia. This is probably the furthest we can go with any speculation about the audience of Euhemerus's work. As Umberto Eco argued about a quarter of a century ago,

> when a text is put in the bottle [. . .]—that is, when a text is produced not for a single addressee but for a community of readers—the author knows that he or she will be interpreted not according to his or her intentions but according to a complex strategy of interactions [. . .].[4]

Although, from what I assume here, Eco is not referring to a conscious knowledge that the author has, he nevertheless indicates the problems arising with texts that deal with issues about which probably every reader has either a personal or a shared opinion, like that of gods (and religion) in the case of Euhemerus's *Sacred Inscription*.

Moreover, throughout the book, I have probably given the impression that I am preoccupied with the author and the text, and ignore or do not value the reader.[5] However, my approach has not been a study of the reception of original euhemerism. The original text is lost, and an examination of euhemerism's reception here only means the reception of Diodorus's, Ennius's, Eusebius's, and Lactantius's euhemerisms. As such, in terms of reader-response and reception theory, euhemerism has a peculiar form and multiple levels. The original work was received primarily by Diodorus, secondarily by Ennius, and then by Eusebius and Lactantius. Strictly speaking, Eusebius and Lactantius are readers of Diodorus and Ennius. The early Christian authors are readers who responded to both pairs, but mainly responded to other authors who responded to the latter pair already from antiquity (for example, Plutarch, Sextus Empiricus, or Cicero). And, finally, late antiquity and modern scholars were and are responding to those early Christian authors. It becomes thus evident that the actions involved in responding to a text, as Wolfgang Iser argued almost half a century ago, which constituted for him the center of reader-response criticism, is not related in the case of euhemerism with the original text.[6] Rather, Eco's 'text in the bottle' here is those earliest authors' texts who incorporated (verbatim, in summary, in translation, or in altered forms) parts of the *Sacred Inscription*. Hence, although the reader's view does matter, I have been more focused on the first level of reception, which most likely contains some information that goes back to the lost original. After that level, as I have discussed, we encounter constant transformations that alter those earliest testimonies, leading us to generalizations about what euhemerism is about, often contradicting or even being irrelevant to those earliest forms of the theory. If those earliest forms of euhemerism are themselves partial or modified versions of the original theory, one can only conceive what modern views of the theory are in such a long process of alterations, modifications, corruptions, and transformations.

The crux of my thesis is not to jettison the study or the utilization of Euhemerus's theory or the term 'euhemerism' for that matter. On the contrary, following Aaron Hughes's basic argument in his discussion about the term 'Abrahamic,'[7] I maintain that the term 'euhemerism' cannot be employed as a tool of analysis and theorizing about any particular set of data without being informed about and acquainted with its history, earliest content, and reception. Failing to do so, as I hope I have showed in this book, we only append further variations and mistreatments of the theory, which eventually produces a theoretical and methodological tool that anyone can utilize in whatever form she or he wishes—such as, for example, further propagating the prevalent understanding of euhemerism being about deified dead humans or about justification of divine kingship,[8] or associating it with any theory of transforming myth into history. If my discussion of Euhemerus's theory has any value whatsoever, then it is my insistence on its use and not its abuse, which can be avoided by simply asking: whose euhemerism? Once an answer has been provided, we must then be conscious that the version of the theory we choose to adopt is not necessarily the theory that Euhemerus himself promoted. Considering that probably the most ancient forms of the theory lie afar from its original articulation, it becomes evident that 'euhemerism' and its usage has different connotations and coloring based on the way it was used by the different actors that decided, for their own reasons, to employ it. Similarly, the modern utilization of euhemerism will have different meanings and subsequently repercussions according to the version one chooses to employ; something that is more often than not overlooked in modern scholarship, which takes for granted that euhemerism is about, for example, 'deified dead humans' or 'turning myth into history,' both partial and essentially mistaken interpretations of ancient euhemerism.

## Notes

1 See Evans-Pritchard 1965, 6–8. Although the term 'primitive' was not in use anymore when Evans-Pritchard delivered his lectures, he informs his audience that he is using the terminology those theorists used, without however sharing their vocabulary (18).
2 See Van den Heever 1999, 351.
3 Kearney 2002, 5, emphasis in the original.
4 Eco 1992, 67.
5 See Eagleton 1996, 64–65 on the three stages of modern literary theory as exemplified by Romanticism and the nineteenth century, New Criticism, and reception theory.
6 See Habib 2005, 724. Generally, on reader-response criticism, cf. 721–734.
7 See Hughes 2012, 100.
8 It is indeed refreshing that the term euhemerism does not appear in a recent collection of articles that deal with kingship and cover different epochs and locations, including the Hellenistic era (see Mitchell and Melville 2013).

## References

Eagleton, Terry. 1996. *Literary Theory: An Introduction.* Second edition. Malden, MA and Oxford: Blackwell.

Eco, Umberto. 1992. "Between Author and Text." In *Interpretation and Over-interpretation,* edited by Stefan Collini, 67–88. Cambridge: Cambridge University Press.

Evans-Pritchard, Edward E. 1965. *Theories of Primitive Religion.* Oxford: Clarendon Press.

Habib, M. A. R. 2005. *A History of Literary Criticism: From Plato to the Present.* Malden, MA and Oxford: Blackwell.

Hughes, Aaron W. 2012. *Abrahamic Religions: On the Uses and Abuses of History.* Oxford: Oxford University Press.

Kearney, Richard. 2002. *On Stories.* London and New York: Routledge.

Mitchell, Lynette and Charles Melville. (Eds.) 2013. *Every Inch a King: Comparative Studies on Kings and Kingship in the Ancient and Medieval Worlds.* Leiden and Boston, MA: Brill.

Van den Heever, Gerhard. 1999. "Finding Data in Unexpected Places (or: From Text Linguistics to Socio–Rhetoric). Toward a Socio–Rhetorical Reading of John's Gospel." *Neotestamentica* 33 (2): 343–364.

# Index